SCATTERING
CHAFF

BEYOND BOUNDARIES: CANADIAN DEFENCE
AND STRATEGIC STUDIES SERIES
Rob Huebert, Series Editor
ISSN 1716-2645 (Print) ISSN 1925-2919 (Online)

Canada's role in international military and strategic studies ranges from peacebuilding and Arctic sovereignty to unconventional warfare and domestic security. This series provides narratives and analyses of the Canadian military from both an historical and a contemporary perspective.

No. 1 · *The Generals: The Canadian Army's Senior Commanders in the Second World War*
J.L. Granatstein

No. 2 · *Art and Memorial: The Forgotten History of Canada's War Art*
Laura Brandon

No. 3 · *In the National Interest: Canadian Foreign Policy and the Department of Foreign Affairs and International Trade, 1909–2009*
Greg Donaghy and Michael K. Carroll

No. 4 · *Long Night of the Tankers: Hitler's War Against Caribbean Oil*
David J. Bercuson and Holger H. Herwig

No. 5 · *Fishing for a Solution: Canada's Fisheries Relations with the European Union, 1977–2013*
Donald Barry, Bob Applebaum, and Earl Wiseman

No. 6 · *From Kinshasa to Kandahar: Canada and Fragile States in Historical Perspective*
Michael K. Carroll and Greg Donaghy

No. 7 · *The Frontier of Patriotism: Alberta and the First World War*
Adriana A. Davies and Jeff Keshen

No. 8 · *China's Arctic Ambitions and What They Mean for Canada*
P. Whitney Lackenbauer, Adam Lajeunesse, James Manicom, and Frédéric Lasserre

No. 9 · *Scattering Chaff: Canadian Air Power and Censorship during the Kosovo War*
Bob Bergen

 UNIVERSITY OF CALGARY Press

BOB BERGEN

SCATTERING CHAFF

Canadian Air Power and Censorship during the Kosovo War

 **UNIVERSITY OF CALGARY**
FACULTY OF ARTS
Centre for Military, Security and Strategic Studies

Beyond Boundaries:
Canadian Defence and Strategic Studies Series
ISSN 1716-2645 (Print) ISSN 1925-2919 (Online)

© 2019 Bob Bergen

University of Calgary Press
2500 University Drive NW
Calgary, Alberta
Canada T2N 1N4
press.ucalgary.ca

This book is available as an ebook which is licensed under a Creative Commons license. The publisher should be contacted for any commercial use which falls outside the terms of that license.

LIBRARY AND ARCHIVES CANADA CATALOGUING IN PUBLICATION

Bergen, Bob, 1949-, author
    Scattering chaff : Canadian air power and censorship during the Kosovo War / Bob Bergen.

(Beyond boundaries : Canadian defence and strategic studies series,
    1716-2645 ; no. 9)
Includes bibliographical references and index.
Issued in print and electronic formats.
ISBN 978-1-77385-030-6 (softcover).—ISBN 978-1-77385-032-0 (PDF).—
ISBN 978-1-77385-033-7 (EPUB).—ISBN 978-1-77385-034-4 (Kindle).—
ISBN 978-1-77385-031-3 (open access PDF)

    1. Kosovo War, 1998-1999—Aerial operations, Canadian. 2. Kosovo War, 1998-1999—Censorship—Canada. I. Title. II. Series: Beyond boundaries series ; no. 9

DR2087.5.B47 2019   949.710315   C2018-906435-8
                                           C2018-906436-6

The University of Calgary Press acknowledges the support of the Government of Alberta through the Alberta Media Fund for our publications. We acknowledge the financial support of the Government of Canada. We acknowledge the financial support of the Canada Council for the Arts for our publishing program.

This book has been published with the support of the Centre for Military, Security and Strategic Studies.

  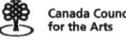

Copyediting by Peter Enman
Cover image: GBU-10's over Croatia. Photo courtesy of Travis Brassington.
Cover design, page design, and typesetting by Melina Cusano

*In memory of Lois,
my Mom,
who taught me to love reading*

Contents

Illustrations	IX
Abbreviations and Nomenclature	XI
Acknowledgements	XV
Introduction—Kosovo: Canada's Unknown Air War	1
1 A Fearsome Aerial Ballet	13
2 Planning for War	37
3 I Cringed Every Time It Rained	59
4 Don't Go to War without It	79
5 The Fog of War	103
6 Prelude to Censorship: Media, Body Bags, and the Persian Gulf War	119
7 Like an Overnight International Courier	145
8 A Blanket of Secrecy	169
9 Friction and Iron Will	191
10 On Body Bags and the News Media	211
11 Canada Missed a Good News Story	221
12 Homecomings	237
13 Context-Less Facts, Ambiguity, Half-Truths, and Outright Lies	253
Afterword	265
Notes	273
Bibliography	313
Index	325

Illustrations

1.1	Captain Kirk "Rambo" Soroka	*34*
3.1	Air Crew Accommodations at Piancavallo, Italy	*61*
3.2	Modular Trailer Accommodations at Camp Canada	*64*
3.3	Protests Against Operation Allied Force	*65*
3.4	Bomb Loader and 500-pound Bomb	*68*
3.5	CF-18 Hardened Shelters	*73*
3.6	Bomb Loaders Working in Pouring Rain	*74*
4.1	A CF-18 Refuelling on a KC-135	*80*
4.2	Lieutenant-Colonel William Allen Flynn Inspects a Smart Bomb	*87*
5.1	Bomb Loaders and a 2,000-pound Bomb	*107*
5.2	Lieutenant-Colonel William Allen Flynn Prepares for a Mission	*111*
8.1	CTV's Joy Malbon Interviews an Unnamed Canadian Pilot	*186*
9.1	CF-18 Cockpit Targeting Imagery—Ammo Storage	*193*
9.2	CF-18 Cockpit Targeting Imagery—Radio Relay	*193*
9.3	CF-18 Cockpit Targeting Imagery—Army Barracks	*194*
9.4	CF-18 Cockpit Targeting Imagery—Industrial Site	*194*
9.5	CF-18 Cockpit Targeting Imagery—Airfield Runway	*194*
9.6	United States Navy EA6Bs	*201*
9.7	CF-18's Afterburners	*205*
12.1	Kosovo Battle Honours	*251*

Abbreviations and Nomenclature

AAA – Anti-aircraft artillery
AAR – Air-to-Air Refuelling
ACC – Air Component Commander
ACE – Aviation Combat Element
ADM (PA) – Assistant Deputy Minister (Public Affairs)
AETE – Aeronautical Engineering and Test Establishment
Air Ops – Air Operations
AMEs – Aircraft Maintenance Engineers
AMIRS – Advanced Multi-role Infrared Sensor
AOR – Area of Responsibility
ATO – Air Tasking Order
AWACS – E-3 Airborne Warning and Control System
BGen. or Brig. Gen. – Brigadier General
CADPAT – Canadian Disruptive Pattern
CANFORME – Canadian Forces Middle East
CANSOCOM – Canadian Operations Support Command
CAP – Combat Air Patrol
Capt. – Captain
CAS – Close Air Support
CBC – Canadian Broadcasting Corporation
CDS – Chief of Defence Staff
CEFCOM – Canadian Expeditionary Force Command
CF – Canadian Forces
CFACC – Combined Forces Air Component Controller
CFB – Canadian Forces Base

CF-18 or CF-188 – McDonnell Douglas F/A-18 naval fighter jet aircraft (CF-18 Hornet)
CFCC – Canadian Forces Combat Camera
Chief MAAP – Chief Master Air Tactical Planner
CNN – Cable News Network
CO – Commanding Officer
COAC – Combined Air Operations Centre
Col. – Colonel
Cpl. – Corporal
C2 – Command and Control
DAOD – Defence Administrative Orders and Directives
DCDS – Deputy Chief of Defence Staff
DND – Department of National Defence
DoD – Department of Defence
EUCOM – United States European Command
FLIR – Forward Looking Infrared
FRY or FY – Federal Republic of Yugoslavia
GBU – Guided bomb unit
Gen. – General
GPS – Global positioning system
Hercs – Lockheed C-130 Hercules four-engine turboprop military transport aircraft
Hercules – C-130 Hercules
Hornet – McDonnell Douglas F/A-18 naval fighter jet aircraft (CF-18 Hornet)
HQ - Headquarters
ID – identify
INS – Instrument navigation system
J-DAMS – Joint Direct Attack Munitions
J5 PA – Joint Operations Public Affairs
KC-135 – Boeing jet-powered Stratotanker
KLA – Kosovo Liberation Army
Lt. Col. – Lieutenant Colonel
Mach 1– the speed of sound, about 344 metres per second
Maj. – Major
MCpl – Master Corporal

NATO – North Atlantic Treaty Organization
MiG – Russian MiG Corporation multi-role fighter jet aircraft
NCMs – Non-Commissioned Members
NDHQ – National Defence Headquarters
NVG – Night-vision goggles
OP or OPS – Operation or Operations
OSCE – Organization for Security and Co-operation in Europe
PGM – Precision-guided munitions
POW – Prisoner of war
RCAF – Royal Canadian Air Force
ROEs – Rules of engagement
ROTO – 0 – First Rotation
SACEUR – Supreme Allied Commander Europe
SAM – Surface-to-air missile
SCONDVA – Standing Committee on National Defence and Veterans Trade
SEAD – Suppression of Enemy Air Defences
SFOR – NATO's Stabilization Force in Bosnia
Sgt. – Sergeant
SHAPE – Supreme Headquarters Allied Powers Europe
snag – Malfunction
sortie – One flight by one plane
strat – Strategic
TFA – Task Force Aviano
TF Comd – Task Force Command
TFL or TF LIB – Task Force Lebeccio
TOT – Time on Target
Triple A – Anti-aircraft artillery
TRP – Timing Reference Points
UN – United Nations
UNSCR – United Nations Security Council Resolution
US – United States
WComd – Wing commander
WO – Warrant Officer

Acknowledgements

This book would not exist if not for the friendship and generosity of three of Canada's pre-eminent scholars, beginning with Dr. David J. Bercuson, who, one day over lunch, offered me the opportunity to pursue a PhD with him at the University of Calgary's Centre for Military and Strategic Studies. Although I thought I knew a lot about the news media after twenty-five years as a journalist, my co-supervisor Dr. David Taras led me to think about journalism in ways I never had before. His wisdom, guidance, and unfailing support have been invaluable. Dr. John Ferris was instrumental in bringing this study to the manuscript submission stage. Brian Scrivener, Director of the University of Calgary Press, is right: a book truly is a team effort.

I am indebted to the Canadian Armed Forces—from the corporals to the generals—for all its help. The assistance of Col. W.R.R. Cleland, Commander of 4 Wing Cold Lake, Alberta, was crucial to this study. Without Col. Cleland's permission to interview his servicemen and women, I would not have received the ethical approval necessary to conduct research involving human subjects. Col. André Viens, Commander of 3 Wing Bagotville, Quebec, made another major component of the research possible by similarly allowing me to interview his personnel there. Cols. Cleland and Viens want Canadians to know what their men and women did during the Kosovo war. Also generous with their time and assistance were Maj. Luc Gaudet and the late Eric Cameron of the National Defence Public Affairs Office, Calgary (Prairie Region & Northern Area). They provided me with numerous records and introductions that, at one point, took me to the highest-ranking officer in the Canadian Forces, Chief of Defence Staff Gen. Ray Henault, who was also gracious with his time. Many of the original Department of National Defence and Canadian Forces documents that fleshed out the bare bones of my ideas about the 1991 Persian Gulf War and the 1999 Kosovo air war were obtained using the federal *Access to Information Act*. I must thank the Department's Director of Access to Information and Privacy, the staff, and the Canadian Forces and National Defence personnel for their responses to my many requests.

Some of Canada's most prominent journalists went far out of their way to share their experiences in Aviano, Italy, during the Kosovo war. Among them were the CBC's Paul Workman in Paris, France; his colleague Neil Macdonald in Washington, DC; and the *Globe and Mail*'s Geoffrey York in Beijing, China. Lastly, I must single out CTV's Washington bureau chief Joy Malbon for her televised interview from Aviano with a Canadian Forces CF-18 pilot—who had his back to the camera—which inspired my research.

INTRODUCTION

Kosovo: Canada's Unknown Air War

Canada is widely and approvingly thought in many circles to be a nation with a purely peacekeeping military tradition, despite its contribution to two world wars. Since the 1964 White Paper on Defence in which the Liberal government of Prime Minister Lester Pearson made peacekeeping Canada's top priority,[1] it has been a myth that has endured for decades. In 2001, the Canadian government contributed to it by enshrining the humanitarian image of the armed forces as binocular-toting female peacekeeper on the back of Canadian $10 bills.

One can easily argue that the myth was shattered in that same year when Canadian forces became involved in the Afghanistan conflict with Operation Apollo, which contributed to America's Operation Enduring Freedom there. But even as late as 2007, after years of conflict in Afghanistan, prominent Canadian scholars Janice Gross Stein and Eugene Lang provided stark evidence of a yawning gap in the public perception of Canadian military history in which the peacekeeping myth was allowed to perpetuate itself. In their controversial book *The Unexpected War: Canada in Kandahar*, claiming the Canadian government stumbled into a protracted combat mission in Afghanistan, they traced the decision-making process that resulted in the deployment of an 800-strong Canadian battle group on the ground in Kandahar. It was sent to help fight the Taliban and al-Qaeda in wake of the September 11 terrorist attacks. Canada, Stein and Lang said, was pressured by the United States for ground troops. They wrote:

The choice that the Cabinet made was neither the best option nor the least offensive option: it was the only remaining option on the table.

The Kandahar deployment signaled a major political shift in political and military thinking in Ottawa. It would be the first combat mission for the Canadian Forces since the Korean War, fifty years earlier.[2]

This book vehemently disagrees with Stein and Lang's contention that there had been no combat mission since Korea. It examines Canada's contribution to the 1999 Kosovo air war authorized by the Liberal government of Jean Chrétien, for which a dedicated campaign medal was struck, and for which Battle Honours were awarded to the 441 and 425 Tactical Fighter Squadrons for their participation in Operation Echo. Operation Echo was the Canadian contribution to Operation Allied Force, the North Atlantic Treaty bombing campaign against Yugoslavia President Slobodan Milosevic's Serbian military and paramilitary forces in Kovoso. It should be noted that Canadian pilots also dropped bombs during the last three days of the 1991 Persian Gulf War, but they were not engaged in protracted combat, flying predominantly escort and sweep roles accompanying coalition aircraft. That is as far as the disagreement with Stein and Lang will go. But Operation Echo does establish a modern baseline departure from Canada's reputation as a purely peacekeeping nation. That this is not general knowledge is not surprising. To put it bluntly, Operation Echo was a black hole from which no light of information could escape by the usual means of mass information dissemination: the news media.

Most Canadians know little if anything about their military men and women who fought that air war and who rightly should be considered modern-day war heroes. Despite the news coverage, Canadians could not have learned how their men and women in uniform dealt with critical equipment shortfalls and personnel problems resulting from years of military budget cuts; the threat levels and the calculated, but terrifying, risks that were taken in combat as a result; the incredible success stories, and the absolute skill, dedication, and bravery of the aircrews.[3]

The reasons for this failure of knowledge are many and are explored in detail in the following pages, but one of the biggest is that an occupational conflict of interest lies at the heart of the relationship between the news media and the military. Journalists like to think that the news media, despite its vagaries, "constitutes the foundation of all freedoms" and that they are one of its principal supports.[4] They are small "l" liberals by nature. They favor openness and think that the news media should provide their readers, listeners, and audiences with the information, ideas, and freewheeling public debate that citizens need to make informed decisions about government and the society in which they live.

There are media scholars and theories aplenty that examine the way the media present the news and what effects that may have on society. In the context of the Kosovo air war, the most relevant scholars are Murray Edelman, Daniel Hallin, and Lance Bennett.[5]

Political scientist Murray Edelman holds that political reality is socially constructed through shared meanings that shape patterns of belief and how we define or "frame" ideas and concepts in our minds.[6] Edelman wrote that during the Cold War, governments successfully created the widespread perception among the populations of North Atlantic Treaty Organization allies that NATO military defences were necessary countermeasures to possible Soviet aggression in Europe. The shared perception was that Russian hawks were dominant in the Kremlin and that aggression was likely.[7] Such perceptions were mobilized in mass publics by political leaders and others skilled in inducing news media coverage that reflected their institutional aims.[8] Edelman wrote that "the critical element in political maneuver for advantage is the creation of meaning: the construction of beliefs about events, policies, leaders, problems and crises that rationalize or challenge existing inequalities."[9] He explained that during crisis, a political leader's strategic need is to mobilize support for the official policy and to immobilize opposition. To that end, the leader must choose language that evokes interpretations that legitimize the preferred course of action and either "encourage people to be supportive or to remain quiescent."[10]

Later, American political science and communication scholar Daniel Hallin wrote about the news media practices and routines during the Vietnam War. Hallin pointed out that when US president Lyndon Johnson lied to the American news media about his intention to increase the number of US troops in South Vietnam to take over the war from the South

Vietnamese, it wasn't questioned. The press simply hadn't been taught to question the president or that a government would lie and cheat.[11]

One clear pattern University of Washington scholar Lance Bennett observed that was thought to affect the level of domestic debate from Vietnam to the Falklands, Nicaragua, and the Persian Gulf wars was that journalistic routines drove reporters to official sources and indexed them within the political hierarchy. As a result, debate in the media over American war policy ended when official debate ended.[12] Bennett found that during the 1991 Gulf War, elite opposition was never prolonged or prominent enough to affect President Bush's leading policy options.[13]

Few, however, address the most fundamental, occupational, and direct questions as Jay Rosen does: What do journalists stand for? Rosen wrote: "Freedom of information, an open flow of ideas, honesty and candor in public business, the people's right to know—certainly. But it is equally certain that none of these things matter unless we have not just the right, but the means to know, unless we show a will to inform ourselves, unless we are given a decent chance to get into the game, put our ideas and experience to use."[14]

In a 2004 Ontario Superior Court ruling, Justice Mary Lou Benotto said:

> It is only through the press that most individuals can learn of what is transpiring in government and come to their own assessment of the institution and its actions. Protecting the freedom of expression of the press thereby guarantees the further freedom of members of the public to develop, put forward and act upon informed opinions about government and other matters of public interest.[15]

In this role, journalists perform an often adversarial watchdog function, holding people accountable, as exemplified by the investigative reporting of the *Washington Post*'s Bob Woodward and Carl Bernstein during the Watergate affair in the 1970s.

Thirteen years after Justice Benotto's statement, Prime Minister Justin Trudeau said during a press conference in China in December 2017 that reporters in democracies perform a valuable challenge function. It is noteworthy that he made the remarks in a communist country where independent journalists who challenge Chinese leaders often end up in jail.[16] "Allow me to take a moment to thank members of the media," Trudeau began. "You play an essential role: a challenge function, an information function. It is not easy at the best of times. These are not the best of times with the transitions and challenges undergoing the traditional media right now and I really appreciate the work that you do."[17]

Military services, on the other hand, are conservative by nature. In that vein, Canadian military men and women adhere to social convention, duty, and a belief that they answer a higher calling. Their business is national defence, security, and war, which are extremely complex affairs. The official media relations policy of the Canadian Forces claims that it strives to be visible, accessible, and accountable to the Canadian public. Yet because the Canadian military's business is national defence, the reality is that its members are given to discretion, if not secrecy.[18]

Few Members of Parliament, let alone the vast majority of the Canadian public, have sufficient expertise to debate or judge matters of national defence. Still, those who study the relationship of militaries to civilians in democracies, or civil-military relations, hold that there ought to be an unbroken line of accountability from Canadian Forces commanders in the field, to the chief of the defence staff, to cabinet, to Parliament and, ultimately, to Canadian citizens who pay for the troops with their taxes and whose sons, daughters, husbands, wives, brothers, sisters, fathers, and mothers participate in combat operations. There is no greater clash between the news media's liberal value of openness and accountability and the military's conservative values of discretion and secrecy than when a country is engaged in war. But, like moths to a flame, journalists and writers have been drawn to military conflicts since Homer composed the *Iliad* and the *Odyssey* chronicling the Trojan War and its aftermath. In that tradition, Canadian journalists have a rich history of informing the country about Canadian Forces operations overseas, despite being hampered by military secrecy and often outright censorship.[19]

But precisely such secrecy and censorship is what happened in the months after 24 March 1999, the day the Liberal government's minister of national defence, Art Eggleton, rose in the House of Commons to make one of the most serious announcements any government official can. He reported that six Canadian Forces CF-18 fighter aircraft had participated earlier that day in NATO bombing operations against military targets in Serbia. Canada's military strategy had quietly been in place for months, but Eggleton refused to use the term "war," preferring to euphemistically call these operations a "humanitarian mission."[20] Canada's military action, Minister of Foreign Affairs Lloyd Axworthy later elaborated, was part of the international community's response to the failure of the Federal Republic of Yugoslavia to provide basic rights to its own citizens in the province of Kosovo. He reported that Yugoslav President Slobodan Milosevic had been using military force to crush Kosovar Albanian dissidents, murdering innocents and destroying their villages, leaving some 450,000 homeless. In the House, Axworthy said: "Humanitarian considerations are the main impulse for our actions. We cannot stand by while an entire population is displaced, people are killed, villages are burned, and people are denied their basic rights because of their ethnic background."[21]

The immediate concern for both Axworthy and Eggleton was the safety of some 130 Canadian Forces personnel based in Aviano, Italy, who were taking part in the action to halt the violence in Kosovo and avert an even bigger humanitarian disaster. Eggleton assured the House that the Canadian Forces in Aviano were well equipped and well prepared for the role they would play in the days ahead. The CF-18s would participate in ground attacks with new precision-guided munitions and could engage in aerial combat with air-to-air missiles.

Notwithstanding the Yugoslav military's sophisticated air defence systems, Eggleton explained that NATO commanders had taken all necessary measures to reduce risk and that the Canadian CF-18s would have the support of NATO escort aircraft on their missions. In other words, the Canadian government's strategy for the deployment of its CF-18s was well underway even if Eggleton preferred to define the conflict as a humanitarian mission, as opposed to a war.

Axworthy had earlier told the House, on 7 October 1998: "No one in Canada and in the international community supports the use of violence to achieve political ends."[22] But according to one of history's most influential strategic thinkers, Carl von Clausewitz, that is precisely the point of war in strategy: the application of military force as an instrument of policy to achieve political ends.[23] That aim was precisely the point of the NATO

War that NATO commanders were never allowed to call the Kosovo military intervention a war, but "of course, it was."[38] Similarly, former US President Bill Clinton does not provide the rationale for his use of the term, but he interspersed the terms "conflict," "air campaign," and "bombing campaign" to describe the military action in the Balkans with the words "war" three times and "air war" twice in his autobiography *My Life*.[39] The nomenclature is central to this book's argument that the Canadians who fought there deserved a warrior's honour for risking their lives in military operations mandated by the Canadian government, even though it was long been denied to them.

Swiss strategic theorist Baron de Jomini's theories, which reduced war to an intellectual fixed order, are generally known only to military specialists.[40] Jomini also wrote about the political nature of war, but he argued that the political direction in the form of a war council of generals and ministers must be limited to only broad general plans of operation. Once a decision is made to go to war, it is up to the general directing the war to decide on the manner in which he should achieve the war's objective. If he is unable to do so, Jomini wrote, "the unfortunate general would certain[ly] be beaten, and the whole responsibility of his reserves should fall upon the shoulders of those who, hundreds of miles distant, took upon themselves the duty of directing the army—a duty so difficult for anyone, even upon the scene of operations."[41]

Because Operation Allied Force was an air war, it also merits briefly visiting the writing of Giulio Douhet, the Italian air war strategist who wrote as early as the 1920s about the importance of air power. It can be argued that many of Douhet's theories set out in his later work, *The Command of the Air*, proved to be true in the skies over Kosovo and Serbia. "To have command of the air," he wrote, "means to be in a position to wield offensive power so great it defies human imagination."[42] Douhet set out systematic, if not scientific, plans for air attacks that took every conceivable variable into account, including: weights of aircraft, armaments, and crew; the air force's organization into tactical groups based on air speed capabilities of the planes; fuel; plans of operations; and the air organizations needed to achieve them. But his one single overwhelming principle for air war, which he said governed warfare whether it was on land or sea, was surprise, and to "inflict the greatest damage in the shortest time possible."[43] Douhet also envisioned strategically targeting cities or major population centres for aerial bombardment, as opposed to strictly tactical military targets, to break the population's support for the war. He wrote: "A nation which at once loses the command of the air and finds itself subjected to incessant aerial attacks aimed directly at its most vital centres and without the possibility of effective retaliation, this nation, whatever its surface forces may be able to do, must arrive at the conviction that all is useless, that all hope is dead. This conviction spells defeat."[44]

Post-Kosovo air war scholars Peter Wijninga and Richard Szafranski wrote that the 1991 Persian Gulf War and the Kosovo air war demonstrated the strategic worth of axiological air operations. The term axiological combines the Greek words "axios," meaning worthy, and "logos," meaning reason or theory, and involves a philosophical investigation into the nature of value. Wijninga and Szafranski wrote that axiological bombing operations go beyond the focus of "utility bombing" of military infrastructure and its war-fighting tools—including industrial capacity, aircraft, tanks, and troop formations—to non-military targets that political leaders value or hold dear. In the case of Kosovo, that included the state-controlled media outlets by which then Yugoslav president Slobodan Milosevic attempted to control his people's minds. Wijninga wrote: "While a totalitarian leader is certain that he can control people's actions, he is uncertain that he has control over their minds. If he does not attempt to control their minds, he knows he may lose control over their actions in the long run."[45]

More recently, Paul Rexton Kan wrote that whereas early air power theorists like Douhet concentrated on the breaking of civilian morale by bombing major population centres, the NATO bombing campaign Operation Allied Force would appear to offer the most persuasive case for axiological targeting. Early in the bombing campaign, conventional military targets were struck by NATO forces without having the desired effect of halting the humanitarian catastrophe caused by Serbian ethnic cleansing. Only when NATO's bombing was broadened to include institutions crucial to Milosevic's rule did he capitulate. Having said that, Kan wrote that it is not clear that such coercive axiological bombing alone resulted in capitulation because, at the same time, NATO ground troops were being assembled on Kosovo's borders while Russians engaged the Serbs diplomatically.[46]

The Kosovo war was NATO's first air war and was the first in which Canada's airmen had fought in Europe since the Second World War, when some 10,200 of the aircrew fought in Royal Canadian Air Force squadrons and some 16,000 others in the British Royal Air Force.[47] The Kosovo war provides a rich opportunity to examine the relationship between the Canadian news media and the Canadian Forces, and the conflict of interest that emerged. It studies an asymmetric power struggle between the Canadian Forces, which commanded all the information, and journalists who attempted to uphold the democratic principle of accessibility. This war occurred three years before Canada's involvement in Afghanistan began and makes it clear that Canadians must shed their peacekeeping view of the armed forces in favour of what those forces were during, and have been before and since, this historic international event: warriors.

This book also examines the notion that the news media plays a vital democratic role in informing Canadians about federal government policies, thereby allowing the government to be held accountable for its military policies. It argues that this expectation went unfulfilled in the case of the Kosovo air war. It challenges fundamental Canadian Forces security considerations that undermined any democratic role the Canadian news media might have played during the Kosovo conflict. It shows that the censorship invoked by Canadian Forces over the news media was driven by myth. It argues that operational security considerations must be based on meticulously documented evidence of security threats, not myth, and that censorship is a government—not a military—responsibility.

At the heart of the book is this question: What could Canadians have learned from their news media about the RCAF's exercise of its military skill in pursuit of the government's policies during the Kosovo air war? The research pursued three objectives: The first was to discover what the Canadian Forces did in Aviano, Italy, and in the skies over Kosovo and Serbia during the Kosovo air war. In the process this portion of the book provides details about that war that never have been made public. The second was to learn what English-language Canadian journalists could have learned about Canadian Forces participation in the air but didn't. The author interviewed military personnel involved in the air war and journalists involved in its coverage. The interviews were conducted in person, by telephone, and through email exchanges. Many of those interviews are quoted extensively because they offer unfiltered evidence about the experiences of Canadian personnel in the Kosovo war, evidence that is otherwise difficult to find. Military ranks used are those held at the time of the conflict or interviews. The third goal was to learn about the interaction between the news media and the military, which held all the information cards about the war close to its chest and actively prevented the news media from learning about its activities in Aviano, Italy, and in the skies over Kosovo and Serbia. This book deliberately makes no distinction between what the different media—print, radio, or television—could have learned because it will be shown that the results were the same for all. It is not what is contained in the news media that threatens the foundations of liberal democracy; it is what is *not* found in the media, that which is absent from the public record. The danger is that a Canadian public ill served by its news media will be unable to make informed judgments about the government and its military policies.

A Fearsome Aerial Ballet

Canadian Forces fighter pilot Maj. Alain Pelletier's thoughts cascaded as he sat in the cockpit of his CF-18 Hornet, its engines idling on a runway in Aviano, Italy, after the tangerine dusk of twilight had darkened around 6:30 p.m. to a deep purple, then inky black, on 24 March 1999. Pelletier was waiting for clearance to lead a package of four Canadian jets on a NATO bombing run into Serbia, marking the first time Canadians had fought in a European war in more than a half-century. Like dozens of other Canadian pilots who would follow over the next seventy-seven days and nights, Pelletier felt inner doubts, thoughts of his family and a dread of the unknown wash over him as he sat alone in his cockpit with little but dead air over his radio. He had spent two decades in the Canadian Forces training for combat, but none of it prepared him for his solitary thoughts in that moment.

"You're: 'OK. I'm ready. Here I am sitting in that aircraft and we'll be launching in a few minutes, but holy shit, you know, we're really going at it.'"[1] Pelletier's mind raced back to when he signed up with the Forces as an unmarried seventeen-year-old with not a care in the world. "Now, here you are married. You've got kids and a family to care for and you're asked to go into a hostile environment."[2] Pelletier mentally checked the briefings about possible threats from Serbian forces that awaited the package as it penetrated Serbian airspace. Would the Serbs have anti-aircraft artillery weapons the briefers hadn't anticipated? Would a surface-to-air missile site be placed on a mountaintop to give it that extra reach that could cripple his airplane? What about enemy aircraft?

Lt. Col. Sylvain Faucher, commanding officer of 425 Tactical Fighter Squadron, who was to be flying on Pelletier's wing that night, had an entirely different set of worries as he sat on the tarmac waiting to take off. In his mind, he was preparing to go to war, regardless of what the politicians in Ottawa might call it back home. "Let's not be shy of saying it, if I'm going to cross some enemy lines somewhere, sorry, I'm going to war."³

As a pilot, one of his concerns was that, despite the numerous Maple Flag joint-NATO air exercises in which he had taken part at Canadian Forces Base Cold Lake, Alberta, and Red Flag exercises at Nellis Air Force Base in Nevada, nothing compared to knowing he was flying into combat.

> You're talking to an individual who was in the Forces for quite a while, who has been looking at many commanding officers (COs) prior to that. All the COs I've looked at in the last—name a number of years prior to that—never showed me an example of how it is to go into conflict. We went to a lot of exercises. We went to Maple Flags. We went to Red Flags and we went to some low-level operations. On the 24th of March 1999, we were about to go to war.⁴

His second set of concerns was for the personnel in his squadron, which is why, mentally, he could not fly lead that night.

> I was now commanding a unit in the field that was about to go to war and I had a lot of people to watch over. I had a lot of concerns about a lot of things. At the time, I couldn't concentrate or put my mind on the mission without forgetting the rest of the folks and, by the time the war started, the conflict started on the 24th of March, most of the pilots in the air force were in situ. The staff, or the amount of personnel that we had, was around 350 personnel or so. There were a lot of issues to think about and to consider so that we don't lose people. When I use the term "losing people" in a general sense, I'm going to give you an example. To an armourer who has been putting bombs on a fighter aircraft for the last twenty years of his life, that bomb has been put on

and probably dropped on a range somewhere, whether it's in Europe, whether it's in North America, for an exercise. Well that night—or in the next few nights that followed or many nights or the seventy-seven nights that followed—the armourer is now putting a bomb on the airplane and the bomb is not coming back. We had to pay particular close attention to some of these folks because that was an issue, a psychological issue, so that's what I mean by not losing anyone.[5]

In the cockpit of a third Hornet sat a twenty-nine-year-old wingman with 433 Tactical Fighter Squadron, the youngest and most inexperienced of the Canadian pilots flying with Pelletier and Faucher that night. Although fully qualified with 500 hours in the CF-18, the airman's hours were a fraction of Pelletier's 1,600 hours. The expectations placed on him were enormous, but if it was not for bad luck that night, he would not have had any luck at all. While Pelletier harboured his innermost thoughts nearby, a system failed on the junior pilot's CF-18. Although snags—as they are called—are routine, it added additional stress to his first combat mission. The wingman explained:

> There's a lot of time built in between the walk time and the takeoff time. You actually spend, if your jet's going when you start, a long time sitting on the ground running. If things don't go well, if you have a systems problem or something, then you have to shut down and run to the spare and then you're in a rush, obviously, in order to make the takeoff time. The jet that I was in started out broke. We had, at the time, a running spare. Someone else had started an aircraft for me and programmed the wave points and everything. All I had to do was shut down, jump from my plane, jump into his, start the left engine and then make sure everything was the way I wanted it. I did make it. I was still pretty busy, as far as where my mind was. I was mostly focused on what I was doing because I just didn't have the time to sit and think.[6]

Capt. Mike Barker, a maintenance officer with 441 Tactical Fighter Squadron from Canadian Forces Base Cold Lake, was on the Aviano air base that evening. He had gone for a walk that night with a buddy to an American mess near the end of the runway. They watched the Canadian CF-18s lift off. The glowing blue-white plumes of their twin-engine afterburners emitted a crackling thunder as the jets soared off the runway. Once the jets were airborne, the afterburners were shut off and the CF-18s disappeared like stars fading in the night. Afterward, reading from a diary he kept while in Aviano, Barker described the fearsome array of NATO coalition warplanes taking off:

> From the Victor Loop mess, which was a mess out on the end of the runway, we saw jets lining up—bombed up—and then they started rolling. It kept up for something like one to one-and-a-half hours, jet after jet screaming down the runway. There were American jets; there were Spanish jets; and us; and there were tankers. There was all kinds of stuff there. The British at one point had an AWACS (NATO's E-3 Airborne Warning and Control System) there. I'm not sure if that was there at this point or not, so a couple of F-16s, the EF-18s, F-15s, C-130s, tankers, everything.[7]

Not until the four Canadian Hornets eased into formation were the self-doubts swirling through Pelletier's mind crowded out by years of training and the familiar routine of being airborne. Pelletier was at home in the cocoon of his fighter's cockpit, thousands of feet above the Adriatic Sea and more than familiar with the lay of the land in Europe.[8] He was among a mixed cadre of CFB Bagotville, Quebec, pilots with 433 and 425 Tactical Fighter Squadrons who had been flying six CF-18s out of Italy since the fall of 1998.

They generally had been flying three sorties per week in two-ship, four-ship, or larger coalition package formations.[9] As a result, Pelletier and his Bagotville comrades were skilled at flying in formations with French, Dutch, British, Spanish, and American allies. After less than an hour of flight down the east coast of Italy, the need to refuel in the air put the Canadians into one of two parallel refuelling tracks that led toward an American KC-135 refuelling tanker over the Adriatic Sea in an area roughly east of Albania. As far as the eye could see, warplanes took up nearly the whole of the night sky over the Adriatic in patterns leading to dozens of air-to-air refuelling tankers

Managing that many warplanes in a confined airspace before, during, and after combat missions is a science and a highly choreographed art of war. All of it embodied even the earliest writing of strategic theorist Giulio Douhet, who systematically mapped out the elements of air superiority. The science began at the headquarters of NATO's Air South Commander, Lt. Gen. Mike Short, in Vicenza, Italy. Short's mandate was to use air power to enforce NATO's direction to halt Serbian president Slobodan Milosevic's military and paramilitary's ethnic cleansing of Kosovars and remove those Serb forces from Kosovo. He began with a planning concept known as centralized command and control and decentralized execution. Centralized command and control meant that Gen. Short and his staff were located at Short's Combined Air Operations Centre in Vicenza. There they controlled the decentralized NATO allied forces at the Aviano, Gioia del Colle, Brindisi, and other air bases down the boot of Italy, in addition to those in the United Kingdom and Germany. Battle space management experts and master air attack planners had predetermined the ranges involved from all the bases to military targets in Kosovo and Serbia and threats that might be encountered and parsed up the airspace into manageable bites. All worked to execute the strategic Air Operations Directive signed by Short.

The NATO planners and pilots followed an Air Tasking Order produced by the Chief Master Air Tactical Planner (the Chief MAAP) following Short's air operations directive. The air tasking order identified targets to be struck; the warplanes available; the location of defensive screens; the provision of an E-3 Airborne Warning and Control System, or AWACS; Suppression of Enemy Air Defences (SEAD) capabilities; intelligence, surveillance, reconnaissance; and air-to-air refuelling.

One of the first things the Chief MAAP did was carve out an area of responsibility (AOR) about 60 miles wide by 100 miles deep, roughly over Bosnia near the Serbian border, and assign two fighters to conduct combat air patrols and provide a defensive screen to protect the bases and warplanes in Italy. Depending on the situation, the defensive screen could be two deep or side by side. This night, they were side by side. Behind them, in a similar orbit in its own area of responsibility, was an E-3 AWACS equipped with an array of radars, communications, and data processing equipment and a command-and-control computer able to detect enemy aircraft approaching at low altitudes down Serbian valleys. Personnel aboard the AWACS also controlled all the Allied aircraft taking part in that night's missions. Two packages of strikes took place that night. The first precisely choreographed wave included British bombers, American stealth aircraft, and cruise missiles launched from the British submarine HMS *Splendid* and from the American USS *Gonzales* and USS *Philippine Sea* in the Adriatic.[10] The second strike package involved Canadian, French, and British warplanes.

Prior to takeoff from Aviano, their air tasking order gave the Canadians directives on targets, radio frequencies, and codes. French Mirages bombed targets next to them in the same strike package, with the British operating on the far side in the same package under one commander. The commander planned the package at the main planning area in Aviano, with the Canadians, French, and British all in the same room. The pilots were assigned altitudes, transit routings, and designated marshalling areas in which they gathered at precisely calculated times before entering Serbia, along with timings for which planes were striking which targets and when.[11]

Once airborne from Aviano, the pilots were handed off from the air traffic control tower to controllers circling near Serbia in the AWACS. Although the Canadian CF-18s were loaded with 16,000 pounds of fuel in Aviano, they burned 1,500 pounds during taxi and take-off or about 1,000 pounds per minute in full afterburner. They burned another 5,000 pounds per hour in cruise, or about 10 pounds per nautical mile flown. With a 500-mile flight to their targets, one of the pilots' first jobs was to refuel midair with another 6,000 pounds of fuel en route to their targets as far south in the Adriatic as possible. That was enabled by an elaborate battle space management plan. Lt. Col. Kirk Soroka, the 4 Wing Operations Officer at CFB Cold Lake, Alberta, who was a CF-18 pilot during the Kosovo campaign, described it as possible to think of battle space management as a ladder superimposed lengthwise over a map of the Adriatic Sea, with its rungs forming six individual "boxes" or areas of responsibility at precisely designated Global Positioning System (GPS) locations. The long left rail of the ladder down the Adriatic close to the eastern coast of Italy behind those individual AORs was an air transit route code named Backstreet. Inside each AOR in the ladder were air-to-air refuelling tankers like flying gas stations. Each airspace was assigned north-to-south code names: Elf, Sonny North, Sonny South, Shell, Johnson, and Mobile. Each individual airspace can be envisioned as a massive three-layer cake. At each layer was a refuelling tanker such as a Spanish Hercules, a French 707, or an American KC-135, or a combination of them at different altitudes. In that airspace control plan, a Spanish Hercules flew a circular counter-clockwise orbit, or tanker track, at 16,000 feet, a French 707 orbiting counter-clockwise at 20,000 feet, and an American KC-135 orbiting counter-clockwise at 25,000 feet. This is known as a tanker stack.[12]

As the warplanes flew down Backstreet to their assigned tanker tracks, the pilots were in radio contact with a controller in the AWACS. Generally, they approached their assigned tanker about 10,000 feet above, descending to 1,000 feet below it and about a mile behind. En route to the mission they entered the gas station box through a GPS position known as the "Window" on the northwest corner. Each refuelling track was set up the same way, with parallel air corridors or "Alleys" between each box like rungs on the superimposed ladder. While the approach to the refueller at the northwest corner of the gas station was called the "Window," the exit on the northeast corner of the box was called the "Porch."

Soroka explained that if the pilot's radio call sign was "Dirk 11," the tanker's "Exxon 35," and the AWACS "Magic," the conversation between the pilot and the AWACS as it entered the refuelling track through the "Window" would go something like: "Dirk 11. Flight Exxon 35 is BRA (Bearing, Range, Altitude) 180 (degrees) for 25 miles at 20,000 feet. Call radar contact." The pilot would reply: "Dirk 11. Radar Contact Exxon 35." And the AWACS would say: "Right, you are cleared to switch boom to contact Exxon 35. Contact Magic prior to exiting at Porch."[13]

Soroka explained the process:

> Because we hadn't crossed enemy territory yet, all of our lights were on so we would see where we were at night. So once we had radar contact, talking to Exxon 35 they would clear us astern. So we would pull up about a mile behind

him, in formation, and then he would clear us to move to the echelon, in formation, depending on which airplane we were going on. (An echelon is a military formation which, in this case, aircraft to follow one another in an offset pattern). As we went out to the echelon as either a two ship or four ship, the lead, the number one aircraft would be closest to the tanker, then number two, number three and number four. The lead would be cleared astern the tanker, the lead would say: "Copy clear astern." He would fly to the right behind the boom and would be cleared to wet contact. He would say: "Copy wet contact." Then he would add power and put his fuel probe in the KC-135's funnel-like drogue. Once he got his gas, the airplane would stop giving him gas. The lights—which are either red, amber, or green—the light would turn red which means you're cleared to disconnect, or they will tell you to disconnect. They would say: "cleared echelon left." The lead would say "copy that," and go to the other side of the airplane. And they would say: "Number two, you are cleared astern. Clear to wet contact." The whole formation went through. When everyone got their gas, the tanker would read out what fuel we took on board. We would respond with our tail numbers so the appropriate nation would get the bill for the fuel and the tanker would say you're cleared to climb straight ahead. The formation would leave the tanker about 1,000 feet above it and head towards the Porch, switch frequencies to Magic and then move to the next stage of the flight which was to the marshal part of the push.[14]

To the north, over Hungary, a second smaller set of refuelling tracks—Texaco, Gulf, and Conoco—supported other Allies' strike missions, under Short's Air Operations Directive. Once refuelled, Pelletier and the Canadians continued through the Porch, exited the gas station box, and flew over Albanian airspace, eventually positioning themselves in a circular holding pattern flying at a predetermined GPS marshalling point and at four predetermined separate altitudes over Macedonia where a strike package of twelve other NATO warplanes was similarly marshalling a few miles back from timing reference points (TRP). Each formation would leave their marshal point to hit their timing reference point at an exact time that would allow them to fly into the target area and deliver their weapons on a predetermined time on target (TOT).[15]

Given the signal from an airborne air controller, the four Canadians established their attack formation with the other NATO aircraft flying north over the Macedonia/Serbia border on their way into Serbia. Serbia is not a big country by Canadian standards: at 88,631 square kilometres, it is only a little larger than Lake Superior. Kosovo is tiny; at 10,887 square kilometres, it is about half the size of Lake Ontario.[16] The package the CF-18s were in was divided into western and eastern elements. Pelletier led the four Canadian CF-18s flying single file and the eastern element as a whole.

Within a heartbeat they were in hostile territory preparing to launch 500-pound laser-guided bombs onto a predetermined military target, a Serbian military base. In a CF-18 engaged in a running procedure on a target three minutes away, combat activities occur in a matter of seconds. As they closed on their target, Pelletier saw anti-aircraft artillery fire, or triple-A, arcing in the night sky toward his formation.

> You're seeing triple-A coming up and then you're wondering still, hopefully, is everything we were told about this, the maximum height of the triple-A is that accurate? So you take a quick look. Where is it directed? It was pretty much a barrage fire, nothing really directed at something specific. They knew that we were coming and they were trying to put up stuff in the air. So we saw it and kicked away from the position.[17]

Some sixty seconds after the triple-A fire, the CF-18 pilots received a radio warning from the E-3 AWACS that two Yugoslav MiG-29 Fulcrum fighters were closing in on them sixty miles off their nose. Pelletier explained: "Initially, you see it on radar. Obviously, nobody's got lights on over there because it's a war and so you don't see it visually until somebody fires a missile or until an aircraft gets shot down."[18]

As formation commander, Pelletier had to make split-second decisions. His package was over Kosovo moving north toward Serbia.[19] Royal Netherlands air force jets flying combat air patrol missions in support of the eastern arm had also picked up the AWACs surveillance signal. The CF-18s also were quickly closing in on their original target 30–35 miles away.

> We were close to our decision range. OK. Do I press to the target? Do I engage the airborne target or do we turn and let the Dutch handle it completely? Just before I had to make the decision to abort the attack and make a formal commitment on that group of aircraft, the Dutch were successful in shooting one down and getting the other one to turn around.[20]

Within seconds, the next thing Pelletier was aware of was the fiery exhaust of a surface-to-air missile streaking through the night sky in their direction.

> We had no indication, initially of the missile coming up, except for the visual pickup, which is easy at night because you see bloom of the missile exhaust coming toward you. Since we were the leading edge of the eastern element, the eastern arm, we could see that it was actually targeted towards us. We did a quick inventory of the spike, we call it, of what the radar warning receiver tells us at the time. Nobody was calling anything threatening, so I made the decision to kick the formation away—not away as to turn around—but to put a vector that would increase the distance between us and the site launch. Looking at the missile, we finally decided that it never made it to the formation. It was one of those lucky shots that didn't turn out lucky for them, but it was like, the first thing you think about was: "What is the best course of action?" After that the training starts kicking in. You do a quick inventory, attempt to put the formation into a defensive position and assess again. It was just one thing

> after the other. You react to the triple-A, you react to the SAM, and then you start thinking about the target things.[21]

As with Pelletier, once Faucher became airborne over the Adriatic, the job at hand overtook everything else.

> At takeoff you become one with the airplane. You forget the rest of your problems in life because you've got a mission to do and everything becomes second nature. Because of the training we did, you're one with the airplane and the procedures, tactics, etc., really sink in and you're just flying and reacting. That night by the time the picture got clear, all these inputs, all these images coming in, well now you know what to expect. You know how to deal with it and we had a job to do which was dropping bombs.[22]

Faucher recalled the very minute when he felt all the years of training gel. That was ninety minutes into the mission, when the Canadians received word that enemy MiG fighters had been spotted on radar headed their way. "That's where your questions about all your training issues and the questions you've been asking yourself for the last hour and a half are answered because the co-ordination, the command and control identified these folks."[23] When the Dutch F-16s engaged those enemy planes, a picture emerged of what it was actually like to be in combat.

> It all adds to the picture that you see which is missiles firing, bombs dropping and, of course, airplanes like our F-16s firing missiles at these MiGs. I remember seeing that twitch in the sky, which after the fact, I didn't know what it was, but now I know. It was the missile impacting the first MiG and then becoming, slowly but surely, a big shooting star until it crashed right in front of us at about eight to ten miles. At two o'clock or at about the same location, there was a missile launch prior to the crash and that's when we quickly realized that these Serbs had a different tactical approach.[24]

Faucher recalls that the 30–40 seconds after the release of his first 500-pound laser-guided bomb seeming like an eternity. That release was the culmination not only of flying into combat but of a harrowing period of trying to identify pre-designated targets on a Forward Looking Infrared (FLIR) pod screen. That display sits on the top left of the CF-18's cockpit array. The roughly 20-centimetre by 20-centimetre digital screen is surrounded by an array of twenty buttons or tiles that let the pilots call up the different functions as required. When the pilot engages the FLIR functions, their infrared sensors identify physical features on the ground miles in the distance and display them as greenish images on a dark screen. The pilots can toggle between a wide display and a close-up four-power magnification display. A selected target can remain locked on the screen even as the pilot approaches and passes over it at hundreds of miles an hour.

What the pilots must do on a bombing mission is find their targets up to ten nautical miles away from an altitude of 20,000 and 25,000 feet by comparing actual features seen on maps programmed into their computers. Once a pilot is certain he has the target, a bomb is released. The pilot guides it onto the target on his screen, during a flight that can take up to forty seconds, through a laser designator, a computer joystick on the left-hand side of the cockpit, precisely at the same time as he manoeuvres the plane at combat speed with his right hand on the flight control joystick. For all the four-power magnification, the targets on the ground appear as flecks of light on the FLIR screens.

> You have to use those laser-guided weapons, put them in the right place at the right time, and during that time of flight, which, depending on where you drop, could be anywhere from thirty to forty seconds. There's not much you can do. You don't want that bomb to go astray on the civilian population somewhere else. At the same time, you'd like to be able to deal with whatever other inputs that could be dealing with you so you try to stick your bomb.[25]

Once in the air, Pelletier's and Faucher's wingman slipped into the routine of flying, but nothing could have prepared him for Serbian airspace. He described it in apocalyptic terms:

> There was plenty to see from the fires from the bombs going off, the whole western air force is basically dropping bombs on this country and it looked like, basically, it looked like hell. You know, there's black on the top and orange on the bottom, like the whole ground is burning. It was kind of difficult to tell what's fire, what's AAA. There's just fire everywhere.[26]

Flying last in the formation, the wingman could see the aftermath of the Dutch F-16 engaging the Serbian MiG.

> I heard the communications, but I didn't see anything until I saw an explosion on the ground. I saw kind of a fireball and it caught my eye and I looked over thinking, "SAM launch." Then I kind of reflected on the communications that I'd just heard and realized that it was the MiG that had just been shot down and the fireball that I was witnessing was the explosion of the MiG hitting the hill.[27]

The wingman also glimpsed what it was like to be on the receiving end of being engaged by the enemy. After three CF-18s had dropped their bombs on target, he picked up an electronic warning of a missile launch.

> Basically, after the target, I got an indication of a SAM launch. It was on me. I didn't see any SAM launch, it may have been ambiguous with a friendly threat radar that caused that indication, but unlikely. I kicked away from it. I deployed chaff and despite it, it came back again and I did the same thing again.[28]

At one point, the wingman said, he fell behind the formation. "I do remember getting stretched, like falling behind, due to I can't remember what, and turning around a corner and not being able to catch up. I'm basically at full power without the afterburners and not being able to catch up."[29]

If that was not enough on the first night of combat, the wingman admits he was the only one of the four who wasn't able to successfully drop his bombs that night.

> I was not able to ID the target. I felt horrible about it. What I just went through, terrifying as it was, terrifying, pushing across the border, I'm like: "This is it." I mean my heart's just going a million miles a minute and I'm thinking: "This is everything I've done, every ounce of training I've done so far has led to this moment." And then I come home having, you know, bringing my bombs back and it's just a, it's just a horrible feeling.[30]

The mission was far from over when Pelletier and his fellow pilots touched down on the runway back in Aviano. It and every other mission that followed concluded with debriefing sessions. The pilots met first within their own group of four and then with the squadron's intelligence officers to report on the success of the attack. Two of the pilots had hit their targets, one missed his target, and one didn't drop his bombs.[31] They had to review cockpit film of the attack on their target, the threats they encountered, and whether there had been any attempts to jam their communications. Only afterward could they reflect on what they had just done. Each saw it differently. Pelletier later remembered: "You really think about this. Hey, first of all we went through it, survived the threat that was out there. You think about it. You think about the positive outcome, but mainly you think about your decisions with regard to those actions or inputs you received in the air and whether they were the right ones."[32]

Faucher recalled that all of his self-doubting questions were answered.

> Is this whole thing going to work? By the time you cross enemy lines, the missiles start flying, airplanes start shooting other airplanes and you go: "Well, I guess what we've been learning really works." It was extremely well synchronized and the stuff that is in the books in terms of co-ordination, command, and control and so on and so forth, was really arriving, was really coming to reality, just like clockwork.

> It was amazing, a ballet in the sky, by the book and you go: "Well, I guess we're doing something right."[33]

The less experienced wingman was left to agonize over being the only one to not drop his bombs.

> I mean I don't think it was a hugely high-priority target. That may have been some of the comments made by some of the other pilots—that we were often fragged against low-priority targets rather than going for the head of the snake. That's kind of a political thing that I, as a wingman, was not really, caring too much about at the time. I mean, obviously, my one hope in life that night was to hit the target and it was just heart rending not to be able to do it.[34]

While the wingman agonized over his failure, his commanding officer (CO) Faucher was singing his praises.

> I'm never going to blame anyone. As a CO, I was never going to blame anyone and say: "You didn't identify the target." You just come back with the damn bomb, which he did, of course. That was the greatest thing on the planet that night because it showed that the guys were professional. They were not anxious to drop anything even if it was the first bomb of his life in a conflict. We were there for a mission and if it didn't work the way they wanted to, they were going to come back and do it the next day. The guys were not going to risk anything, whether the lives of the folks on the ground or their own, for no stupid reason.[35]

Meanwhile, Canadian CF-18 pilots and ground crew from CFB Cold Lake were all over the world. They were ordered to reach Aviano, as soon as possible by any way they could. Now-retired Lt. Col. William Allen Flynn—call sign "Billie"—commanded Cold Lake's 441 Tactical Fighter Squadron and led an advance party to Aviano on March 20 to replace 425 Tactical Fighter Squadron from Bagotville. Within three days of his arrival, his Cold Lake pilots were being integrated into the operational team. Flynn recalled there were twelve Bagotville pilots and eight Cold Lake pilots in the beginning. "Once we realized we were in for a longer haul, the Bagotville pilots in place were rotated out by Cold Lake 441."[36]

One of those 441 Squadron pilots, then-Capt. Kirk Soroka, was in France the morning of March 24, when he received a phone call to report for duty in Aviano as soon as possible. Soroka was in France to co-ordinate 441 Squadron pilots' involvement in Exercise Brilliant Foil, a massive exercise involving about 300 jets that was to take place over the English Channel in the first week of April. Soroka had been working with the French air force on the exercise for a year and had planned that the Canadian planes would arrive at the Soesterberg Air Base in the Netherlands on March 27. "We were going to be like coalition forces against coalition forces where there'd be blue forces versus grey forces and there would be about 300 jets flying at any one time. It was going to be an awesome exercise."[37]

Those plans went out the window with the beginning of the NATO bombing campaign on March 24.

> I told the French air force that the Canadians were withdrawing from Brilliant Foil on the morning of the 24th and I reported down south [to Aviano]. A few days later the jets showed up in Holland and sat there. There were six ships sitting there waiting for orders to either come back to Canada or swap out with the jets in Aviano which was the intent of Brilliant Foil.[38] We would finish the exercise then my squadron was going to take over in Aviano from 3 Wing or 425 Squadron. Their planes would go back to Canada and our planes would step into the fight.[39]

Soroka arrived in Aviano by a commercial flight as the first wave of Bagotville pilots was dropping bombs in Serbia. A Bagotville pilot, who goes by the radio call sign "Tubs," was 433 Tactical Fighter Squadron's weapons and tactics officer when the war broke out. He was at home in Bagotville when he received a phone call March 23 to catch a commercial flight that would take him to Aviano. He had spent about eight months in Aviano previously in various rotations and was on ready reserve when the phone call came. "I was on notice to move, so when it looked like it was going to happen, I just hit the airport and off I went."[40] Twenty-four hours later, he arrived in Aviano and watched the first four CF-18s led by Pelletier launch into the evening sky. The policy was that he had to have thirty-six hours of down time after a trans-oceanic flight, so he was unable to fly his first combat mission until night three of the air war.

441 Squadron pilot Capt. Brett Glaeser, who goes by the radio call sign "Laser," recalls vividly how he received notice to report to Aviano. Twenty-seven-year-old Glaeser was at home at Cold Lake having dinner with his wife and another CF-18 pilot and his wife on March 25. They watched news of the aerial bombing campaign unfold on television.

> What was memorable for me: We were having dinner, watching CNN and our wives were kind of giving us a hard time because we weren't really paying attention to the dinner conversation. We were looking over our shoulder at CNN, what was going on. When the bombing started I just remember them saying: "The United States has attacked Serbia. Bombs are falling." We both, him and I, both stood up and walked over. We were glued to the TV for about a half an hour and then we decided we better go back and eat with our wives. So, we go back to sit down and no sooner did I sit down than the phone rang and it was my CO over in Aviano. He said: "Laser, can you and Brass, which is another guy in my squadron, can you two guys get an airplane as soon as you can, or get two airplanes and bring them over as soon as you can? We want you guys to come over right away." So the next day we were in to work, we took airplanes and left.[41]

Glaeser, a newly qualified combat-ready wingman, had been with the squadron for only about ten months and knew his rookie status compared to other, more senior pilots. He was in the process of upgrading his qualifications, but he hadn't yet qualified to lead a two-ship element or four-aircraft formation into combat.

I was being sent over into a combat environment as a wingman basically, so I was a confident, capable wingman, not a qualified lead yet. I was totally happy to go, like pumped up. All the guys I flew with I totally respected. They had way more experience than I did. At the time, my squadron, 441, had so much experience on the CF-18 it was ridiculous. The average hours flying time on squadron at that time was probably 1,500 to 2,000 hours in the airplane. I was one of the least experienced guys.[42]

The other 441 pilot that Glaeser's commanding officer Lt. Col. Flynn mentioned in his phone call to Glaeser was Capt. Travis Brassington—"Brass." Brassington remembers everyone thinking that the bombing campaign would only last three days and by the time they arrived in Aviano they might miss the action. "We thought we were going to miss it and then it would be over. In fact, we thought they wouldn't even let us land at Aviano because we had visions of wave after wave of airplanes taking off and landing and that they wouldn't be able to tell us to land."[43] Brassington and Glaeser married up in the hangars on March 26 with another CF-18 pilot who was to fly a third CF-18 with them as far as Goose Bay, Newfoundland, as a spare, in case one of the jets "snagged," or became unserviceable. Brassington recalled both the feeling of uncertainty he had and the emotions he was experiencing as they prepared to taxi their jets for takeoff. "We didn't know what was going to go on. When we taxied, I actually asked for a taxi with ground here because it was pretty emotional. I said, you know: 'Hey ground. Taxi three Hornets for God, Queen and country.' And off we went."[44]

With all of the US refuelling tankers tied up with America's own strategic lift and combat needs, the pilots had to rely on the least two preferred options to fly their CF-18s to Aviano: air-to-air refuelling on a Hercules and island hopping. They left Cold Lake and air-to-air refuelled off a Canadian C-130 Hercules, which let them fly to Goose Bay, Labrador. From Labrador they flew to Keflavik, Iceland, where they stayed overnight. From Keflavik they flew to Ramstein, Germany, via Kinloss, Scotland. They couldn't fly directly from Germany to Italy because a landing couldn't be scheduled due to the bombing campaign. Instead they stayed overnight in Germany and eventually flew into Aviano on March 29 after three days of flying. Glaeser remembers the sobering evening he and Brassington spent on March 27 in Iceland when the reality of heading off to war finally hit home.

> Normally when we go on the road and we land somewhere it's, you know, we'll go out for dinner. We'll kind of go out late. This night we were just like, "Nah. let's just have dinner in the hotel and just hang out in the hotel." We started watching CNN again. There wasn't really anything special going on, so we decided we were going to go to bed early because we had a big day the next day. Then, as I went to bed in my room, CNN came on and said: "The American F-117 has been shot down. The stealth fighter has been shot down." I immediately went back to Brass's room and I said: "Did you see that? I think a Stealth just got shot down." We were both like, there was a moment of clarity. We were both like: "Oh my God. We're actually going in. This is for real you know." At that point it was like: "All right. This is real. This isn't just a game. That airplane's supposed to be, it's the Stealth fighter, come on that airplane's supposed to be fairly hard to detect and shoot down. How did they do that?" The fact that we're bringing F-18s over, it was just like: "OK. We're really going to have to be on our game." I called my wife right away and said: "Did you see that? The Stealth got shot down." She's like: "Yeah." But we never questioned the fact that we were going to do our job.[45]

Upon arrival in Aviano, one of the first people pilots like Glaeser and Brassington had to talk to was Soroka, the Canadian pilots' expert on survival training. Soroka was referred to by his colleagues by his call sign "Rambo." Pilots' call signs are picked for them by their colleagues. Soroka was tagged with the "Rambo" call sign because he is an ex-infantryman who spent six years with the 3rd Battalion Princess Patricia's Canadian Light Infantry before joining the air force as an officer cadet in 1989. Tough as nails, Soroka took advanced combat training, learned how to parachute from transport planes, and trained in jungle warfare in Panama and in winter warfare in Alaska in January. As the squadron's combat search-and-rescue officer, his biggest concern was that the Canadian pilots had never trained in combat search and rescue and didn't have the capability to recover and extract a pilot shot down by the enemy.[46]

Soroka had identified escape-and-evasion problems in the Canadian air force long before the bombing campaign began, starting with their standard-issue blue flight suits. About the same colour as blue jeans, they had bright zippers and patches. They were the transport aircraft pilots' flight suit of choice, but no fighter pilot who could be forced to bail out deep in enemy territory was comfortable with them. They were dangerous. They stood out. The other problem was the survival pack in the CF-18 seat, which would hang by straps below the pilot in the event of an ejection. Soroka discovered its problems when he took escape-and-evasion training in the desert in 1998 with Americans out of Holloman Air Force Base, New Mexico. For two days, he had to avoid a hunter force of fourteen with search dogs. In the seat pack was Lypsyl™, Kleenex™, fishing line, glow sticks, and, originally, a little beacon that was replaced by a radio. The first and major problem with the seat pack was its colour. Soroka explained: "It was all based on peacetime survival in the boreal forest, maybe even the Arctic. Everything was wrapped in bright orange shiny tinfoil. When I was down in the desert, any time I took it out, I was afraid that it would be like a mirror and the enemy would come get me. So, I buried it and left it."[47] The other problem was the radio's location in the seat pack. The radio had to be on the pilot's body, because during ejection, if the seat pack line snapped, all the survival equipment, including the radio, would be lost.

Upon his return to Canada, Soroka reported on what pilots needed in their search-and-rescue packs, based on Canada's NORAD and NATO commitments. Among the recommendations was that pilots needed survival equipment sufficient for three days, including water pumps and radios that could be carried on their person in a combat vest. His recommendations went to the Canadian Forces Aeronautical Engineering and Test Establishment (AETE), which started developing the vest in 1998.

The first problem to be rectified was the blue flight suits. In 1998, the CF-18 fighter squadron commanders in Cold Lake and Bagotville bucked the chain of command and ordered green Nomex® fire-resistant flight suits used by the US military.⁴⁸ The chain of command was displaced. Soroka explained: "We were told that we could wear these flight suits interim only. When they basically wore out, you could start wearing the Canadian ones. Well, guys are still wearing them five years later, because they refuse to wear the issue."⁴⁹ The seat pack and its contents, however, remained a bigger problem. Soroka recalled that, more than a year later in Aviano, "when the shooting started, pilots were still flying with the peacetime boreal forest seat pack, the Lypsyl™, the Kleenex™, the tin foil wrapping and the bright orange bags."⁵⁰

There was another set of search-and-rescue problems: the radio in the seat pack. With no indigenous rescue capability, the Canadians would have to rely on their allies, but their radios were incompatible with NATO allies' equipment. The Canadians needed PRC-112 combat search-and-rescue radios, complete with internal global positioning systems.⁵¹ An alternative to putting their survival radio in the seat pack was to put it in one of their flight suits' leg pockets, but that wasn't much of a solution at all, because during ejection, that was likely to be lost as well. They needed proper, robust combat vests.

The radio problem was the first to be rectified in theatre. It began with a phone call to Brig. Gen. David Jurkowski, the Canadian military's Chief of Staff, Joint Operations, in Ottawa who phoned the Challenger flying unit, gave them his (government) credit card number. He ordered them to fly to the manufacturer's location and to buy forty of the radios and have them delivered. A day-and-a half later the pilots were training on the radios and flying with them. Brig.-Gen. Jurkowski recalled that, in Ottawa, they were vaguely aware of the search-and-rescue radio limitations but acted quickly when asked for the PRC-112s.

> We kind of suspected they weren't there before but, you see, you throw away the plans as soon as you go to war or as soon as you go into combat. You develop things. There is a requirement that pops up that nobody thought of before and so you fix it. You get onto what the hell it was that you need to do. In terms of search and rescue, of course, the Americans basically were the only ones with a robust capability; therefore, we had to be one with them in equipment.

1.1. Captain Kirk "Rambo" Soroka outfitted in a new green flight suit, a laser visor and new combat survival vest he argued was necessary to carry out search and rescue radios mission in the event a pilot was shot down. To his left is a 500-pound GBU-12 Paveway II laser-guided bomb. Photo courtesy of the Department of National Defence.

> But it was fixed, you know, that's why you have a task force commander on the ground.[52]

At the same time, Soroka called the AETE staff in Canada, saying, "We've got to get these vests over there now. We needed them yesterday."[53] Soroka flew his first combat mission from Aviano on the night of April 3 and was in Aviano when the PRC-112 radios arrived, with four of the urgently requested combat vests arriving the third week into the campaign. Once they arrived, two problems had to be resolved immediately. None of the pilots had ever worked with the radio before or trained with their allies on the NATO search-and-rescue protocols. Although everyone knew that an American F 117A Nighthawk Stealth fighter had been shot down, there wasn't a structured search-and-rescue training plan in Aviano. The solution was to have Soroka arrive early on the days the pilots planned their flights and brief his fellow pilots as best he could.

> I would come in early and I would grab a vest and I would look and if I hadn't talked to a pilot yet, I'd say: "OK come with me." We'd sit down on a couple chairs and I'd say: "Here's your vest. You just got shot down in Serbia." I'd show him on the evasion map where he was and I'd ask him: "Okay, so talk me through what you're going to do." And that's how I taught them. I also confirmed that they learned the information they needed to know.[54]

The second problem was that the AETE staff had manufactured only twenty of the new combat vests. The pilots had to pair up with someone the same size who flew on an alternate day. That was possible because each pilot flew one day and planned flights the next day. To say that the CF-18 pilots were as confident as Soroka in their ability to carry out their own rescues vastly overstates the case. It became a running joke in the preflight briefings. One pilot said, "We used to say, 'If I get shot down, your job is to shoot down Rambo, so he can come and save my ass.'"[55]

On a more serious note, the prospect of getting shot down still weighed heavily on the pilots' minds. Canada had not declared war on Serbia, a fact that had important legal implications for pilots shot down and captured. One pilot explained:

> As pilots, we could have benefited from what's associated with being at war but we were never given that. In fact, the government never admitted that Canadians were at war. Based on the laws of armed conflict and war, if I'd been shot down after attacking a sovereign nation, I'm essentially a criminal. If I was at war, I'm entitled to the protection of the Geneva Convention and that was something that, depending on where you were shot down, determined how you were treated. If you were inside Serbia, you claimed POW status. Outside of Serbia, you claimed mission specialist status. I didn't know what mission specialist status meant, but that's what the guys were told to say. That's what was written down. To me that was the most terrifying thing.[56]

2

Planning for War

The year 1998 began with good news for the Canadian Forces. Some 15,000 personnel had been deployed to southern Quebec, eastern Ontario, and rural New Brunswick after massive ice storms wreaked havoc in the two provinces. Power lines were knocked out by ice and falling trees, leaving one million people without heat and power, including residents in Montreal and Ottawa. Soldiers from across Canada assisted power crews in the biggest peacetime deployment of the country's history. They helped to evacuate the most desperate and feed people in shelters and were given emergency policing duties to foil looters. Their efforts encouraged media outlets across Canada to report on local soldiers who were deployed in the Herculean rescue effort.

This was a huge morale boost to the men and women in the Canadian Forces. In the five years since a Canadian Airborne Regiment soldier, Master Cpl. Clayton Matchee, tortured and killed a sixteen-year-old Somali prisoner Shidane Abukar Arone, most of the news about the military had been bad. Media inquiries, court martial proceedings, the disbanding of the Airborne Regiment in disgrace in 1995 and a Commission of Inquiry into the Deployment of the Canadian Forces to Somalia and its hearings and witnesses, and news about document destruction and resignations all provided headline fodder for two years that portrayed a military in disarray.[1] When the tired soldiers finally returned home from the icy disasters in New Brunswick, Quebec, and Ontario, they were able finally to bask in the glow of local media outlets that eagerly portrayed them as hometown heroes.

The early months of 1998 were also a busy time for the Canadian military. In February, the Canadian Forces launched a recruiting drive to attract more women to military jobs. Overseas, a Canadian Hercules aircraft completed its first operational air-to-air refuelling mission involving two US Navy F/A-18 jet fighters in the Persian Gulf. In April, the Canadian Forces deployed forty-five soldiers to a United Nations peacekeeping operation in the Central African Republic. The government also announced it would spend $750 million to acquire and modify four diesel-electric used submarines from Britain that, it said, would ready the navy for the challenges of the twenty-first century, sparking a lengthy debate on the wisdom of the purchase. In May, the Canadian government sent thirty military personnel and ten front-end loaders to Sarno, Italy, to help clean up after heavy rain triggered massive mudslides that killed some 135 and left another 1,500 homeless.

But much also was going on elsewhere in the world as winter moved into spring in 1998 that pushed even the best news stories about the Canadian military to the media's back burner. Sex sells, and there were plenty of opportunities for news outlets to titillate readers and viewers with lurid details about a sex scandal developing in the United States involving President Bill Clinton. In early January, he was required to testify under oath about allegedly exposing himself to former state employee Paula Jones and asking her for oral sex while he was still governor of Arkansas. Things got much worse in the coming months as old problems with Jones were overshadowed by an avalanche of new allegations of presidential sexual activity that threatened his marriage and presidency. In "Zippergate," a play on the Watergate affair that saw President Richard Nixon resign rather than be impeached, Clinton faced impeachment on perjury and obstruction charges related to the Jones case and his affair with a twenty-one-year-old White House intern, Monica Lewinsky.

Meanwhile, moviegoers set box office records flocking to see *Titanic*, directed by Canadian filmmaker James Cameron. In January, it captured Golden Globes for best dramatic film and best original score and song for "My Heart Will Go On" by Canadian songstress Celine Dion. In March, Cameron and Dion won Academy Awards in the same categories and the movie tied an industry record, winning eleven Oscars.

Canadian sporting fans' plates were full with the news the best player ever to play in the Canadian Football League, Toronto Argonaut quarterback Doug Flutie, had signed with the Buffalo Bills in America's National Football League. Flutie won Grey Cups with the Calgary Stampeders in 1992 and the Argos in 1996 and 1997. In February, the Canadian men's hockey team, led by Canadian legend Wayne Gretzky, arrived amid pandemonium in Nagano, Japan, for the 1998 Olympic Winter Games. The star-studded men's team, expected to win a gold medal, was knocked out of contention in a controversial overtime best-of-five shootout with the Czech Republic. The Czechs scored only once, but the Canadians could not score on Dominik Hasek. Astonishingly, Gretzky, the most talented hockey player and prolific scorer ever to lace up a pair of skates, sat on the bench during the shootout. The men's team came home empty-handed, while the women's hockey team settled for silver. Easily one of the most surprising Canadian newsmakers during the Olympics was unknown Ross Rebagliati, of Whistler, BC, who won a gold medal in giant slalom snowboarding. Rebagliati, stripped of his medal after urine samples tested positive for marijuana, claimed he had only been exposed to second-hand smoke. His medal eventually was reinstated after the amounts detected were found to be so minute they could not have affected his performance.

In late February, political leaders headed off a series of pre-emptive strikes by Israel or America against Iraq's developing missile program by brokering a deal to give United Nations inspectors unfettered access to its weapons sites. But the major international concern in the spring of 1998 was the news that India had set off three underground nuclear tests, enraging its neighbour Pakistan and defying the world community with a celebratory announcement that it was capable of making nuclear weapons. Speaking at a G8 summit in England, Prime Minister Jean Chrétien publicly feared an arms race in south Asia and thought it was just a matter of weeks before Pakistan—which had previously fought wars with India in 1948 and 1965 over the disputed region of Kashmir—set off its own series of nuclear tests.

Given the staggering magnitude of events globally, it would take a lot for the Canadian military to crack newspaper front pages and television network news lineups, but it did. An avalanche of news reports of rape and sexual harassment of female Canadian Forces members dominated the headlines and news reports across Canada for months. These reports were sparked by two in-depth reports in *Maclean's* newsmagazine's May 25 and June 1 editions. The first reported on thirteen women who claimed they had been sexually assaulted while in the military. The second edition carried reports of eleven more women who came forward after the first, who told tales of sexual harassment, assault, and rape. The June 1 edition led with a front-page picture of former CF-18 pilot Dee Brasseur, with an insert picture poised in front of her jet fighter, who claimed she had been forced into sex by her Canadian Forces flight instructor.

The cartoons in the May 12 *Globe and Mail* and the June 1 edition of the *Vancouver Sun* about the Canadian Forces said it all. The *Globe* cartoon showed a helmeted soldier with a pony tail with a pair of groping hands from soldiers to her left reaching toward her. The *Sun* cartoon showed darkened images of a tank, a jet fighter, a submarine, a missile, an attack helicopter, and a curvy outline of a woman it identified underneath as "BABE." For a proud but notoriously thin-skinned institution like the Canadian Forces that doesn't take criticism—let alone ridicule—well, the reports of some military members' sordid sexual behaviour drove the relationship with the Canadian news media to a new low.

It was on a hot, muggy day with a light breeze in Ottawa, 11 June 1998, when Canadian air force Col. Benoît Marcotte had been summoned to DND's grey headquarters at 101 Colonel By Drive. As with so many recent days, the news reaching Canadians about their military was all bad. Headlines in newspapers across Canada screamed out allegations of the rape of a female army recruit, Ann Margaret Dickey of Oromocto, New Brunswick, at a military base in St. Jean, Quebec. But the subject Marcotte would talk about at National Defence Headquarters (NDHQ) had nothing to do with the sex scandal and everything to do with Kosovo, the tortured Serbian province half a world away.

The average Canadian could be forgiven for knowing little about Kosovo, home to about 1.75 million Muslim Albanians and 200,000 Orthodox Serbs. The ethnic (Muslim) Albanians, by 1998, had been struggling for years for independence following the collapse of the Soviet Union and the breakup of the former Yugoslavia in 1991, but nationalist Serbs considered Kosovo their historic homeland. Impatient with the political progress toward independence, militants formed the Kosovo Liberation Army (KLA) to fight for it. Serbian police and military units under the command of Slobodan Milosevic responded with brutal ethnic cleansing, which by August 1998 saw up to 230,000 displaced and other 50,000 homeless. Ethnic cleansing had been widespread from 1992 to 1995 in Bosnia. Unprecedented North Atlantic Treaty Organization bombing attacks on Bosnian Serb positions around Sarajevo in August 1995 led to the establishment of NATO Stabilization and Implementation Forces and a NATO-enforced no-fly zone that eventually brought stability to Bosnia.

The emerging humanitarian crisis in Kosovo in 1998 was but the latest chapter of misery inflicted on the long-suffering people of the former Yugoslavia. But, given the world events elsewhere, it is not surprising that a news report of the deaths of sixteen Albanians and four Serbian policemen in a six-paragraph Reuters News Agency report on March 2 was the first to crack the pages of Canadian newspapers, however tepidly. It was buried on page A11 in the *Globe and Mail* beneath a story on India's new coalition government. That ranking would change, however, as the rampage of ethnic cleansing of Albanians reached crisis proportions and world leaders woke up to a new humanitarian disaster looming in the Balkans.

By June, Canadian newspapers regularly carried prominent, often front-page reports of the escalating violence. The seriousness of the situation prompted NATO defence ministers to meet in Brussels. By June 3, they considered deploying 20,000 troops to Macedonia and Albania, given mounting fears that the clashing KLA and Serb soldiers and police, coupled with ethnic cleansing, could cause a military crisis. By June 8, one of the world's biggest news stories was that Britain's prime minister, Tony Blair, and US president Clinton expected to seek a United Nations Security Council resolution to set the stage for NATO military action to halt the bloodshed in Kosovo. One day later, the fifteen-member European Union imposed economic sanctions on Belgrade, while Blair raised the possibility of NATO air strikes to push Serb leader Milosevic to the negotiating table in order to secure an end to the ethnic cleansing and autonomy for Kosovo.

Col. Marcotte was the former commander of Operation Mirador, Canada's contribution of six CF-18s from CFB Cold Lake to the NATO-enforced no-fly zone over Bosnia-Herzegovina, which ended on 15 November 1997. The notes in his personal Day-timer show that he was called to NDHQ on the afternoon of June 11 and told of NATO's request that Canada join the planning for Operation Echo, an aerial bombing campaign for Kosovo that was already being considered in June by NATO defence ministers.[2]

"I was informed at that time", Marcotte said, "that Bagotville was selected as the operational wing which would deploy—if Canada accepted the invitation—and, strong of the experience the previous year as the Commander of Op Mirador, a similar deployment of CF-18s into Aviano, I was being asked to lead the initial phase of this new operational deployment."[3] At that time, 3 Wing Bagotville started planning and polished off its training requirements in anticipation of the deployment of six CF-18s. Although Canada had been invited to join the coalition, an air base had not yet been designated for Canadian warplanes. But discussions were already taking place among Canadian, NATO, and Italian officials for the return of the CF-18s to Aviano, Italy.

Marcotte recalled:

> That base was already very busy with early operations linked to the growing Kosovo crisis and places to park coalition aircraft were at a premium. Also, within Canada, while the planning was going on, our government had to determine if we were going to accept the invitation. This planning was progressing well, and late on Thursday June 18, the advance party was put on twenty-four-hour readiness to deploy.[4]

The government's quiet approval for Operation Echo on Saturday, June 20, came two days after the House of Commons had adjourned for the summer. Marcotte and his advance party were told to deploy to Aviano soon after. That night they boarded a Canadian Forces Airbus to Europe.[5] The first six CF-18s were scheduled to deploy to Italy on June 24.

The sprawling air base at Aviano was at that time headquarters for the US 16th Air Force and two F-16 squadrons with the 31st Fighter Wing, which had the Mediterranean Region as its area of responsibility. It is in the scenic Po Valley where the Dolomiti Alps loom in the distance. Lush vineyards and wineries dot the rich agricultural and industrial plain surrounding it. Also a popular tourist destination, Aviano is about twenty kilometres from the internationally renowned ski resort of Piancavallo and fifteen minutes away from the historic city of Pordenone.

Within hours of Marcotte's arrival in Aviano on June 21, he met the 31st Fighter Wing Operations Group Commander and left most of the advance party in Aviano in the hands of a major from his wing. The advance party was to work out the Canadian contingent's operational and logistics details, including arrangements for CF-18 parking, hardened aircraft shelters, maintenance areas for the aircraft, and the contingent's living quarters. After lunch, Marcotte and two others were on the road for the two-hour drive to Vicenza, an inland city about 100 kilometres west of Aviano near the northern tip of the Adriatic Sea. Vicenza was home to the US Army's Southern European Task Force and NATO's Combined Air Operations Centre (CAOC). Marcotte was responsible for setting up the Canadian contingent in the CAOC.[6]

Starting on June 22, he had meetings to secure facilities for Canadian headquarters in trailers in Vicenza, access to all operational areas, and the insertion of the Canadian contingent aircraft into NATO air operations out of Aviano. He had to familiarize himself with operational plans and the rules of engagement and work on national activities such as the Canadian terms of reference for the operation and the less strategic local contracts for required services such as rental cars for the deployed contingent. He worked with NDHQ in Ottawa to set up the terms for the Canadian military personnel's deployment, including allowances, sports facilities, recreation, amenities, laundry, and dry cleaning. In Ottawa, the role that Canadian CF-18s would have within the coalition was discussed among NATO officials while discussions took place with Italian officials to secure approval for the Canadian CF-18s' flights from Italian airfields and in Italian airspace.

In Canada, Aviano, and Vicenza, the air force activities continued at a pace set on edge by the potential for participation in the first protracted combat campaign involving Canadian pilots since 1945.[7] On June 24, three days after MPs adjourned to their constituencies across Canada for the barbecue circuits during the dog days of summer, six Canadian Forces CF-18s assigned to Aviano took off from CFB Bagotville. They were already three days late. Just four days after the government's approval for

Operation Echo, the cracks in the readiness posture the Canadian Forces maintained were beginning to show.

In 1998, the auditor general of Canada reported that the Canadian navy was seriously deficient in its projected need for four support ships on the east and west coasts to provide strategic sea lift capability. The navy was operating with only three support ships.[8] Canadian Forces Hercules C-130 strategic and tactical transport aircraft could provide airlift for passengers and cargo and some air-to-air refuelling.[9] The aging CF-18 fighter aircraft procured by the Canadian Forces in the 1980s, the auditor general noted without being specific, lagged in advanced technology available in other aircraft that represented a potential threat. However, it noted that CF-18 squadrons had acquired precision-guided munitions and associated delivery systems.[10] In fact, for all its criticisms of the Canadian Forces, the auditor general's report was overly optimistic in assessing its strategic capabilities.

For example, despite the auditor general's observation that the Hercules C-130 could provide "some" air-to-air refuelling capabilities, both before and during the Kosovo air campaign the lack of an indigenous air-to-air refuelling capability created critical deficiencies. Canada had a core capability of air-to-air refuelling only until 1997, when its fleet of Boeing 707s was retired.[11] That retirement limited air-to-air refuelling capability, which restricted the deployments of the original six CF-18s and the force package increase from six to eighteen aircraft. Given the limited air-to-air refuelling capability, the Task Force Aviano commander was compelled to approach NATO allies to develop "tenuous operational planning and scheduling to achieve the mission."[12] Details beyond this limited observation were exempt from *Access to Information Act* release, citing international affairs and defence considerations.[13]

Canada's limited air-to-air refuelling and sea lift capabilities manifested themselves from day one with the first deployment of six CF-18s from Bagotville on 21 June 1998. The problem was this: Canada's thirty-two C-130 Hercules transport planes were and are the workhorses of the Canadian Forces. They are used for troop transport, cargo and equipment transport, and on search-and-rescue missions. They can also be reconfigured to carry up to 100 planeloads of fuel that enables air-to-air refuelling of fighters. However, they have a maximum ceiling of 10,770 metres and a propeller-driven maximum speed of 556 kilometres per hour,[14] whereas the CF-18 jets have a ceiling of 15,000 metres and a top speed of Mach 1.8, or nearly twice the speed of sound.[15] The lumbering Hercules C-130s reconfigured to an air-to-air refuelling role were woefully inadequate for refuelling CF-18s on transatlantic flights. A CF-18 fighter pilot who flew in the Kosovo air campaign explained:

> The Hercs are not strategic tankers, they're tactical tankers, so they cannot fly very high. They don't fly fast. We can't just stay on their wing forever. They fly at about, I don't know, 230 to 250 knots, and they stay at lower altitude. Lower altitudes, most times, means worse weather and you can't climb above the weather [with the Hercules]. It's not a place we [the CF-18s] want to be. There's altitudes we cannot fly at because of the equipment, so just being on the wing of a Strat tanker is just so easy for us.[16]

The other option for pilots on transatlantic flights was to island hop: to fly from Bagotville to Goose Bay, Labrador, where they would refuel; then to Keflavik, Iceland, where they would refuel; and then to Germany, where they would refuel again before flying to Aviano. That is only a marginally worse option than flying with a Canadian Hercules tanker. They do it, but they don't like it.

> Every time you stop a jet and you shut down the engine there's a chance there might be something breaking with it. Those are pretty high-tech systems so if you keep a jet running, it just keeps running, but when you shut down and stop, now you might have a hydraulic leak. You might have a snag between the time you shut down and start again, so something might go wrong and so, for us, not having to stop is a big plus. If you're stuck in Keflavik, then you have to have a mobile repair party and so on. It makes things more complicated, for sure.[17]

As a result, Brig.-Gen. David Jurkowski, the Canadian military's Chief of Staff, Joint Operations, was on the telephone in Ottawa to his American counterpart in the Pentagon for help. His counterpart in the Chairman of the Joint Chiefs of Staff office, was able to assist thanks to long-standing co-operative arrangements established by the Permanent Joint Board on Defence during the Second World War[18] For the For the Kosovo air war, Jurkowski was number two in the Canadian military's operational chain of command. The Chief of Defence Staff was Gen. Maurice Baril, but the day-to-day operations of Canadians overseas—including eighteen different missions—was the responsibility of Deputy Chief of Defence Staff Lt.-Gen. Raymond Henault. Jurkowski reported directly to Henault.

Jurkowski recalled his interchange with the Americans:

> It was brilliant, you know. The kinds of conversation would be: "Hey, so-and-so, how are you doing? Me again. Listen, we want to send half a dozen F-18s over to Aviano. We need a tanker because we no longer have strategic tankers and there's nothing on the horizon. Can you help us out?" "When do you want to move?" "Tuesday." "Okay, stand by. We'll call you back." Call back about an hour or two later. "Listen we're really sorry we can't do it on Tuesday, but how about Wednesday?" They were brilliant, they were really supportive, really helpful. We would rendezvous with them and they'd take care of us.[19]

Jurkowski's negotiations resulted in arrangements for American KC-10 air tankers to rendezvous with the Bagotville CF-18s over the St. Lawrence and mid-Atlantic. However, it took three days to conduct those negotiations. The CF-18s eventually took off from Bagotville on June 24, three days after their original planned departure, reaching Aviano, at 8:45 p.m.[20] Baril signed the Canadian terms of reference for the military contribution to Operation Echo in Ottawa on 25 June 1998.[21]

However, the military's air transportation problems were not over. The Operation Echo after-action report notes heavy-air lift deficiencies rendered the Canadian Forces totally dependent on commercial sources. That dependency caused significant expenses and formidable limitations on the ability to commence rapid operations. For example, the air force had to abandon the Hercules for transport of its supplies and equipment. Instead, it contracted two An-124 Antonov civilian aircraft from a Russian firm to move its equipment from Bagotville into Aviano. Unfortunately, the Italian government was reluctant to let commercial aircraft on a military air base even though it was operated by the American military and the two cargo planes were loaded with military equipment.[22] Hence the two Antonovs and their Canadian non-commissioned officer escorts were stuck in Greenland for a week after leaving Canadian airspace.[23]

Cpl. Patrick Savoie, an aviation technician with 3 Wing Bagotville's Air Maintenance Squadron at the time, was sent to Aviano on a Canadian Forces Airbus CC-150 Polaris in the Canadians' bomb dump/missile lab group. Upon arrival, there was nothing for those in second-line support for weapons and munitions to do for upward of two weeks due to the Antonovs problem.

> We went over there with minimum stuff, our own personal baggage. Everything else—trucks, tools, equipment, munitions, boots, screwdrivers, extra towels, aircraft jacks—those two Antonovs had everything on them. I had a laptop computer from the shop with me to do the weapons inventory because I carried it with me on the Airbus to go over. If I had not brought it along and said, "Oh, I'll put it with the tools, I don't want to carry it," I wouldn't have had a computer to work with to do the weapons inventory.[24]

A Canadian government diplomatic intervention was required to authorize the deployment of the OP ECHO main party and the logistical equipment into Aviano via heavy lift Antonov cargo planes chartered by the Canadian government. Otherwise, the Canadian Forces operational readiness in Aviano could have been severely delayed.[25] Col Marcotte recalled some of the negotiations involved in finally getting permission for Antonov aircraft to land in Aviano to complete this deployment. "These negotiations were being done by NDHQ and likely other Canadian government departments and agencies. I was involved from Vicenza and served as a conduit with the operations' group in Aviano to find a compromise on the Antonov landing times which would meet the requirements of all parties."[26] His personal records showed the following:

> NATO and Italy finally accepted on June 24 that AN-124s would be allowed to land into and take-off from Aviano during nighttime but that they could support only one Antonov per night. The resolution of this deployment hurdle was welcomed to finally get the full contingent on the ground and minimize the charter costs which were adding up while landing clearances were being negotiated.[27]

Once Marcotte set up the basic logistics for the establishment of Canada's Task Force Aviano, it needed a full-time commander. The problem was where to find one. In the end, Lt. Col. Jim Donihee gave up command of 410 Tactical Fighter (Operational Training) Squadron, a CF-18 fighter training squadron at CFB Cold Lake, to take the job. Donihee, promoted to colonel, assumed command of the newly formed Task Force Aviano in Aviano on 5 August 1998. He held that position for four months. Donihee recalled commanding Task Force Aviano as being a particularly frustrating experience.

> The first part of my duties really was to get the unit stood up, to get them bedded down, to get the local operating procedures established, to get the rules and regulations and administrative procedures all in place. One of my disappointments, which was one of the greatest indicators of where Ottawa was at with a lot of these things, was that it took me longer to get permission for the alcohol policy than it did to get permission for the rules of engagement surrounding the employment of deadly force. I think that was really just all the aftermath of the Somalia affair and so much sensitivity and so much concern about having an occurrence of that nature. It actually consumed more of my time and effort than getting the unit established on an operational footing.[28]

Cpl. Savoie understood why Donihee was so frustrated over the alcohol policy. Savoie was sent with the first wave of about 100 Canadians and arrived with the main contingent on June 25. The senior officer on the plane, most likely a major, told everyone that Aviano would be "dry" for the Canadians. There would be no drinking. However, the advance party members sent to Aviano to prepare the ground for the main body were already familiar with Aviano's hot muggy weather. In the interest of boosting their comrades' morale upon arrival, they had water and a table full of free beer ready for the troops when they landed. Savoie recalled:

> When we first went in there, we were just sitting around waiting and there was free beer sitting there, so what did we do? We drank. Most people just took a beer or two—a few of us took a little more. One guy did a three-point landing in the dirt. We picked him up, carried him out and took care of him. Unfortunately, he did it in front of everybody, including the senior leadership, so right away it was obvious this could become a problem.[29]

Complicating the senior leadership's development of an alcohol policy was the fact that upon their arrival, the Canadians were housed in modular "shacks" like the portable trailers used by civilians as construction offices. They were part of a huge tent city set up by the American military. It comprised about 200 shelters, each of which housed between eight and ten people. Although they were cramped, most felt the trailers were better than sleeping in a tent or, worse, a trench. The American base also housed some fifty tents, a Burger King, and a Base Exchange tent where soldiers could rent videos, shoot pool, play bingo, and, most importantly, buy beer. The American base also was not far from a little town, replete with Italian restaurants and world-renowned wine.

Savoie says the technicians in Aviano were no different than many soldiers past or present. "The 425 technicians were party animals. They got the work done, but they enjoyed a good party. So, our idea was to work hard, party hard. Everything's fine as long as the work gets done."[30] Sometimes, Savoie said, the soldiers had a few beers after their shifts, but more often than not, a group would get together in one vehicle and "go to a good Italian restaurant and order good Italian wine. You know, it was quite normal. We acted and treated it the same way as we do when we go down to the southern United States to use one of their training facilities. We weren't at war."[31]

Savoie said: "The [drinking] policy pretty much came up to no drinking eight hours before you use a military or rented vehicle. Also, don't get into trouble because if it becomes a problem, everybody will be dry. The military always has this problem of you're allowed to do something until somebody screws up, then nobody's allowed to do it."[32] The Canadians in Aviano officially went dry as a matter of policy three months later at the end of August. Unofficially, the troops still found time to indulge after hours. "The same happened during the [1991] Gulf War. I mean, we're in Italy. There's vineyards surrounding the base. Have you ever heard of a military unit anywhere succeeding in keeping dry? Never, ever."[33]

Back in Ottawa, the Chief of Defence Staff's alcohol policy considerations all were driven by a scandal four years earlier, a result of the torture and killing of a Somalia teenager in March 1994 at a Canadian Airborne Regiment camp near Belet Huen, Somalia. Jurkowski recalled:

> To my recollection, possibly driven above his level, the CDS invoked the policy. There was a lack of appetite for the obvious deleterious effects that alcohol could have on operations and, frankly, in the minds of the Canadian public. We had a good statistical sense of the number of incidents that occurred that were almost always traceable to too much alcohol. I mean guys accidentally getting killed in other theatres, you know, falling off buildings and doing stupid things in an operational theater. That was not acceptable, so there was a limit on that and there was a challenge for the task force commanders.[34]

In Aviano, Donihee didn't view the alcohol policy problem so much a challenge as an exercise in frustration.

> That's the kind of to-ing and fro-ing that went on between ourselves and Canada, because they wanted it to be like

> Bosnia, dry. I said: "Look, first of all it doesn't work. In Bosnia you have a captive audience. The only time the guys are not in garrison is when they're out on patrol, and they're certainly not going to be drinking while they're out on patrol." The situation for us was obviously totally different. I mean you've got people living right next to the American mess and it's simply not going to work. On top of that when they're off duty they're heading out into the Italian villages and every place else and we had no intention of restricting that freedom of movement to them, because I mean it's simply not warranted. I finally won the argument because I said: "Look, unless you want to send me a company of military police in order to try and police this, it just ain't going to work."[35]

The alcohol policy finally put in place allowed the Canadians at Task Force Aviano to drink if they abstained twelve hours before working. "You know, twelve hours prior and a responsible approach to drinking. If you are ever caught at the point of being inebriated to the extent that you bring embarrassment to the Canadian Forces, you will be charged and there is no tolerance. You will be sent home."[36]

By comparison, Donihee said, the rules of engagement for the CF-18 pilots were straightforward. In August and in the later fall months, the pilots were flying in a fairly benign environment.

> Ultimately, it was self-defence that was the primary consideration. If your own defence is ever threatened, you had the right to employ force up to and including deadly force, but, in any of those situations, your first act should be to withdraw from the encounter, as opposed to going looking for a fight in the name of self-defence.[37]

Back in Ottawa, our Rules of Engagement (ROE) process was so well refined and efficient that it routinely took less than an hour for the Chief of Defence Staff to approve requests from the Task Force Commander in the field to modify his originally issued ROE. Jurkowski said:

> Only the CDS is authorized to issue or change ROE. They are classified, carefully crafted numbered lists for the use of force up to and including lethal force based on operational needs, Canadian and international laws. It got so we could receive, analyze, send a courier to the CDS's residence at say, three o'clock in the morning, get his sign off and transmit the approvals back out the TFC within 25 minutes. It was that slick.[38]

In Aviano, meanwhile, NATO aircrews had been flying missions from the base over former Yugoslavia since the beginning of Operation Deliberate Force on 30 August 1995, when they attacked Serbian military targets in response to a Bosnian Serb mortar attack on civilians in Sarajevo. US military planners viewed Operation Deliberate Force as proof that air power could play a decisive role in achieving clear policy objectives.[39] A succession of NATO non-combat air operations took place after Deliberate Force in support of NATO's stabilization force in Bosnia (SFOR), including: Operation Deny Flight, Operation Decisive Endeavor and Operation Deliberate Guard. Deliberate Guard, which ended 20 June 1998, was replaced by Operation Deliberate Forge in the wake of SFOR's extended mandate in the Balkans.[40] Over the summer, behind the scenes in Aviano and in Canada, the Chief of Defence Staff considered force generation for limited air operations as early as August 27. The air force, meanwhile, readied in mid-September for a proposed aerial bombing campaign in Kosovo, assessing Canadian munitions inventories and storage.[41]

During the summer months, the armed conflict in Kosovo had resulted in hundreds of civilian casualties and nearly 300,000 ethnic Albanian refugees. On September 23, the UN Security Council adopted Resolution 1199 demanding that all parties end hostilities, backed by the threat of NATO air strikes.[42] From day one of their deployment, the 433 Squadron pilots dispatched to Aviano on June 24 knew the reason for their mission. Despite the vague references to Kosovo by the defence and foreign affairs ministers, the CF-18 pilots knew as early as June that they were not there to participate in Operation Deliberate Forge's demonstration exercises. Instead, they were in Aviano and flying over the Balkans to familiarize themselves with the lay of the land and to prepare for an aerial bombing campaign against Serb military forces in Serbia and Kosovo. One pilot recalled:

> Oh yeah. The Canadian detachment, the reason Canada deployed there was for Kosovo. Even that early in June, we knew the main reason was for Kosovo. We didn't go there to support Deliberate Forge, but we were on site, so we might as well practice and do something and learn about the airspace and all that, keep our skills up, so we did participate in Deliberate Forge.[43]

Although the theatre was benign, the missions flown over Bosnia were no longer practice runs or Maple Flag exercises. The Serb military had sophisticated aerial defence systems that included sixty surface-to-air missile (SAM) sites and 1,000 Soviet-made SA-2, SA-3, and SA-6 surface-to-air missiles.[44] Those three missiles are radar-guided weapon systems that lock their radars on targeted aircraft. While older systems, they had high ceilings. The SA-6 medium level missile system could be guided by radar from the ground onto aircraft engaged in evasive manoeuvres and had brought down a US Air Force F-16 in Bosnia in 1995.[45]

Yugoslavia also had 1,850 anti-aircraft artillery pieces and 240 warplanes, including fifteen Soviet MiG-29 and sixty MiG-21 fighter interceptors.[46] Those threats changed everything for the pilots, including their relationships with the ground crew. Bravado and jocular humor in the hangars and on the flight lines went by the wayside. Cpl. Savoie recalled:

> I mean for them [the pilots], all of a sudden this is real, eh? It wasn't just strutting around wearing the G-suits anymore. It was actually going for real. I mean they would get into their planes and the technicians would have to be careful how they spoke to the pilots. I mean, normally, you know the pilots a little bit. The pilots are so good. We're only technicians, right? In Aviano, we had to be careful with them. They were over flying Bosnia, right? Doing air patrols. The pilots came back pretty white, scary, not the same thing

doing training and actually, "Oh, wow. I've got a SAM site pointing at me."[47]

Back in Ottawa, the House of Commons began sitting on Monday September 21, carrying through with sessions on September 22, 24, 25, 28, 29, 30, and October 1, 2, 5, and 6. During those sessions, nothing was said about the air force operations in Aviano, where the CF-18 pilots and ground crews were getting ready for all-out war. On September 27, National Defence Headquarters gave Task Force Aviano clearance to use a 2,000-pound smart bomb in an air campaign in Kosovo.[48] The training and certification of load crews would begin with the bombs' arrival in Aviano.[49] Maj. Stéphane Hébert was deputy weapons and tactics officer for Bagotville's 433 Squadron in Aviano as the situation in Kosovo deteriorated in October. During the three months Hébert was there, the situation was "fluid," in the words of SACEUR (Supreme Allied Commander Europe) US Gen. Wesley Clark, with some NATO countries repatriating their planes and pilots.[50] Hébert described what "fluid" meant for him personally:

> I spent about four months there pre-war. I was there in October for the first time until just before Christmas. Then I was home for three weeks and then I was there until just before the war started on Easter weekend. I got home probably around March 15 or so. I had gone to Montreal where my family is. On Easter Sunday, I got a phone call at about 7 o'clock saying to jump on the next plane. I took a Dash-8 to Bagotville and the next morning I was flying out of Bagotville on a Challenger with six pilots aboard.[51]

During that period Hébert was prepared to fly his CF-18 into battle several times before Christmas 1998. Meanwhile, the problems in the Yugoslav province of Kosovo had been roiling following violent clashes between Serbian soldiers and the guerilla Kosovo Liberation Army (KLA), which had emerged in 1997. The KLA had assassinated Serbian officials, police officers, and Albanian collaborators with the Yugoslav regime in Belgrade, which wanted to crush it. In September of that year, the Contact Group of six nations—the United States, the United Kingdom, France, Germany, Italy, and Russia, that had first come together years earlier over Bosnia—issued an appeal for negotiations to end the escalating conflict. Their proposals and a proposed observer mission by the Organization for Security and Co-operation in Europe (OSCE) were rejected, because Belgrade deemed Kosovo an "internal affair."[52]

After an arms embargo and a round of UN sanctions imposed by the UN Security Council against the Yugoslav regime in March 1998, NATO increased its presence in Macedonia and Albania in June 1998 and threatened air strikes. Amid a humanitarian crisis, with 200,000 displaced ethnic Albanians by September, NATO enacted Resolution 1199, an activation warning of an air campaign on September 23. That was followed by an October 12 ultimatum for a withdrawal of some Serb forces and the establishment of an OSCE 2,000-personnel verification mission. Despite mild success, sporadic fighting between Yugoslav forces, paramilitary forces, and police against the KLA led to a complete ceasefire breakdown by Christmas.[53]

During that time, Bagotville pilot Maj. Alain Pelletier said the pilots were on a readiness roller coaster.

> We experienced two ramp-ups during the times that we were there. The first ramp up was in October, end of October. When I was there for my first tour in theatre, activities started increasing and then the diplomatic activities had a positive ending. We didn't have to use force to actually get to the means and we were able to get the diplomatic staff in with the Serbs and to actually calm things down.[54]

But it was between January and March 1999, when the Canadians moved from preparing for a potential war to a war footing, that they began to feel real pressure. From the day the first Canadian aircrews arrived in June 1998, security at the American base was tight. Cpl. Savoie remembers how daunting the American military was.

> It was kind of funny leaving base, going downtown, going to a restaurant and coming back in wee hours of the morn-

ing. Here is this Hummer with a big 50-calibre machine gun pointing at you as you come in. You showed your ID card and they would say: "Yes. OK. Y'all come on in." This 50-calibre machine gun would follow you in. Then it would point back at the next vehicle. And behind that gun is this tiny little girl, you know, this very same girl we had a drink with the night before. If the guy says "no" and you floored it, she'd shoot you down.[55]

The ground crews that arrived in Aviano in early January 1999 to perform routine maintenance on the CF-18s' complex electronics, avionics, and weapons systems had a typical day's work. The CF-18s flew from four to six missions a day, which required their shift to begin around 6:30 a.m., with a shift change around 4:00 p.m. A maintenance supervisor with the rank of sergeant typically supervised a team of eighteen first-line technicians. Eight of those would be armament specialists responsible for loading the aircraft with missiles and bombs as required and preparing them for their missions. The remaining ten were responsible for fuelling the aircraft, start procedures, and conducting basic inspection and maintenance of the aircrafts' electronic and mechanical systems, including radios, radars, and hydraulics systems. Second-line maintenance saw two technicians conducting X-ray testing of the aircraft to ensure they were structurally sound.[56] That daily routine lasted until the Rambouillet negotiations on the legal status of Kosovo began on 6 February 1999. Pilots moved from flying four to six missions a day to eight to ten missions. Major Pelletier explained:

When we started seeing more activities again at the diplomatic level, we, as a coalition, once again started exercising a little bit more. We were doing packages, a series of airplanes that took off and went flying as a group, as a wave. We exercised pretty much the routine in the event of hostilities, except we were doing it over Bosnia as a rehearsal. So, this is the kind of activities that we ended up doing in preparation for the hostilities.[57]

The more the jets flew, the greater the workload became for the ground crews. They began working twelve-hour shifts, seven days a week, with no increase in personnel to accommodate the increased workloads. As February 1999 worked its way into March, talks with the Federal Republic of Yugoslavia (FRY) broke down completely. That could not have come at a worse time for the Canadians in Aviano. There were plans afoot to move all of NATO's air operations out of Aviano for a period for runway maintenance. The Canadians also were just conducting a wholesale change of personnel from 3 Wing Bagotville to 4 Wing personnel from Cold Lake.[58] As with just about everything in the military, a mountain of paperwork was also building. As a rotation such as 3 Wing's ends, the Forces normally conduct a board of inquiry that measures and investigates all aspects of its operations, including documentation of the force's status, bookkeeping, supplies, and money accounts. The annual reporting season for personnel evaluations was also just ending. But that was only part of the complicated events that were developing. The rotation of 120 personnel from 4 Wing to replace those from 3 Wing was to take place in what would become the first week of the bombing campaign.

3

I Cringed Every Time It Rained

A group of about eight aviation technicians from CFB Cold Lake was in Leeuwarden, Netherlands, when the Kosovo bombing campaign began on March 24. They served as part of 441 Squadron's Capt. Kirk Soroka's planning group for Exercise Brilliant Foil.[1] After the Canadians pulled out of the exercise, that group was left in limbo while the job of transferring the flying missions from Bagotville pilots to Cold Lake pilots was complete. While they awaited orders, defence minister Art Eggleton announced on March 30 that Canada was committing six more CF-18s to the NATO bombing campaign. One of those technicians, "Cookie," said they were finally told late in the first week of April to travel to Aviano because they were running out of ground crew to service the increased number of jets.[2] The problem was, the military had no plan to get them to Aviano. Each had to find his or her own way. "Cookie" and a master corporal made their way to Amsterdam, where they tried to catch a commercial flight to Aviano. They ran straight into a tangle of red tape at the airport.

> They weren't going to let us go because you couldn't go anywhere in Europe unless you had a return ticket. We weren't getting a return ticket. After some discussions with the airport people, one of them realized that we were Canadian service members heading for Aviano so they finally cleared us and let us leave the country and go to Italy.[3]

In what would become a routine occurrence in the weeks to come, "Cookie" produced a Canadian government credit card issued to squadron members to pay for the two one-way seats. The ticket agent told the pair that they were flying business coach, but it never occurred to the technicians, used to travelling on service flights, what that meant. They soon found out: "We went to war first class."[4]

Within days of their arrival in Aviano, the Cold Lake pilots began integrating into the NATO bombing packages while the Bagotville pilots gradually returned home, although some of them and their ground crew remained working with the Cold Lake crews. Capt. Mike Barker was a maintenance officer with Cold Lake's 441 Squadron when he arrived in Aviano on March 21. He later recalled that some of the transitions did not always go smoothly:

> When it started, I was not officially part of the team because I was the guy who was coming in to take over and pretty quickly they [the Bagotville commanders] froze the existing chain of command. They said: "OK, the people that are here, they're the guys in charge. You guys from Cold Lake help out wherever you can but stay out of the way." So that was frustrating because we were coming in full energy ready to go save the world, ready to do everything right because, of course, the guys from Bagotville had been doing everything wrong. To be put on the sidelines to watch, that was very frustrating and there was tension between some of the different groups on that kind of thing.[5]

Alongside problems of command, the ground crews laboured on twelve-hour shifts night and day seven days a week, keeping the CF-18s ready for war in appalling working conditions. When the bombing campaign began in March, a typical workday for most began at least an hour before their shift with a drive to the Aviano air base from Piancavallo, northwest of Aviano in the southern ranges of the Eastern Alps. The Canadians had moved into a four-star hotel, condos, and two-bedroom ski chalets at the picturesque Piancavallo ski resort in September 1998 to accommodate construction at the Aviano air base.

3.1. A hotel located on the Via Barcis at Piancavallo, Italy, which accommodated Canadian air crew and pilots. Photo courtesy of Travis Brassington.

Piancavallo is renowned for its vistas that stretch from the craggy peaks of the Alps on the Slovenian border to the Adriatic Sea. It is also famous for its après-ski restaurants, discos, cafés, and, to a lesser extent, the hordes of bats that flit through the night air as revellers make their way to the resort's nightclubs. Although their accommodations sounded glamorous, they were little more than a place for the Canadians to sleep. A Cold Lake's sergeant explained:

> The plan was to put up everybody in that big hotel we were in. That was the easiest way. You have to remember a four-star hotel in Europe is not up to the standard of a four-star hotel in America or Canada. Like in Europe, a four-star hotel is when you've got your shower and your toilet in your

room. If you've ever lived in Europe, you know that from the end of March they've got the heat off no matter how cold it is. Some people wouldn't have heat in their condo but we tried to take care of that. The hotel owner tried to get the heat back on but some people had it pretty bad. There was another hotel, they had carpet that was mouldy, so that was a problem. But it was not as bad as the guys in Bosnia. Those guys would have been laughing at the accommodation we were in. See, I served on a ship for four years, like when you sleep about fifty-four guys in a room. I can't complain about the hotel, and I was lucky because I was given one of the staff rooms. It was not, let's say, as nicely furnished as the rest of them, but it was a lot bigger so I had a table. My brother he would call and laugh at me that I'm on the wine and cheese tour.[6]

A 416 Squadron's sergeant said that, four-star hotel or not, he was not impressed. "I can remember the European standard hotel rooms are nothing like the North American standard hotel rooms we were staying in. I've been in military barracks better than some of those hotels."[7]

The air force crews travelled back and forth from the hotels in rented cars and nine-passenger buses. To a man and woman, they remember the drives as excruciating thirty-five-minute ordeals at the beginning of their workday and hour-long ordeals at the end. The base of the Piancavallo ski resort is on a plateau on the edge of the Italian Alps, some 1,300 metres above sea level. That elevation required drivers to follow a twisting turning series of switchbacks that snaked up the steep hills leading to the resort. Capt. Barker, one of the first to make the trip, recalled:

> When we first got there, it snowed and rained and there was thunder and lighting and, of course, there were sheep on the road, rally cars and bicycles. They had rally races on the weekend. I'm surprised we survived. It actually wore us out more than anything because you had to go up the mountain every day and down the mountain every day on switchback roads. I actually had people sit beside me and get sick, pull

off their T-shirt and get sick because of doing this, swinging back and forth on these hills.[8]

On top of that, the aircrews had to find time to eat and sleep. Barker recalled the daily routine:

> It was a crazy, crazy drive. I remember the first time we drove up thinking: "Are they kidding? Are we lost?" And we're still going up this crazy hill. It was dark at the time so we had no idea how far we'd gone, anything like that. So your twelve-hour workday rapidly expanded to a fourteen-hour day minimum, you know, generally kind of fifteen hours, at least. If you wanted to fit in eight hours of sleep, that's your day.[9]

A 416 Squadron weapons loader said that they worked twelve-hour shifts in name only. "Twelve hours, that's what your shift is called. But by the time you do hand over or debriefs, there's lots of times when you're there and you're in the middle of a job and you're not going to drop it to another crew. It's a lot easier to finish it yourself, so you can be there for fourteen or fifteen hours just for the sake of getting something done."[10]

Yet it wasn't so much the pace of the work that wore on them: it was that the work never, ever, ended.

> Actually, it's the pace of work that armourers enjoy. We were always loading. We like that. It's just, it starts to wear on you. Your shift at work is twelve hours, but when you're talking the driving and all the rest of it, you're actually up for more like eighteen hours. There wasn't a whole lot of downtime for sleep and recuperating after the harrowing drive up and down the mountain.[11]

The hardships caused by travelling back and forth from Piancavallo to Aviano were resolved about four weeks before the war ended. The Canadians were moved back to the American base after 2.5-metre-wide modular buildings were set up for them near a runway.

3.2 Modular trailer accommodations at Camp Canada or "Tin City" air crew moved to in the last days of the bombing campaign. Photo courtesy of Travis Brassington.

Even though the spring weather got progressively hotter and the runway location was insufferably noisy, making sleep difficult, most saw it as the lesser of two evils. The logistics non-commissioned officer "Cookie" recalled that when the portable trailers arrived, air crewmen and women were desperate to get into them, and it wasn't for security reasons. "People were begging to go into those eight-foot trailers because they were so sick and tired of going up and down that mountain."[12]

During the trip from Piancavallo to Aviano, the Canadians routinely had to drive past thousands of chanting placard-waving Serb supporters gathered at the gates to vent their rage at the NATO bombing campaign. One protestor working from a tent erected a white cross every single day of the campaign. Death threats were painted on garbage cans and stop signs.

On one weekend, 20,000 people gathered outside the gates to protest the war. The Canadians' security precautions were heightened. No protesters were going to get past the heavily armed American guards, but

3.3. Protests against the North Atlantic Treaty Organization bombing campaign Operation Allied Force took place daily outside the entrance to the American 31st Fighter Wing at Aviano Air Base, Italy. Photo courtesy of the Department of National Defence.

it was outside the gates where the Canadians were most vulnerable. A master corporal recalled a potential terrorist threat, not at Aviano but in Piancavallo, where they were staying:

> Our only real threat that we had was a terrorist threat and we knew that it was there. A lot of people say that living up in Piancavallo, which was where we originally stayed in the ski hills, was a good thing. In my eyes it was a very bad thing. We were only lucky, in my mind, that we didn't lose somebody to a terrorist act. We drove up the mountain at night time. We saw cars. Every day in the same spot there was a guy on a cell phone sitting in his car. Every day we saw the same guy, same car. The threat was there.[13]

A sergeant was aware of potential threats, but he didn't give them much thought. "I knew I was going to be pretty safe. We were in Aviano. There was a little bit of terrorist threat every now and again—watch for this, watch for that—but I wasn't that worried being in Italy."[14] If there was a terrorist or Serb threat to the Canadians, it was minor at best, explained retired Brig. Gen. James Cox, who was posted to the intelligence staff of the Supreme Headquarters Allied Powers Europe (SHAPE) in Mons, Belgium, during the war.

> In my job in SHAPE, I had never heard a threat against Canadians per se, but we had intelligence and we often acted on it in terms of the force protection of guerrilla or terrorist—call them what you will—threats against installations of the coalition and even at SHAPE. In Mons, there were a few times that we closed up the base and closed all the stores and the shopping centre for a day or two because there was a perceived threat for a period of time against the base. It was always particularly against Americans, because Americans were the ones who were running the show. The threat against everybody else would have been incidental. I can't recall anything ever that said there was a threat against Canadians, but a threat against an installation and the Aviano air base was an obvious thing. I mean if you're at war you can anticipate that the enemy's going to try and get at your base and anybody on the base will be at risk.[15]

Still, as an added precaution, the Canadian aircrew were ordered to wear civilian clothing when travelling to and from Piancavallo to decrease their visibility and potential exposure to harm. Some thought that security precaution was silly. Explained one ground crew member: "The same five people would be in the same cars every day. They told us to change the route because there was two ways to get to the base from where we were. Anybody who went up there on a daily basis saw the same vehicles, saw the same people taking basically the same routes."[16]

A weapons loading supervisor with CFB Cold Lake's 416 Tactical Fighter Squadron seconded to 441 for Operation Echo. He was given orders to report for duty in Italy on March 27 the day the US Stealth fighter was shot down. In Aviano, he worked in the squadron operations centre and saw the transition from Bagotville to Cold Lake personnel as the bombing campaign kicked into high gear. His job on the midnight to noon shift was to make sure the weapons technicians knew what weapons to assemble and where to deliver them. He also had to ensure that those on the flight line knew what weapons were to be put on which aircraft and what the weapons configuration of each CF-18 was. He remembered that the transition to the bombing campaign workload shocked the Bagotville crews, but by the time most of the Cold Lake crews began arriving they had a better idea of what they were getting into. Still, the workload astonished them. He explained:

> There is no need to train to that level, twenty-four-hour operations. On the weapons side, we train for timings where we have to do each job in a certain amount of time and we train to meet that time. The weapons build-up people are a little bit different. When we load the plane, we're under time constraints. We trained for that kind of stuff, but we hadn't actually seen it before. Some guys trained for twenty years before they went. It was just the intensity of what we were doing there. It was a little bit higher than we thought it would be.[17]

Master Cpl. Edelman, with 441 Tactical Fighter Squadron, was a thirty-three-year-old load crew chief supervising a team of bomb loaders in Aviano. Edelman thinks the most physically demanding part of the crew's job was reconfiguring the CF-18s to drop unguided munitions, or dumb bombs, when cloud cover prohibited the use of smart bombs. In order to reconfigure the jets that way, the crews had to install vertical ejection racks on the CF-18s' wing pylons. The racks allowed the crews to load two dumb bombs on the pylon instead of one smart bomb. What made the job so demanding was the physical exertion and frequency. Edelman explained:

> It's all manhandling. You're not doing this with an MJ1, your bomb loader, you're doing it by hand.[18] We would download

3.4. A Canadian Air Force bomb loader inspects two Mark 82 500-pound General Purpose Bombs, so-called "Dumb Bombs" which are not laser-guided. Photo courtesy of the Department of National Defence.

> one type of weapon, put up the vertical ejection racks, manhandling them, lock them into place and then reload the aircraft. There was one day that I remember we reconfigured four times. Considering we were working twelve-hours-on and twelve-hours-off, you really had a lot of configurations that happened over that twelve-hour period.[19]

The Canadians' work routine carried on seven days a week, often without a day off, for more than forty days. "Cookie" thought the ground crews were not burned out so much as becoming impossibly tired.

> We got tired because you'd get up—I'd get up at 9:00 o'clock at night—and have a coffee. I'd prepare to go into work with a shave and a shower and everything else. We'd go down the

mountain. By 10 o'clock at night you're saying good morning to people. I'd debrief with the other warrant officer till 12 p.m., he'd go up the hill then he'd come down the next morning at about 11 a.m. Quite often our debriefs went to 1 p.m. and then we'd have to get something to eat. Then we'd try to get to sleep at 2 o'clock in the afternoon. It was almost impossible. In the first forty-three days, we had one day off, but that didn't do you a helluva lot of good. You couldn't go anywhere in one day.[20]

One of the hardest lessons the ground crews learned was that after years of cutbacks to the Forces' budgets, the inability to recruit younger workers into their ranks exacted a physical toll on the Canadian servicemen and women in Aviano. Loading bombs and other weapons onto airplanes is hard, heavy work. Although they have machines to help them, they were still dealing with 500- and 2,000-pound bombs. Most of the older corporals who would have been promoted to a supervisory position in years gone by were frozen in their line jobs doing physical work. As one aviation technician who supervised a crew of fifty-five explained: "If you look in the hangar you finally see some privates now that are in the eighteen, twenty, twenty-two-year range. In '99, in Aviano, we had no privates. Everybody was at minimum rank of corporal."[21]

One sergent explained why that was a problem:

> The armament world is a young man's world because you move things. You lift things, you push things. That's why, by trade, armourers have always been bigger and stronger. In Aviano, most of us were, the average, I think, about thirty-five years old and a lot of people were getting hurt. Old guys, like me, we had bad backs or bad knees. So, we went over there and we worked twelve hours a day, seven days a week for a while. Then we switched to six days a week. But old injuries will flare up, especially on the loaders. I think that was one of the main problems. We were older people. We were too old to do our work.[22]

Many of the weapons loaders ended up being medical evacuees sent back to Canada with knee, shoulder, and back problems. Among them was a corporal, who understood that the military was egalitarian. She was out in the cold and rain in Aviano with the men, putting in up to fourteen hours on the night shift in the dark and in the rain. She was just doing her job as part of a team until she was returned to Canada at the end of April with a herniated disc in her back.[23] The ground crews agreed that they had never worked so hard and that they had never been as close as a team as during their experience in Aviano. One 416 sergent explained. "As a result of ten or fifteen years as a weapons loader, they'd all do the same thing. The weapons people, we work together as a group. It's just our nature and I'm sure that most of them, most of the old armoured people would say they don't regret being an armourer, bad backs, knees and all."[24]

The spring weather brought a relief from some of the winter cold, at least, but it also created another problem: heat. Although the hottest Italian weather is in July and August, it was still hot enough at 40 degrees Celsius by the end of May and early June that the wheels of the 23,832-pound CF-18s routinely sank right into the asphalt sitting on the tarmac at Aviano.[25] A technician explained:

> There were a couple areas that they just built for us, eh, like elephant ears we call them. They were just round circles, enough for three jets. They'd start to melt into it. That would make extra work because we could turn them real tight to park them, get them in there, and you'd just tear it up. It'd be like an old piece of driveway that's not finished, just rock and no asphalt. You'd have to sweep it out of the way because now it can go up the engines.[26]

The second problem the heat caused was with the CF-18s' sensitive electronic equipment. The CF-18s were not designed to sit idle in the heat, but that was precisely what they had to do in Aviano because of the tight windows for takeoff times to rendezvous with the refuelling tankers and then join the strike packages. Edelman explained the problem and what that meant for the ground crews. "The avionics system wasn't prepared to be sitting for long without getting cooling air through it. Honestly, apart from the armourers, like the loaders and the bomb dump guys, the avionics guys probably worked the next hardest, continuously changing out boxes because they were overheated."[27]

That was on the outside. On the inside, the second-line maintenance technicians were coping with heat problems of an entirely different nature. The electronic testing equipment they used generated a lot of heat on its own. One sergent elaborated:

> When you touch your TV, you feel how warm it is. Your TV, your stereo, all that kind of stuff generates heat. Heat is the worst enemy of electronic equipment. We had problems finding air-conditioning to bring the heat to a normal level. Like the tire bays, we didn't get the tire stuff until pretty much the end of the war.[28]

The Canadians' lack of equipment was an ongoing story. Despite the defence minister's calm assurances in the House that the aircrew in Aviano were well equipped, that was anything but the case. Much of their equipment was borrowed on the fly from the Americans. The maintenance and bomb loading crews said it was humiliating, always going to the Americans with cap in hand. The biggest embarrassment was that they had to borrow the Americans' MJ loaders, forklift-like tractors that lift bombs for loading onto the CF-18s. They also had to use the Americans' testing equipment. One sergent of 1 Air Maintenance Squadron from Cold Lake, said: "The lack of equipment we went in with was embarrassing."[29]

On 17 April 1999, Defence Minister Art Eggleton announced in Ottawa that Canada was increasing its commitment of CF-18s in Aviano by six, bringing the total number to eighteen. However, the ground crew in Aviano didn't know what to do with them. 441 Squadron's Capt. Barker, who managed a midnight-to-noon shift of eighty aircraft technicians, noted the problems the additional six jets created.

> When they sent the last six, everybody in Aviano is going: "Huh? What are we doing?" We never ended up truly using those six jets. We weren't sure where we were going to park them. We were looking at all kinds of things like roll-

ing out runway mats and stuff and it seemed like the commander was then trying to find a role for them because we had them, so let's send them into the fight. But they weren't fully equipped. They didn't have the targeting pods so they couldn't do smart bombing. All they could do was combat air patrol missions, which, if we wanted to truly integrate them into the operation, we couldn't.

The way they were configured for air-to-air missions was very different than the way they're configured for air-to-ground. Air-to-ground, generally all we had to do was put the bombs on, take the bombs off, put the bombs on. But with the air-to-air role, there's all different kinds of pylons and monitors and stuff that all needed to be tested with an associated workload, so we had two sets of jets. We had one set for the bombers and one set for the air-to-air. The air-to-air were parked on the other side of the airfield with all the related problems of commuting and back and forth.[30]

Barker, however, identified one bright spot in having six extra warplanes on the tarmac. The $35-million jets could be cannibalized for parts. "They turned into a ready parts bin because we had far more airplanes than we needed for the operation. I think we almost always did have one airplane on the ground as a parts bin. We'd pull whatever we needed off that."[31] When the necessary replacement parts eventually arrived in Aviano on a Hercules transport plane, Barker said the aircrews would then rebuild the cannibalized aircraft, only to cannibalize it again when something else went wrong. "So, having all those extra jets did help us, which was good, because our supply line back to Canada was pretty long."[32]

Some Canadians toiled in and around a series of cement bomb-proof aircraft shelters positioned on either side of a semi-circular loop. Located on the south side of the Aviano airport, the shelters had a rounded half-moon roof and a floor space the size of a small outdoor hockey rink. A shelter generally housed one CF-18, but two could fit in with delicate manoeuvring. With such limited space, however, the ground crews responsible for aircraft inspections between flights mostly had to work outdoors, all too often in the rain.

3.5. A CF-18 emerges from a half-moon shaped hardened shelter at the Aviano Air Base, Italy. Photo courtesy of the Department of National Defence.

Canadian soldiers fighting in Italy during the Second World War learned all about the rain that drenched them, turned streams into angry torrents that washed away Bailey bridges, and transformed slit trenches into cold, miserable mud holes.[33] Four decades later, everyone who worked on CF-18s in Aviano remembered the rain. Master Cpl. Edelman was one of them.

> We really weren't prepared for the climate and environment that we would be working in. I never saw so much rain in my entire life, that place. I lived in a big swimming pool. It rained from the moment we got in to the moment we left, so we were soaked. We were soaked right through. The saving grace is that was it was warm. There were cold times but, had it been raining and cold all the time, then we would have been in a world of hurt. I think from the armament perspective, one of the saving graces in all of this is that

3.6. Canadian armorers working in pouring rain carry an AIM9M8/9 Sidewinder Missile that locks onto and tracks Infrared energy emitted by an enemy aircraft. Photo courtesy of the Department of National Defence.

> you're sitting there and you know that you've got a job. This is the one time in your life that you have the opportunity to make a difference. So, from our perspective it kept us going. If you had too much time on your hands then you'd sit around and you worry about how cold you are or how wet you are, or whether your clothes are nice or not.[34]

A sergeant who spent most of his time indoors, said his heart bled for the crews working outside in the rain:

> When I was a master corporal, I loaded with them so I knew every loader that was there. A lot of them were my friends. I knew what they were going through, although not to that level. Fortunately for me I was in a building most of the time and I stayed dry most of the time. I cringed every time it rained.[35]

Edelman noted that the Canadians weren't prepared for the climate. The publicly released after-action report on Kosovo by the Canadian Forces ignored the clothing issues, but the standard-issue boots were totally inadequate for the Aviano weather. Their misery nearly repeated the experience of the First World War, when Canadian soldiers found out that their boots could not handle the mud of an English winter and there was no chance to either dry them or waterproof them.[36] While the Canadian boots held together in 1999, that wasn't the problem.

> The biggest problem we had was that our boots were not made for that kind of weather. What we had was Canadian-standard safety boots. They were very thick and insulated. They were made to work like in November, December, for outside in Canada, not in Aviano. I suffered from what they called Aviano rot, my feet both covered in blisters because you were working for twelve hours, without you know, without removing your boots.[37]

One technician recalled: "I remember that people were having a lot of problems with their feet over there with the poor boots. You got to remember that the focus over there was getting weapons on targets so for the ground crew, a lot of our annoyances they'd sort of just say: 'That's OK. They can live with that.'"[38] While war is hell and asking the troops to live with an inconvenience like sore feet makes sense to some, it damaged morale. Capt. Barker recalled:

> I can sit back and see the other things that had to get done like, "Hey, make sure we don't run out of bombs before the war ends." Some pretty important things were occupying people's attentions. But it was a significant morale issue for the guys on the line. They saw it as just their needs not being looked after. All they wanted was a decent pair of boots to do their work with.
>
> Everyone seemed to agree that the solution to the problem was a steel-toed, steel-shanked hot weather boot that the Americans were selling over the counter at their Base

> Exchange. They were canvas-sided like the Canadian military's desert boots, but they had steel toes which are one of the fundamental safety requirements for working around airplanes. Everybody agreed that, yeah, these boots were an important thing to get but nobody wanted to pay for them. So it went up and down and around and through and everybody who came, every general who came, I said: "Hey, Sir. You know, things are going good over here, but what we would really like is boots."[39]

A solution finally came in early June, just days before the air war ended on June 10. "I can't remember how much it was, but they just went to the American base exchange and bought everybody a pair of boots. They asked you your size and went over there and bought them."[40]

Whether cold and wet, or hot and wet, exhausted and often injured to varying degrees, ground crew personnel said that seeing bits and pieces of the situation in Kosovo on television and talking to the pilots helped keep them motivated.

> We had CNN playing every night, all the time, you know, 'cause there's some military things the military is not going to tell everybody. But CNN had a bit of an overview, so we watched the cars from Kosovo pulling up to the border—moving out of the trouble zones—and they'd get their licence plates taken off and their passports taken so they couldn't come back. Now we're thinking: "OK, that's pretty bad." But the image that got me was the picture of this guy pushing his grandmother or mother-in-law or mother in a wheelbarrow. She was an old lady—wrinkles, the works—being pushed across the border to get away from the trouble zone. I'm thinking: "Well, you know, maybe we're doing some good here. Maybe we're going to stop this kind of stuff, so the Canadian people could maybe know that we were there for a reason." I think we helped.[41]

Capt. Barker explained that talking to the pilots also helped boost morale:

Everyone out there was working real hard. People were taking a great deal of satisfaction from the job that was being done. The pilots would come down and say: "Yeah, you know, hey that one went great." The guys would feel good about that. Every once in a while the pilots would be able to show their tapes from the FLIR pods to folks and say: "Hey. Here's what I just did. Here's what you helped me do." They'd tell them whatever the target was and, you know, we're doing our bit to end this thing and guys would feel good about that. They'd mark the number of successful bombing missions on the side of the airplanes and get a sense of pride out of that.[42]

As tough as the work in Aviano was, ground crews also knew that what the pilots were going through was equally so. One technician explained:

> Some guys were pretty shaken up. We had to help them out of their cockpit. They tape everything. They can see where their bombs are going with their pods. I saw one tape—you see it's an air base and you see people. You can actually see people running around, then see the bomb drop, a big explosion and no more people running around. They just weren't used to bombing people.[43]

For Edelman, seeing the tapes after the pilots returned made him think about soldiers, their roles, and the difference between an infantryman and the ground crews servicing CF-18s:

> I have a lot of respect for infantry men and engineers. They see the results of the war. We never really saw that. I saw a bridge blow up on an odd day. I saw a building blow up, but it's not the same thing. I speak at schools and that on Remembrance Day, and when I talk I don't know if it will ever settle in me that we actually killed people. It's kind of surreal, like you were there. The jets came back without bombs.[44]

4

Don't Go to War without It

The dangers that Canada's CF-18 pilots faced each time they flew into combat began high over the Adriatic Sea about ten or fifteen minutes before their final push to targets in Serbia and Kosovo, through a date with the "Iron Maiden." The Iron Maiden was the pilots' affectionate name for the American or French KC-135 air-to-air refuelling tanker the Canadians call a strategic tanker.[1] To take on a load of jet fuel, the pilots had to approach KC-135s from behind with their fueling probe extended toward the Iron Maiden's 8.5-metre boom with a 68-kilogram cast iron basket attached to the end of a 2.4-metre rubber hose.

The pilots had to insert their probe into the basket and then delicately manoeuvre their jets so a 90-degree bend occurred in the rubber hose. That bend let the fuel flow.[2] The task could be jeopardized by jittery or uncertain pilots who missed the basket and tipped it into the KC-135's slipstream, causing a violent swinging motion that could flail the basket into the jets, tearing their skin or shearing off vital sensors. That was known as "the kiss of the Iron Maiden."[3] Capt. Brett Glaeser recalled his first terrifying date with the Iron Maiden the night of his first mission on 5 April 1999:

> Being a Canadian fighter pilot with 350 hours, I'd never had a chance to fuel from one of these things. The brief was like: "OK, has anybody here flown on a 135?" I said: "Yeah. I've never done this before." The brief from the flight lead was: "OK, you know you need to do this, this, and this. These are

4.1. A CF-18 refuels mid-flight on a KC-135 during a "date with the Iron Maiden." Photo courtesy of Travis Brassington.

the cues that you're going to want to look for and this is how you're going to want to approach the airplane and get your fuel." Probably five minutes he spent just talking to me. I remember I was the last guy in the formation. It was in the dark and in the clouds and I had the least amount of gas when I arrived on the tanker. If I was unable to get gas then I was diverting and I would have been landing somewhere in southern Italy where I'd never been before in my life, but I got my gas and the airplane didn't get damaged. Nobody got hurt. It was a heck of an experience. I'd never air refueled on a KC-135 before; I'd never carried a live GBU-12 before and I'd never been shot at before. These are all things that I've never done before in my life and I'm doing them all on the same night, but probably 50 per cent of the stress was going to that tank.⁴

Whether with Glaeser on his first mission or Maj. Alain Pelletier on his third tour of duty flying out of Aviano and refuelling on many different tanker aircraft, the experience could be harrowing. Pelletier explained:

> There was one night during the actual conflict itself where Rambo and I showed up and tanked out on a KC-135, an American KC-135, between two cells—two thunderstorm cells—that were extending up to about 35,000 feet. So, we were between those two cells. Just seeing the lightning coming from the right or from the left as you're actually hooked up to an aircraft that carries about 135,000 pounds of fuel makes you think about what you're doing. It's like lighting a match right next to a fuel cell or fuel tank.⁵

Just as Pelletier remembered almost every detail from the night of his first combat mission on March 24, pilots like Glaeser vividly remember what was going through their minds:

> Really, like I had no real fear for my safety, for my life or being shot down. My biggest fear was: "OK, did I pay attention enough in my training, you know, and whether or not I could actually pull it all together and make it happen. If not, then really it's life or death so it was like, OK, I need to be on my game tonight."⁶

Glaeser's first mission was a Battlefield Air Interdiction (BAI), or bombing mission attacking army barracks, in the town of Prizren, barely into Serbia about twenty miles north of Kosovo's southern border.

> We got gas and waited for the whole strike package, the whole mission that was going into theatre to push into country. We crossed the border and we were in bad guy

land, as we call it, for probably no more than five minutes. We dropped our weapons, turned around, came home.[7]

By the time one Bagotville pilot of 425 Tactical Fighter Squadron arrived in Aviano on 1 May 1999, Canada's air-to-air refuelling limitations were beginning to fully manifest themselves. He had been in Aviano for three months in 1998, but he wasn't in Aviano for the first night of bombing on March 24, because his pregnant wife was due to deliver a baby. When he flew off to war, he left his wife and newborn in the care of both sets of grandparents. He was sent over with seven other pilots flying an eight-pack of CF-18s to replace those that had reached their serviceable limit in Aviano. Unfortunately, the Americans' KC-135s were fully committed to the war effort and were unavailable to refuel Larouche and his fellow pilots mid-ocean. Hence, they had to fly the operationally least preferable transatlantic route to Aviano. They hopped to Goose Bay from Bagotville; stayed overnight in Goose Bay; met a pre-deployed Hercules refuelling plane off Iceland and flew to Germany; stayed overnight in Germany and reached Aviano on May 1.[8]

On a more optimistic note, the Canadian Forces had obtained precision-guided munitions capabilities for the CF-18 after the 1991 Persian Gulf War. The Canadian Forces' after-action report on the Kosovo air campaign addresses this issue in only the most opaque fashion. The Canadian airmen and their support crews had to "adapt to difficult and unfamiliar operating environments with equipment that was new, unproven and incompletely documented" while maintenance personnel had to cope with "new software versions that were introduced without documentation that made troubleshooting and fault code analysis difficult."[9] To understand those cryptic observations, one must consider how the Canadian Forces developed precision-guided munitions capabilities for the first time.

Air forces worldwide began to view precision-guided munitions as the way of the future after the 1991 Persian Gulf War. During that war, US commanders appeared on television sets around the globe in post-operation briefings showing cockpit footage of so-called "smart bombs" guided to their targets with pinpoint accuracy. Lt. Col. Don Matthews, who commanded the Canadian "Desert Cats" during the 1991 Persian Gulf War, came within two hours of being the first Canadian pilot to drop precision-guided munitions in February 1991. The American navy had supplied Canadians with the bombs, which would have been buddy-lased or guided on to their targets by Americans flying A-6E Intruder carrier-based aircraft training their lasers on designated targets. Those bombs were never dropped because a ceasefire was agreed to and the war ended.[10]

The Canadian air force did not acquire precision-guided munitions until six years after that war ended, for several reasons. Most had to do with Department of National Defence budget cuts following the collapse of the Soviet Union. In 1991, the Mulroney government announced that it would close the Canadian air force bases at Lahr and Baden-Soellingen, Germany, by 1995 and that the Forces' overall strength would fall to 76,000 from 82,000. In years to follow, the finance ministers began plucking the low-hanging fruit that was the national defence budget in the name of the peace dividend and deficit reduction. Defence spending was slashed by 23 per cent to $9 billion in 1998–1999 from $12 billion in 1993–1994. When coupled with inflation, the effect was a 30 per cent reduction in real terms.[11] With no indication in the 1994 White Paper on Defence as to what the budget cuts would mean for the air force operationally in the coming years, fighter-related overheads were cut, including annual authorized flying rates, the CF-5 fleet was retired, fighter pilot training was modified, and operational aircraft were reduced to between forty-eight and sixty from seventy-two.[12]

The 1994 white paper also indicated that the CF-18s' multi-purpose capabilities would be enhanced with the acquisition of a small number of sophisticated precision-guided munitions.[13] However, the air force did not receive the so-called smart weapons for years. Matthews explained: "The peace dividend was going to be pulled out of the military come hell or high water. Precision-guided munitions went into a long list of capabilities that were shelved."[14]

The air force eventually began to receive the long-sought precision-guided munitions capability six years after the 1991 Gulf War. It began with the delivery of Forward Looking Infrared (FLIR) pods and NITE Hawk B laser targeting in 1997.[15] FLIR pods enable target identification at night using four-power magnification and heat-sensing equipment. NITE Hawk pods enable pilots to home smart bombs onto their targets by directing laser energy at them, which the bombs follow.[16] Also, six years after the Gulf War, Matthews was back in Canada commanding the military's Aerospace Engineering Test Establishment. He flew on the final missions to clear the NITE Hawk laser designating pod and 2,000-pound precision-guided munitions for the CF-18. The work configuring the CF-18s' computers for that capability spoke volumes about the state of the Canadian air force. There was a six-year hiatus between the time the Canadians saw that precision-guided munitions were the way of the future and their eventual clearance for use. By that time, the CF-18s' mission computers had become the equivalent of computing dinosaurs, like obsolete early 1980s–vintage Commodore 64 computers.[17] Matthews explained the problem:

> The mission computer on the F-18 could barely handle the NITE Hawk. I mean it's sort of like saying you know, "let's buy the best target designating pod on the market." So, it's like buying the best peripheral for your computer. If you've got a Commodore 64, do you think the latest piece of software from IQ is going to work on it? No, so that's the issue. We diddled our software so badly and under-funded our software so badly that we really had to tweak it up. By really tweaking it, we screwed some things up badly. One of the missions I was on, the bomb went Pffft. I don't need to bore you with all the details, but that was indicative of where we were as an air force.[18]

When Canada acquired the technology, it bought only thirteen FLIR pods. Immediately upon acquisition, two were taken out of service to be cannibalized for parts, while the remainders were allocated to Canada's two fighter wings for training.[19] Former 4 Wing Commander Lt. Col. Jim Donihee did not have positive memories of the experience. "You basically had two wings attempting to shuttle six or eight pods back and forth on a recurring basis in order to try and maintain readiness levels. It was almost whimsical that it could ever be achieved."[20]

When Canadian CF-18s were committed to the Kosovo air campaign, eight pods were committed to Aviano, while three remained in Canada to train pilots who replaced the CF-18 pilots in theatre. Canada could only escalate its sortie commitment to twelve CF-18s by borrowing four earlier-generation FLIR pods from the Australian air force.[21] After Canada had increased the number of CF-18s to eighteen, Task Force Aviano never had enough pods to equip the last six jets that arrived, rendering them useful only for air defence or for missions that did not require smart bombs.[22] Bagotville pilot "Tubs" of 433 Tactical Fighter Squadron described what it was like working with a FLIR pod during combat:

> It really depended on the environmental conditions. They are very susceptible to humidity, but on a nice dry night you can see for fifteen or twenty miles. Generally speaking, you had to be inside of ten miles to identify your target area. You have to have familiarity with the pod to sometimes interpret what you're seeing. What you're looking for is heat difference, heat differential, and to recognize the pattern. You learn what things cool off faster if you're at night and what things heat up quicker if you're in the daytime, if it's sunny, if it's not sunny, if it's cloudy, what grass looks like, what buildings look like, roads, concrete—they all look different on a FLIR. I was pretty fortunate. I had a lot of training with the pod, but there were some folks that weren't as comfortable with predicting what things would look like through the pod, so certainly that was a shortcoming.[23]

Another of the shortcomings with the FLIR pod the Canadians were using was its four-power magnification. Of the FLIR pods available to NATO militaries, the Canadians had the poor-cousin variant. During the Kosovo air war, the Americans used FLIR pods with eight and ten times' magnification, with integrated global positioning systems (GPS) that allowed for precise bombing through cloud cover.[24] In the event of cloud cover that made it impossible to deliver their bombs, the Canadians simply returned home with them. One Bagotville pilot, for example, flew six missions and dropped his bombs only once.[25]

Instead of the Americans' GPS, the Canadian FLIR pods were equipped with an Instrument Navigation System (INS) that reduced their effectiveness. There is always a certain amount of drift in an airplane's flight path. That drift could put the CF-18s up to two miles off the path the pilots intended on their bombing run approach, increasing the workload of pilots as they tried to determine where they were and if they were about to bomb the right target. A CF-18 pilot explained:

> Before we dropped we had to update that INS to make sure our FLIR was looking in the right place. The problem is—because of the limitations of the system and the equipment—the problem now became for the pilot, in addition to having reduced magnification, you may not even be pointing at the target. You may be two miles away when you're looking at your FLIR. We used to call it blobology. If you are pointing at something that's two miles off the target, now you're cueing in terms of what you have as a [different] reference from your visual picture and the one from your map. Now it becomes totally skewed, you're not seeing what you expected to see. If I was expecting to see a river, a bridge, a building target and the FLIR is now pointing two miles off, well I'm not going to see a river, a bridge, a building target. I'm going to see a field that looks nothing like what I'm supposed to be looking at so, that in itself causes us some problems. When you look at the Americans, if they have a GPS system, they know that their system is good. They have much more confidence that when they designate a target and when they launch a bomb that it's going to land in the vicinity and not two miles away.[26]

"Blobology" was a far cry from Chief of Defence Staff Gen. Maurice Baril's description before the House of Commons Standing Committee on Defence and Veterans' Affairs (SCONDVA) on the Canadians' precision bombing capability. More than a month into the war, on 28 April 1999, Gen. Baril told SCONDVA: "From very far and very high, our pilots can choose which window of this building to drive the bomb into with precision-guided ammunition."[27] That was not the truth. So, too, with the ordnance or bombs the Canadians were dropping. Deputy Chief of Defence Staff Lt. Gen. Ray Henault told an Ottawa press briefing on March 25, the

4.2. Lieutenant-Colonel William Allen "Billie" Flynn examines a 500-pound GBU-12 Paveway II laser-guided bomb during a pre-flight inspection. Photo courtesy of the Department of National Defence.

day after the bombing campaign began, that acquiring the precision-guided munitions got Canada "back into the club again."[28]

The standard bomb in Canada's inventory before the Kosovo air war was the Mark 82 500-pound free-fall bomb, so-called iron or "dumb bomb," dropped by the Canadian Desert Cats on the "Highway of Death" in the final days of the 1991 Gulf War. One laser-guided technology Canada acquired after the Gulf War coupled a FLIR pod and Mark 82 bombs equipped with MAU-169 Paveway II control units. Those control units turned the Mark 82 bombs into GBU-12 bombs able to follow laser light beamed at targets by the FLIR pod, making them smart.[29]

Canada also acquired a later-generation Paveway III laser-guidance technology for the GBU-24, a 2,000-pound bomb. The GBU-24 was provisionally cleared by the Department of National Defence for use with the CF-18 on 15 July 1998.[30] The differences between Paveway II and Paveway III determined the technology Canadians used during the Kosovo air campaign. Paveway II technology simply let bombs follow a pilot-aimed laser line off the airplane. If the laser beam encounters a cloud, because there is no laser energy for the bomb to follow the bomb falls off the laser beam and misses its target. That is not necessarily a bad outcome, explained Lt. Col. William Flynn, commander of CFB Cold Lake's 441 Tactical Fighter Squadron in Aviano, who assumed command of Task Force Aviano's Canadian fighter operations sixteen days into the war.

> At least you know that if you drop in on a certain line, and you've figured out where your tack is, and if there is something in the way of this bomb when you drop it—if it loses laser energy—it's going to drop short by some distance and blow up a couple of trees. You're not going to have the same risk of collateral damage as you might have with a bomb that you don't know where it goes once it comes off your airplane.[31]

Not knowing where a bomb might land was the problem associated with the Paveway III technology. The Paveway III had a four-program mode capability that let pilots determine how it would fly. When released up to ten nautical miles away from its target, the GBU-24 falls off the airplane and establishes itself on a pilot-determined mid-altitude cruise profile, for example, at about 10,000 feet. The bomb cruises along to a point where it opens its "eyes" and looks for laser energy to dive into the target. The technology was ideal during Desert Storm when there were no clouds over the desert.[32] If the laser beam runs into clouds, however, the GBU-24 doesn't simply fall off the beam like a GB-12; it keeps on flying beyond the intended target. The pilot who launched it has no idea where it is going.[33] However, the weather for much of the Kosovo air campaign wasn't comparable to that of the Persian Gulf, where American pilots launched their bombs from seven miles away, hitting their targets every time because in the desert, nothing was in the way. Flynn explained:

> This was April and May in the Balkans. It was pouring rain—horrible weather—and we had to be very careful about throwing these bombs away arbitrarily. We also had

to deal with the collateral damage issue which is: "You better make sure you know where this bomb is going to go and if it doesn't hit the target, you better have some idea of where it might fall." We didn't want to accept the risk of collateral damage by launching these bombs and having no idea where they were going to go.[34]

The tactical conditions dictated that the only suitable bombs for the Canadians were the lighter 500-pound GBU-12 bombs. There was nothing wrong with them, given appropriate targets. In the most successful bombing mission of the early part of the war, four Canadian pilots—Flynn among them—dropped six 500-pound bombs each on fifty or sixty Serbian army vehicles assembled on a hilltop one Saturday morning. "We dropped twenty-four bombs exactly on target. We destroyed the entire assembly area and vehicles and, obviously, the Serb army soldiers with our attack."[35]

Choosing the right bomb for targets is not up to the pilots. Mission planning aids and computer programs match weaponry to targets.[36] A 500-pound bomb is appropriate for a soft-skinned communications tower, whereas a 2,000-pound bomb is not. Flynn explained:

> A big bomb isn't always exactly what you want when you drop two bombs at a time. Dropping 2,000 pounds of ordnance every time can be serious overkill. When you talk about the lethality of a bomb, it is not linear in the level of destruction from a 500-pound bomb to a 2,000-pound bomb. It is exponential. A 500-pound bomb is basically a poof, a little flash. A 2,000-pound bomb is incredible destruction. You don't always need to be dropping 2,000-pound bombs everywhere you go.[37]

However, three sets of problems emerged as the result of the Canadians only having 500-pound smart bombs in their inventory. The first problem was only cryptically hinted at in the publicly releasable declassified portions of the secret Operation Echo lessons-learned report. "At times during OP ECHO, TFA came close to depleting vital consumables that could have significantly limited operations."[38] Stated in less bureaucratic language, two weeks into the war the Canadians in Task Force Aviano were running out of GBU-12 bombs.[39] A weapons load standards and training officer with 1 Air Maintenance Squadron assigned to 441 Tactical Fighter Squadron in Aviano, saw that shortcoming when he arrived in Aviano two weeks after the bombing campaign began on March 24. He later recalled: "We could still meet mission requirements, but we were using them up pretty quick."[40] Canadian military personnel are reluctant to give specifics about the seriousness of their supply problems, but they were down to one day's supply at least twice.[41]

Brig.-Gen. James Cox was Canada's Deputy Assistant Chief of Staff for Intelligence posted to NATO's Supreme Headquarters Allied Powers in Europe (SHAPE), the NATO military headquarters responsible for all NATO operations in Europe in Mons, Belgium in July of 1998. He officially worked for a Dutch Major-General WHO reported to the Chief of Staff, a very able German four-star General. However, being Canadian, he was the senior "Five Eyes" military intelligence officer in SHAPE, and in that role occasionally had direct access to American Gen. Wesley Clark, NATO's Supreme Allied Commander for Europe. He also had British and American colonels on his staff, as well. Between the three, they had links to their national intelligence organizations and shared intelligence products appropriately. Cox recalled the morning when the Canadians began running out of the "key consumables". He was in the room that was equipped with video screens for teleconferences between Clark and Lt.-Gen. Mike Short, NATO's air south commander who commanded the air war's operations out of Naples, Italy. Cox recalled:

> This one morning, we were there and they were talking about the problems of the targeting and clearing the targets. It was becoming a problem in the Alliance, and General Short happened to say, on screen: "and this morning I had a problem with, of all people, the Canadians." So, I sat up and I perked up as I heard him say "the Canadians." He said: "Yeah, there was a problem in getting clearance for the bombing of targets." I mean, he just happened to throw in the glib phrase of, "and I think it's a problem with their Parliament." Now where he heard that from I have no idea, but

that's what he said. General Clark, in exasperation, because he was having a hard time on target clearances, he threw his pen down on his notepad on the desk and he turned to me a couple of tables over and he said: "Could you please straighten out your Parliament?" So, I had all sorts of ideas in my head, you know, "Jesus, how can I do that?" But, I said, "Yes, Sir."[42]

Cox left the meeting and began making phone calls. "I got an answer out of Aviano that, in fact, the only problem that we were having is that we were running out of bombs and needed more. It was a thing I was happy to take up and report to Clark to say, 'Here's what really happened. The only problem in all this really is we need some more bombs.'"[43]

The only ally Canada could turn to in order to obtain more precision-guided bombs was the United States. A flurry of diplomatic activity occurred between the Canadian embassy in Washington and the Pentagon. On April 8, two weeks after the bombing campaign began, Public Works Canada and Government Services Canada in Washington filed an "extremely urgent" request for an emergency supply of 100 GBU-12 laser-guided bombs.[44] In Ottawa, Brig. Gen. David Jurkowski was back on the phone to his Permanent Joint Board of Defence counterpart in the Pentagon. "It was very quick to call up the Pentagon and say to my buddy: 'We need this. Can you help us?' It happened in a heartbeat. So that's actually a very, very positive capability as well as development."[45]

The clearance happened so quickly that the Canadian Forces' weapons technician in Aviano responsible for acquiring the GBU-12 bombs, at a cost of $25,000 each from the Americans, had no problem at all. Giving added meaning to the expression "Don't leave home without it," he produced his Canadian government–issued credit card. "I can buy military equipment with it. Wherever I need it, I can buy it."[46] In Canada, that is what Gen. Henault told SCONDVA on 28 April 1999 was "the normal replenishment process." He did not say what the process was, only that "we are replenishing or re-supplying the ammunition stocks as we go along."[47] That explanation did not begin to come close to revealing to parliamentarians how ill equipped the Canadians were during the bombing campaign and how reliant they were on the Americans.

The weapons technician said it was easier buying bombs from the Americans than it was to get them back to the Canadian storage area at the southwest end of the Aviano air base. The American ammunition control building, where all ordnance was tracked, was miles from the airfield across the main north–south public highway. When the Canadians needed materiel from the Americans, the east gates of the airfield would be opened and Italian civilian police, the carabinieri, would stop vehicular traffic so military vehicles could cross the road. The technician explained:

> It was actually quite comical. We had a car come right through us, right through the convoy. Like, there was a truck and then two trailers and a truck and two trailers and the car came right between the two trucks and barely missed one of the explosives trailers by about two inches. The carabinieri was quite shocked. All he could do, he sort of looked at us and shook his head and waved us through. It's pretty funny. It wasn't at the time, but when you look back: "Oh, that was close."[48]

Moreover, as the campaign wore on, the quality of the American bomb stocks being supplied to the Canadians dropped noticeably. The weapons technician described what happened:

> When we first went over there, the first ones were basically pristine looking, you know, like they'd never been out of the box. But we ran out of what we bought so we had to buy more from them and the stuff that they were basically pawning off was dregs. The oldest one I saw was made in like 1974. It was really old stuff. Some of them, for me to get them to work, I had to hit them with a hammer. What happens is the little wing hubs that steer the weapon to the target, over time sitting in storage, they sort of tighten up and the "O" rings would dry up a little bit. To get it to work you would have to whack it with a hammer, that's actually in the American technical orders to do that. It's pretty funny actually.[49]

Even more, for the older bombs, the Americans didn't have documentation for the laser-guidance kit codes. A Persian Gulf War veteran, a sergeant, found a solution to that problem, burning out specific lines in the older laser-guidance binary codes to make them compatible with newer guidance systems. "In fact, none of the Americans knew how to do that."[50] He showed the American military how to reconfigure their own old weapons, enabling them to salvage more than 90 per cent of bombs they thought were unserviceable, saving them tens of millions of dollars.[51] Even so, he often felt uncomfortable as a Canadian going to the Americans with his cap in hand.

> We'd always have to go to the Americans to get stuff. It was: "Yep, we're running out of bombs." So I felt like an arms dealer going to the guys and going: "Hey, what do you got, do you have anything left over that we can use?" You know, making deals with them, having to use their forklifts because we didn't have any, and then using the diesel forklift inside a magazine where all the bombs are stored. Then you get fumed out because there were fumes where we should have had an electric forklift in there, or something with better air quality. We ended up putting a strain on the Americans by having to use their stuff.[52]

He says that making do with few resources is the Canadian way. "You work with what you can, and instead of saying, 'No, we can't do it.' You make it happen. There's normally always a way to get work done." Scrounging has become the Canadian way of war.

Shortly after the beginning of May, the Canadian ground crew in Aviano took to naming themselves the "Balkan Rats," because it rhymed with the Deserts Cats, the nickname for the CF-18 pilots who flew during the 1991 Gulf War. It also carried a pack-rat connotation well suited to their ability to scrounge sufficient equipment to keep the CF-18s in the air.[53] To acknowledge their nickname, the crews painted a "Balkan Rats" emblem on the top outboard of each CF-18's forward-facing fins.[54] They also used a stencil cut from cardboard to paint a bomb on the CF-18's forward port fuselage after each successful bombing mission. Once, after a pilot had to jettison a hung bomb into the Adriatic due to a malfunction in the charge that deploys the bomb from the jet, the ground crew painted a fish on the CF-18's fuselage.[55] Despite the hardship, they retained a sense of humour.

At the outset of the air-bombing campaign, SACEUR Gen. Clark aimed to blind the Yugoslav military by crippling their radars and destroying their missile launchers and anti-aircraft missile systems, expecting Milosevic would capitulate in short order. On the first night of bombing, NATO warplanes hammered airfields, an aircraft repair facility, electronic intelligence collection and distribution sites, and army headquarters.[56] However, Milosevic did not capitulate and the bombing campaign became protracted. Generating enough approved targets beyond the initial planned 100 became a problem for NATO commanders, not because there were too few places to hit but because of the approval process.[57] Initially, the plan gave Clark the power to approve targets. When the campaign began, however, Washington and other countries' governments and their politicians wanted to shape the target approval process.[58]

Clark held two command functions in Europe. He was NATO's Supreme Allied Commander Europe, responsible for taking command from NATO's North Atlantic Council, and the US Commander in Chief, European Command (EUCOM). In EUCOM each target was assessed for location, military value, possible casualties, potential for collateral or accidental damage beyond the intended target, and what might happen if a bomb missed its target. The proper weapon had to be found for each target, and once that analysis was done, it was sent off to Washington, where it underwent further military review before ending up on US president Bill Clinton's desk for approval.[59] The US chain of command ran from Clark in Mons, to the joint chiefs of staff, to defence secretary William Cohen, to Clinton and then back to Clark. Individual countries also had their say, frustrating NATO commanders and slowing the bombing campaign. French president Jacques Chirac ruled out strikes against Montenegro, which was viewed as less hostile to the west than Belgrade.[60] The target approval process put Gen. Clark in an impossible position: responsibility without authority. As de Jomini predicted, if the unfortunate general directing the war was unable to decide the manner in which he was to achieve the war's objective, the responsibility for that inability would fall on the shoulders of those responsible hundreds of miles (in this case thousands of kilometres) away.

Canada's ambassador to NATO in Brussels during the bombing campaign, David Wright, sat on NATO's North Atlantic Council. He was one of nineteen ambassadors taking political direction from their countries but empowered to make decisions on behalf of their governments. He wrote that the North Atlantic Council had the authority to decide on categories of targets and used it during the various phases of the bombing campaign, but that politicians did not micro-manage the bombing campaign by deciding on individual targets. The first phase, for example, targeted Serbian anti-aircraft installations. The second phase was launched against tactical Serb targets in Kosovo. The third phase, which was never formally adopted but began anyway, started just six days after the bombing campaign began. It included selected strategic targets such as the state-run television station and other targets at the heart of Slobodan Milosevic's power. Wright denied there were political motivations behind the target selections, insisting that it was military authorities alone who decided on the targets.[61] Wright's account directly contradicts Gen. Clark's and others' accounts. For example, on the first night of the war there were fifty-one targets struck by 366 aircraft. By the war's end, nearly 1,000 targets had been identified as targets for 900 NATO aircraft.[62]

Lt. Col. Sylvain Faucher saw politics shape the target selection. It was never believed around the planning table that the NATO bombing campaign would be protracted.

> Everyone thought it would be over in a matter of days. Every morning I was sitting around the table with X number of nations—the nations that were in Aviano—to plan what was going to happen today. At that point in time, the political inputs, i.e., what would the political leaders want us to do with the conflict, it was their conviction, it was obvious to me, that this conflict would be short. That's what their beliefs were and that's where the number-of-targets issue came into play. A lot of people were convinced that with this amount of targets the military would have accomplished its mission. So initially, the targets were restricted to a certain

number and a certain category. It became fairly obvious after a few days that the aim would not be accomplished with that amount of targets.[63]

Post-mortems concluded that the problem with the bombing campaign was not the NATO mechanisms for using air power but rather with political leaders who believed that Operation Allied Force would end in two to four days. So certain were they of that end, they identified just three days' worth of targets.[64] As a result, the bombing efforts seemed under-sourced, the targeting process erratic, and the aircraft too few. Moreover, the combined air operations centre (COAC) in Vicenza had no flexible targeting cell that could authorize an expanded target list.[65]

The Canadian government documented the targeting process during the air campaign,[66] but those documents are exempt from disclosure under the *Access to Information Act* because their release could damage the conduct of international affairs and the defence of Canada.[67] However, Operation Echo's after-action report showed that the targeting process evolved over time and was briefed to and approved by Gen. Baril in early June of 1999, near the war's end.[68]

Further, long before any Canadian pilot donned his Nomex® flight suit, his targets had to be approved for their military value by Canadian military lawyers in Aviano who vetted them. Lawyers could veto missions based on a target's military worth or proximity to civilians based on the CF-18s' flight paths if bombs fell short, as was the planned fail-safe case with Canadians' use of the Paveway II GBU technology. For some pilots, that vetting was a source of frustration, for others a source of comfort, and, for more, a source of stress. There were flight recorders in the cockpits of every CF-18 that were turned on as soon as the pilots went "feet dry," or, in other words, passed flying over the Adriatic Sea and began to fly over land. The flight recorders record up to three hours, so everything the pilots did was scrutinized by lawyers upon their return, including where the bombs landed and what they hit.[69] Pilot radio call sign "Chimp" explained:

> That was something new for us, to actually have a lawyer with us in Aviano looking over the targets. Every country has a list of declared special sites, religious sites, historically

significant sites, and they're obligated to not hide their military equipment at any of those sites. We make every effort to spare those sites. The lawyers would be looking over our shoulders to be sure we're keeping that in mind and that we didn't use a bigger bomb than we had to.[70]

One pilot who goes by the call sign "Midas" explained that he felt better having lawyers vet his targets first:

> Some people would complain probably that it was a bit of a pain in the ass having them there, but they really sanitized the targets. I was quite confident that I wasn't personally carrying out any atrocities or anything that was questionable. They were quite careful, at all levels, to ensure that there was no collateral damage, the things you see on TV where markets are blowing up. They were quite careful to make sure we didn't do that. It wasn't just legal, it was more of a humanitarian and less of a military approach, which sat well with me. You knew what you were doing was horrible, but at the same time it was for the right reasons. It was sanitized to a point where the people who were getting it deserved it.[71]

Pilot radio call sign "Mur," the 4 Wing weapons officer in Aviano, was happy to have the Canadian Forces lawyers involved in the targeting approval process.

> I personally found it to be a comfort having the lawyers there. Rules of engagement and the validity of military targets is a very, very legal-based thing. It's a bit much to ask an air warrior to be expert in that system of interpreting the legality of rules of engagement and target validity whilst also maintaining the ability to execute that mission. That's a pretty broad spectrum so I was happy to have a lawyer say: "This is a valid target. These are the restrictions you have to apply when attacking a target and these are the areas

that are potential areas of collateral damage avoidance. We should avoid that." I thought that enhanced our mission. It made it easier for me to achieve the commander's intent with their input.⁷²

Not all the pilots were happy that lawyers vetted their targets, however. Pilot radio call sign "Willi," flying with Bagotville's 433 Squadron, explained the frustration:

Some of the times I felt that the lawyers were there more tying our hands than they were helping us. I can come up with a particular instance. We were targeting a facility and all our targets had to go through the North Atlantic Council, which Canada was a member of, so the council cleared all the targets. We have to assume our highest level has cleared this to be a legal, valid target. The target was tasked to us and our lawyer in theatre said we couldn't hit that target because it wasn't a valid target, it was a civilian target. He couldn't see the relation of what this would be for military operations. Twice we targeted the same thing and twice he told us we couldn't target this facility until somebody else destroyed it. It was that level of frustration I felt with the lawyers. By the same token, the lawyers were there absolutely to keep us safe, but sometimes they tied our hands significantly in the belief that, you know, always looking for the 100-per-cent solution. Much of the time we don't deal in the 100-per-cent solution because often, we don't have the time for the 100-per-cent solution.⁷³

Once pilots returned from their missions, the Canadian Forces lawyers stood in the debriefing rooms, reviewing flight tapes to ensure the bombs were dropped on their targets exactly as planned. The pressure the lawyers put on the pilots to avoid collateral damage illustrates just how far modern strategic thinking had evolved from Giulio Douhet, one of its key originators, who argued major population centres should be subjected to strategic targeting to break the population's support for the war. Despite those modern human rights objectives, Capt. Kirk Soroka said the pressure that the lawyers brought to bear on the pilots was almost unbearable.

> The problem is that war's not fought like the Second World War anymore, it's fought on CNN. It's fought with the lawyers hanging over your shoulders and everybody in the chain of command can see your videotape and know every single mistake in action that you make. The pressure on each pilot when he shows up in theatre to fly his first combat mission is incredible. You're not only applying pressure on yourself to deliver weapons so you don't run away from the enemy, but you get pressure from your peers, pressure from the ground crew, pressure from the lawyers, your leaders, all to go out there and destroy your target. That type of pressure can make you ineffective. There were a lot of missed attacks due to this pressure. Everything was being recorded. We were being micro-scoped every day, so you make a mistake and they want your tapes. The guys were afraid if they did make a mistake that the lawyers would basically testify against them. In fact, one lawyer told me right to my face that she'd testify against any pilot she saw that mistakenly dropped their bombs into the target area.[74]

One Bagotville pilot recalled a terrifying night that illustrates the dangers the pilots faced, how their years of training came into play, and why there were times they couldn't give a second thought to the lawyers reviewing their flight tapes and assessing the appropriateness of their actions. After being tasked to bomb an ammunition depot just north of the Serbian city of Nis, he and the pilot flying lead missed their target on the first pass through southern Serbia and returned to re-attack. Although they couldn't see it on their radar, they were shot at by an SA-6 radar-guided surface-to-air missile that was travelling at more than twice the speed of sound.

> The flight lead, he called the SAM launch, right, two o'clock. We didn't talk to each other until everything was over, but we did the same actions at about the exact same time with-

out talking to each other. We both emergency jettisoned all our tanks and bombs and everything. We hit the panic button, if you wish. Everything fell from the aircraft so we have a manoeuvrable aircraft and this SAM, it just climbed. I remember really vividly, it just climbed. Then it was aiming. I was just about to do my last-ditch manoeuvre there so the missile just misses you a little bit, then it just flamed out. So, it became all dark. It was night so I went: "Oh, OK."

Foolish me. I assumed the thing was just gone, but it was still doing over Mach 2 heading my way. So I stopped manoeuvring. I just levelled the wing. I don't know how close it came, but the motor stopped running. Then I talked to my lead. We started talking: "Hey, what's your position?" He was below me, but I put on the afterburners to get some energy. We exited Serbia via Macedonia and came on home. It was quite an experience, not just because they launched some SAMs. This one, it was guided. I'm thinking they had some kind of optical sensors like NVGs or something and were tracking us optically.[75]

Having explained how close the pair came to being killed that night, the pilot explained how, with a guided missile streaking toward him, the concern for civilian casualties and the involvement of the lawyers all went out the window. Self-defence is always the first Rule of Engagement.

No doubt in my mind, saving my bacon comes first. Really, I feel bad if there's somebody underneath who gets the fuel tanks on their heads or the bombs. But, no, we're not going to take a vote here. It's just, OK, I'm either going to die in the next minute or I'm going to drop this stuff.

After the fact it's funny because when I parked my jet, the ground crew's marshalling me in—it's maybe three or four in the morning—and I can see his look wondering why there's no tanks or bombs left or nothing. Usually you come back with your tanks. I shut down and he's coming up the ladder he says: "Airman, what's going on? You have no more tanks." I said: "I know, I know. I got rid of them." I said: "We were shot at by an SA-6." He says: "Oh really," then he runs and he gets the other ground crew to come and look at the jet. I stepped down from the aircraft and I said: "Oh, I think I need a beer." He goes: "Oh, yes. You do go definitely have a beer."[76]

5

The Fog of War

The Clinton administration's strategy, which envisioned only gradually escalating air strikes and negated a commitment of NATO ground troops, was deeply flawed from an airpower perspective. By eliminating a ground threat, it ruled out surprise.[1] By seeking only to compel Milosevic, rather than destroy him, it complicated measurement of the campaign's coercive effect.[2] The rationale for not committing ground troops was that the air campaign was supporting a humanitarian operation. Clinton reasoned that civilian casualties from a ground campaign would be greater than those from errant bombs.[3] Soon, however, Gen. Clark realized that a limited bombing campaign aimed at the Serbs' air defences and military facilities alone wasn't achieving the desired strategic effect: to end ethnic cleansing.[4]

Clark pushed to attack targets deeper in Serbia, including police headquarters in Belgrade, that were directing ethnic cleansing. The kidnapping of three American soldiers on March 31 convinced Clark that he must strike Serb ground forces.[5] "In war, the art is to focus as much combat power as possible at the decisive point. One of these decisive points was the destruction of the Serb ground forces."[6] NATO planners drew up a list of Phase Two targets including Serb forces, armoured vehicles, troop transporters, support trucks, and petroleum storage facilities.[7]

Capt. Travis Brassington remembers the push by Clark:

> The big press from General Clark was troops, artillery and tanks, army in the field kind of stuff, not classic close air

support. We were after parking assemblies which proved to be very difficult. They were pretty good at hiding their stuff. I remember hearing a couple of times about fielded forces, but we'd have so many aircraft in the stack waiting—by the stack I mean waiting in position to drop bombs—but my number never came up. To ensure that we were doing something, we'd always have back-up targets, so the plan was to go and try and destroy fielded forces or find vehicles out there but, if not, we'd move to pre-planned strategic targets like repair facilities or ball-bearing factories. It is kind of a common thing for fighter guys to do. You always have a back-up plan.[8]

NATO planners eventually received approval for more progressively strategic targeting aimed at disrupting Milosevic's ability to command. Phase Three targets constituted axiological air operations aimed at not only targets Milosevic valued—such as his vacant home in the exclusive Belgrade suburb of Dedinje, and TV stations that spewed out his propaganda—but also electrical transformer yards and bridges over the Danube. The assumption was that disrupting the Serb population's quality of life by interrupting electrical service and jamming up civilian and military traffic flows would force a capitulation.[9]

With the targeting changes, the Canadians increasingly were called upon to attack bigger, tougher objectives. 441 Tactical Fighter Squadron Capt. Todd Sinclair—who went by the call sign "Piper"—recalled that his missions' targets ran the gamut from barracks buildings to radio relay stations and bridges.[10] Pilot radio call sign "Chimp" of 416 Tactical Fighter Squadron also recalled the approved target list:

> The other guy's military infrastructure and equipment was number one; then we started going after things like fuel that keeps the tanks running and the jets in the air. "Let's blow that up and then they're unable to operate, and ammo dumps." We wanted to pin them down so they couldn't move about freely, take out antennas and what not, stop

them from speaking and communicating. So that was the nature of it.[11]

Pilot radio call sign "Tubs" of 433 Tactical Fighter Squadron from Bagotville recalled that early in the war, the Canadians spent much of their time bombing Serbian radio relay sites, barracks, and other military infrastructure. "Later on, towards the third week, we started looking at some of the airports, some of the airfields; some of the infrastructure around the airfields; supply-type areas; storage areas; storage facilities; and petroleum, oil and lubricant storage areas. That sort of thing."[12]

The pilots discovered, however, that the GBU-12 didn't have sufficient punch to take out the larger fixed infrastructure targets such as bridges and buildings. As Lt. Col. "Billie" Flynn said: "We have a 500-pound bomb that doesn't knock the paint off the buildings you're trying to bomb."[13] However, pilots were asked to bomb the same targets repeatedly, with insufficient weapons for the job.[14] The Canadians did have a 2,000-pound bomb with more advanced technology, the GBU-24, but its Paveway III guidance didn't suit the tactical conditions over Serbia and Kosovo.[15]

That risk was unnecessary. As early as September 1998—long before the bombing began—Task Force Aviano requested clearance of a third bomb in the Kosovo theatre, a 2,000-pound GBU-10 bomb that used the Paveway II guidance system already in use with the GBU-12.[16] By October 1998, it was noted that "a wartime clearance to carry GBU-10 weapons within a restricted flight envelope is obtainable with minimal analysis and stores certification testing at this time."[17] That clearance never was approved. As Flynn said, "Remember, in peacetime, you don't get anything you want. There's nothing new about that and when war happens, people jump, and they jump pretty quickly."[18]

On 20 April 1999, deputy minister of national defence Jim Judd recommended that the minister approve spending $8 million to obtain 200 GBU-10 bombs from the United States at a cost of $40,000 per bomb.[19] Art Eggleton signed off approval through foreign military sales the same day. Those 200 GBU-10s were listed as an additional procurement, while the operational tempo and length of the conflict might necessitate further procurements.[20] Shortly afterward, near the first week of May, the weapons technicians in Aviano were back across the road at the American weapons dump, using their government credit cards to buy GBU-10 bombs. "I was actually there when we went to buy it. We went in there literally and said: 'We want 200 of this and 200 of that and 200 of this.'[21] The Americans said, 'here you go.'"[22] The actual cost of the bombs came in at US$8,615,753.[23]

Flynn said that once the GBU-10 was approved, the pilots had them within days. "My compatriots from AETE [the Aeronautical Engineering and Test Establishment in Cold Lake] did all our checks and gave us clearance to go with the bomb in about a week, which is unheard of. They flew over, checked how the bomb would fit on the airplane, confirmed the engineering that it would be okay, and gave us a clearance."[24] Back at the Canadian base, the workload ramped up again for loads standards and trainings officers. Once the Canadians had the GBU-10s, it had to be determined how to configure the CF-18s' antediluvian computers and train the crews in their use, while the other weapons in the Canadian inventory had to be assembled and built. The ground crews' efforts were stellar given that staff was over-stressed and the unit undermanned.[25]

Since none of the Canadians in Aviano had ever flown with or dropped a GBU-10, they had to learn how to use them literally on the fly. As Capt. Kirk Soroka said: "No one had ever flown with those except for the test pilots and they basically walked us through a quick how to-in the hangar. You know how to walk around them. They said: 'Just treat them like a GBU-12 and go drop 'em.' So that's what we did."[26]

Out of necessity, innovation on the ground and in the air characterized the Canadian contribution to air war as much as scrounging. As one sentence about the first night of Operation Allied Force in the first chapter notes: "Pelletier positioned himself in the lead of the four Canadian CF-18s flying single file and leading the eastern element." The fact is, they were forced to fly in single-file formations to avoid collisions because they lacked night-vision goggles that allowed them to see in the dark. The "Balkan Bats" flew as blind as the bats that flittered through the night air at their Piancavallo resort accommodations. That absence of night-vision goggles created a host of problems that were the result of budget cuts and the timing of requests to incorporate them in the CF-18s. To use night-vision goggles, the CF-18 had to be modified. The jet's instrument panel was illuminated to be seen at night with the naked eye. With night-vision

5.1. Canadian bomb loaders use an MJ loader to lift a GBU-10 Paveway 2,000-pound bomb on to a CF-18. Photo courtesy of the Department of National Defence.

goggles, that would become a problem, because the instruments could not be dimmed with a knob or a dial like a car's dashboard lights.

Pelletier explained that flying with lights out was less effective, but most of the Bagotville pilots had trained in night flying with all lights out except the red strobe, which was similar to flying in total blackout.

> It was a requirement to carry out one lights-out intercept, not a bombing run, but a lights-out intercept which is fairly similar. The only difference that it does for you is you get to see the strobe. At night, perception is not there so you don't get to see really or to perceive how far away the other guy is. A strobe at one mile is pretty much the same as a strobe at ten miles, the same thing as a strobe at 6,000 feet is about the same as a strobe at 15,000 feet, so to me it, it does make a difference in the confidence factor. So, guys did train with

it, maybe not as often as we should have, but I think the safety factor was there.[27]

The senior Canadian military commanders knew that the pilots in Aviano did not have night-vision capability. Jurkowski visited an American F-16 squadron in Aviano to understand what night-vision capability could give the CF-18s. He thought three considerations likely were behind the absence of night-vision goggles in the Canadians' cockpits when the air war began: an understanding of how complicated developing that capability was; a misperception of its true importance; and "typical sluggishness of the bureaucratic process to buy these things in the midst of a whole bunch of other priorities. There's never enough goddamn money."[28]

Henault, deputy chief of defence staff at the time, had confidence that the pilots had the skill and equipment necessary to conduct their Kosovo missions without night-vision goggles.

> That equipment, although it had been integrated in many other coalition aircraft, was not in Canadian aircraft and could never had been fitted in the short time that we were talking about given the complexities. For example, fitting a fighter aircraft cockpit with night-vision goggles is not nearly as simple as strapping the goggles on the helmet. There's a significant amount of cockpit modification that has to be done and so on. So we were aware of those limitations.
>
> I was also aware that direction had been given to our Canadian pilots not to undertake any missions that they did not feel they could undertake given some of the equipment limitations they had. Indeed, all of their missions were undertaken with the clear understanding that they would do the job with the equipment that they had on the aircraft, do it to the best of their ability or not do the mission, if that was the case, and to ensure that—as time progressed, as part of the follow-up to the Kosovo air campaign—we would inject this into the lessons-learned process for the updating of the F-18.[29]

Flynn, once retired, described the issue differently four years after the war: "It was a huge fuck up. Let me use the words properly: Huge Fuck Up. It was incredibly stupid and typically Canadian."[30]

To understand the complexity of the debate one must understand the "typical sluggishness of the bureaucratic process." In October 1997, Flynn and his 441 Squadron pilots had developed an elaborate case for acquiring night-vision goggles. They reasoned that since the Second World War, about one-third of all air-combat missions had flown at night, to reduce detection. They identified ground school and simulator training needs, aircraft lighting modifications, the different types of kit available, and the types of mission training that would improve as the result of acquiring night-vision capability.[31] The squadron received approval from a supplier that month to provide two to three sets, and assurances that two to three other sets could be purchased for $60,000–$70,000 from the CF-18 risk management program. Wing operations officer Lt. Col. J. M. Ouellet had promoted Flynn's night-vision goggle initiative to his wing commander. Despite engineering and funding hurdles, Ouellet wrote: "I believe that NVG is a force multiplier at night and offer significant safety benefits."[32] Then–wing commander Col. R. W. Guidinger recommended the idea to the director of air requirements at NDHQ in late October 1997.[33]

By November 1997, 441 Tactical Fighter Squadron developed a planning document setting out a concept of operations for the NVGs. It included obtaining six contractor models at US$9,000 each. The study showed how the CF-18s internal and external lighting could be modified with off-the-shelf lighting upgrades involving minimal modification to the jets' existing structure and wiring. The type of goggle that was being considered for testing was a lithium battery–powered binocular-type that mounted on a pilot's helmet by a detachable bracket. The battery life was ten hours. A spare battery would be secured in the cockpit's right-rear console. The document detailed pilot procedures in the event of vertigo, when they would revert to unaided visual use of instruments, and NVG failures. Combat training rules also were developed.[34]

By 28 April 1998, a night-vision goggle committee was struck and met for the first time at NDHQ in Ottawa. The costs of a trial program had grown to about $207,000. Six sets of goggles were purchased at a cost of $97,000, leaving $110,000 for aircraft modifications, trials, and incidentals.

Ground trials were expected to be completed by August 1998 and flight trials to commence by October 1998.[35]

An undated revised timeline pushed back the test date and trials. After contract modifications were completed, the test plan process could be in place by November/December 1998. Flying trials with NVGs would occur from February to May 1999 and reporting on the trials would take place by June 1999. However, the process was frozen with the deployment to Aviano in June 1998.[36] Flynn was livid at the bureaucratic inertia that delayed the program's development.

> The air force shuffled its feet on it. It was an incredible fiasco. That we never killed anybody is a miracle and we had a handful—at least—of near misses, nearly having guys kill themselves on sorties because you couldn't see anybody. And there was no ability once the war started to ramp up and use night-vision goggles. I'm sure the commander of the air war never knew that we were really flying around totally blind at night as we were. It was incredibly stupid. We could have admitted we couldn't see anything and then we would have been pulled out of the night war.[37]

Before Flynn and the 441 Fighter Squadron pilots replaced the Bagotville pilots, they flew at night in formations in anticipation of acquiring them. But from the first night of flying on 24 March 1999, the goggles were not available, forcing them to abandon all the training they had conducted for the previous two years. Flynn remains adamant that it was a mistake to send the pilots flying into some of the most difficult and dangerous parts of the air war without night-vision goggles:

> Every night-mission was lights out, and more than half of what we flew was at night. Of the 678 missions, half were at night. Me, I flew five night-missions before I became a day guy, and it was terrifying. It was really an incredible workload trying not to hit the guy in front of you, trying not to have the guy in back behind hit you and, oh, by the

5.2. 441 Fighter Squadron Commanding Officer Lieutenant-Colonel William Allen "Billie" Flynn in his CF-18's cockpit prepares for a combat mission. Photo courtesy of the Department of National Defence.

> way, you're going to go bomb somebody which was no small feat in itself.[38]

Other CF-18 pilots who flew the night missions have strong feelings about flying without NVGs. Soroka was one of them.

> That was nuts. My squadron, 441, had been training to fly at night for two years because our tactical expertise determined that when we went to war it would probably be at night. So, we started conducting night training and, so much so, that we were really comfortable flying at night. However, the training we were doing was with our lights on because we didn't have any NVGs. We were flying all the NVG formations, but with our lights on because it was unsafe otherwise. We had no training rules at the time to

fly with our lights off. Training rules are set so that we can conduct our operations in peacetime safely and as close to wartime conditions as we can get. We were ready to fly at night, at least we thought, until our first night into Kosovo.[39]

At least seven sets of problems resulted from the pilots flying without NVGs.

First was their inability to see each other. It forced the Canadians to develop flying procedures that enabled them to fly into combat without running into each other. They abandoned the conventional mutually supporting formations they would have flown. In a mutually supporting formation, four CF-18s fly in a box or a rectangle, depending on their objectives. In battle formation, two lead aircraft line abreast with two wingmen each trailing about forty-five degrees off their wings.[40] Those formations went out the window along with the mutual support they provided. Instead the Canadians flew in an entrail formation, basically a straight-line formation with three Hornets following the lead—each several miles behind the jet in front of it—and separated by different altitudes.

Second, flying into combat in a single file compromised their effectiveness because the Canadians could not bomb targets en masse. Glaeser explained.

> Ordinarily, we overwhelm the enemy by all coming in all at once in line-abreast formations, maximizing our weapons' effects by putting our bombs on target all together, all at the same time. But when you come single file into a target the lead will drop his bomb. A couple of minutes later number two will drop his bombs. A couple of minutes later number three will drop his bombs. You're better off to put all the bombs on the target at the same time to maximize the effect. Night-vision goggles allow you to do that.[41]

Third, flying four or more CF-18s dropping bombs on targets, one at a time, all coming from the same direction, made it treacherous for the trailing pilots. Glaeser said:

> When you're the last guy in a train of four guys, it isn't a good feeling. If I can make an analogy, if you've got a bunch of police and they're going to go into a building, they're going to do it all at once. That's kind of the idea. Overpower them. Everybody comes in at once. Everybody goes out at once. Overwhelm the enemy. They're not going to go in one at a time, through the door single file because, eventually, somebody's going to get picked off. That's what you don't want to do and that's what we had to do.[42]

Glaeser found out first-hand out what it was like to fly fourth in formation when enemy gunners knew three pilots before him already had dropped their bombs. On the night of May 30, he flew last in a file of four CF-18s on their way to bomb army barracks in Nis, Serbia's second-largest city.

> Everybody was to bomb these barracks and I'm the last guy in the formation. A captain from Bagotville was the lead. As he was going in he reported heavy AAA in the target area which means heavy anti-aircraft artillery. I was like, OK, I've heard that before. Number two said heavy AAA also. I think three was Rambo and these guys—remember, because I was four—by the time they came off the target they were actually heading south out of Yugoslavia back down towards Albania. I was still heading north into the target because I was a couple of miles behind them. These guys remember. They looked over their shoulder and all they saw was just massive AAA coming up and it was all at our altitude—like it was getting into the 20,000–25,000 foot altitudes, our altitudes—which is incredible for anti-aircraft artillery. It was pretty heavy calibre; they think it was 90-millimetre AAA. I could actually see it in my FLIR on the horizon, kind of like popcorn exploding. The guys, when we landed, we kind of laughed about it. They said: "Oh, Laser, man, we didn't think you were going to make it." That was the worst AAA I've ever seen.[43]

Pilot call sign "Hooker" of 441 Tactical Fighter Squadron's weapons and tactics officer, agreed that flying single-file formations provided less mutual support for the trailing members, but for a different reason. "I would have to agree that flying entrail formations—not the result that you are leaving number four hanging out there to some degree—but the fact that I think you're flying at night makes you perhaps more vulnerable because you're not able to actually check the other guy, you know, visually."[44] Having said that, "Hooker" also said an argument could be made that the night pilots were somewhat more protected "simply because it's dark and it's more difficult for the bad guy to find you and to shoot you than would be the case in the daytime."[45] Night-vision goggles would have given the Canadians greater capabilities and more support, "Hooker" says, but the Canadians had no other choice but to play the cards they were dealt. "Under the circumstances, our feeling in theatre was we had a job to do and we had really only one way of going about doing that and we did what we had to do."[46]

Fourth, because the pilots had to fly in single-file formation, the trailing pilots did their best to use their radars to "see" the leading CF-18s in the dark. However, Soroka explained, ordinarily, the CF-18's on-board radar is used to look for air-to-air threats, not to stay in formation.

> The three [trailing] formation members relied heavily on the radar to stay in position. But because we had to use our radar to ground map the target area, too, and hand that off to our Forward Looking Infrared targeting pod, there were periods of time when there was no radars looking into the air-to-air threat out there. It did exist, particularly with the targets we were going into that were heavily defended and known positions for MiG-21s and MiG-29s.[47]

The pilots also became skilled at training their FLIR pods—ordinarily used for acquiring their targets—on the jet in front of them as another way of seeing in the dark and staying in formation.

Fifth, no battle plan—including a compromised one that required the pilots to fly in single file—withstands the first encounter with the enemy. Capt. Brassington said, despite planning as best they could, staying in formation and trying to dodge surface-to-air missiles when the pilots couldn't see each other was a haphazard affair at best.

> I don't think there's a guy that can't tell a story of swapping places in the middle of the night as you went into the target or come out on the other side because he just couldn't see. You just kind of cross your fingers and hope for the best, you know, when you go into the target area, especially when things get demanding. I can plan it and say we're all going to go 400 miles an hour and, at this point exactly, we're going to each turn at this heading so that we can keep the train following each other around. The second that one person deviates in air speed or heading then it starts to fall apart.
>
> We had specific procedures in place that if someone got lit up by a SAM threat or a triple-A threat, there were manoeuvres that we would do en masse to try and keep the formation together, but the variables are so great. It doesn't take much for an aircraft to drift out of position. One degree of heading change in sixty miles equals a nautical mile out and we move pretty fast. It's called the one-in-sixty rule. If you're two degrees off and you fly 30 miles you'll be one mile out. Sixty miles is not a lot.[48]

Sixth, with the single-file formation under attack, the evasive manoeuvres they had to execute put them unnecessarily at risk. Capt. Neil McRury, a CF-18 instructor with Cold Lake's 416 Tactical Fighter Squadron, explained:

> If we were all going in one after the other at night and the second guy in a train of four had a threat to react to, then the entire formation had to threat-react, because you can't see each other. You basically go on certain on-board devices to determine your separation. We had to watch for things coming up off the ground. The guy in front of you, you had to check a third instrument to make sure you weren't closing in or opening up. If you were No. 2, for example, and I

started stretching away from the guy in front of me, then it goofed up the guys behind me, because they now compressed in on me. If my target reacted, then they're going to be in a world of hurt. Yeah, it was a serious detriment to the safety and effectiveness on behalf of the guys in Kosovo, not having them [night-vision goggles].[49]

Seventh, the crowded battle space over Serbia or Kosovo—which can only be described as controlled chaos—put the night-blind Canadians flying in single formation at risk of collision or being bombed by their own allies. One Bagotville pilot explained:

> What's going on is everybody is lights out. Everything is dark. Where you're going, it is just black, but you know there's about fifty or sixty airplanes in the air. All you look at is the black, because everybody is lights out. They all can see each other because they have NVGs, but we cannot see anybody unless you see them on your radar. So, some guys were coming off target, turning towards you, climbing about, whatever, and you see them on the radar. That's good, but if your radar's busy painting the ground, and you're not looking at the sky then you don't see. So, you just hope everybody's following the flow, there's no clowns there that are going to turn in your face at your altitude.[50]

In the fog of war, Glaeser nearly collided with an allied plane, which he attributes directly to the lack of night-vision goggles.

> A really huge thing about the night-vision goggles isn't safety from enemy fire, it's safety from running into friendly airplanes. You can make the best plan in the whole world, deconflicted altitude wise, deconflicted everything for safety, but the fact is that the lights are out. Somebody is going to mess up the plan and come flying right through the middle of your formation at night. It happened to us where an American guy, or a Spanish guy, or a Brit, I don't know

> which country, but another country. Another allied country flew right through the middle of our formation with one of their airplanes and maybe they saw us, maybe they didn't, but we sure didn't see them. It's a big surprise when another airplane flies right through your formation at night. If you had goggles on you could see that for miles and do things a lot safer.[51]

Apart from colliding with an allied warplane, Soroka was almost bombed by one.

> I almost got killed during a night strike on April 30 because of that formation and the way we were ingressing on the target. Whenever people start shooting at you, the first thing you do is you go faster. You just want to get into the target area, get out of there, dodge the bullets, and then leave the target area safely. The problem is you have to fly the same speed and we weren't flying the same speed in the formation. There was a turn in the routing to the target and the element behind us overflew me and delivered their bombs right through my element. I'll never know how close they were, I just know that, by virtue of the attack access and the formation we were in, it was pretty tight.[52]

Yet another shortcoming of the Canadian CF-18s' standard equipment affected not only Canadian operations but those of the entire NATO coalition air fleet. The whole coalition effort had to use single-frequency jammable radio equipment to accommodate the Canadians because the CF-18s lacked jam-resistant radios, radios that operate on multiple frequencies at the same time. As Capt. Neil McRury explained:

> It illustrated the fact that our aircraft, albeit capable, was dated. It forced us to operate in an environment that was compromised insofar as verbal communications. We didn't have a secure radio system to talk to other coalition fighter aircraft. We could talk to the AWACS in a secure manner,

> but we couldn't talk to the other coalition aircraft in a secure manner.⁵³

That made it easy for the enemy to determine which frequencies the Canadians were using and then jam them. Not only were coalition communications not heard, but unless they turned their radios off they were forced to listen to whatever was being used to jam their frequencies. Capt. Brassington said:

> Anybody with a Radio Shack scanner could eventually find out what frequency we were transmitting on. If you have a really big transmitter with lots of power you can jam out that signal frequency, making it difficult for guys to talk on. Whoever has the most powerful transmitter essentially wins. I'm serious, they were jamming us. Now what that meant was there was nights when, and everybody thinks it's funny, but I listened to Celine Dion. It's a very poignant memory. Yeah. Celine Dion. How appropriate. How do they know it's us out here tonight?⁵⁴

With such powerful and compelling stories to tell, what Canadians could have learned about the heroics of the pilots in combat and ground crews servicing the CF-18s—or not—from the news media during the Kosovo air war—and why—requires a brief departure or glimpse back in time to eight years earlier, a prelude if you will. Central to it is learning what key Canadian Forces personnel remembered from the 1991 Persian Gulf War to understand the dynamics that shaped what the media and—by extension—Canadians writ large could know about the Kosovo bombing campaign. It is somewhat akin to watching sausages being made: unpleasant truths can emerge.

6

Prelude to Censorship: Media, Body Bags, and the Persian Gulf War

The image was chilling and the intimidating thought behind it appalling. The *Vancouver Sun* reported in January 1991 that the wife of a Canadian Forces naval officer had discovered a body bag dumped on her front lawn in Esquimalt, BC. Her husband was among those aboard HMCS *Huron* preparing to take part in Canada's contribution to Operation Friction, the naval blockade of Iraq prior to the Persian Gulf War. The report specifically identified the body bag as the type used by the military but did not indicate how a civilian could have obtained one. The victim's family allegedly was targeted through names published in local newspapers identifying those aboard the destroyer about to relieve others already serving in the Gulf. Canadian Forces spokesmen vowed that no effort was being spared to find out who was responsible for this and other harassment.[1]

Reportedly, more incidents occurred, including callers identifying themselves as insurance salesmen advising the families to buy life insurance for their husbands. Others claiming to be military officials phoned military wives to inform them of the death of their spouses.[2] The following day the Vancouver newspaper took an editorial position stating that the perpetrators "defile the ideals of the peace movement."[3] The *Sun* did not indicate how it knew the alleged perpetrators belonged to the peace movement.

The day after the body bag report, on 22 January 1991, Parliament voted 214 to 47 to support United Nations resolutions for the use of military force to drive Saddam Hussein's Iraqi troops from Kuwait. Iraq had invaded its neighbour some five months earlier.[4] Canada's military contribution included twenty-four CF-18 Hornet jet fighter/bombers and 700 personnel. Over forty-three days, from January 17 to February 28, the 1991 Persian Gulf War—known as Operation Desert Storm—became the world's first real-time televised war.[5] Operation Friction was Canada's contribution. Daily—from the comfort of their living rooms, offices, and wherever televisions could be found—audiences worldwide could tune into a war that featured the devastating strikes of laser-guided smart bombs destroying their targets with pinpoint accuracy. How the American military and governments managed the news media during that war and since has been studied extensively.[6] Little, however, is known about the Canadian Forces' management of the Canadian news media before and during the war, including the reported body bag incident. It is fertile ground for study and explains in large part the security considerations and decisions during the 1999 Kosovo air war.

Five months before the Gulf War's outbreak, Canadian Forces public affairs planners already had developed little-known but elaborate communications strategies for the Canadian news media. It was announced on 10 August 1990 that three Canadian ships—HMCS *Protecteur*, HMCS *Athabaskan*, and HMCS *Terra Nova*—would be sent to the Gulf to enforce UN-mandated sanctions against Iraq as soon as possible. Just five days later, on August 15, a prototype Canadian Forces public affairs plan setting out methods of dealing with the heightened news media interest in the Forces was forwarded to National Defence Headquarters in Ottawa.[7] Major Canadian news outlets already had submitted requests to accompany the warships on their deployment to the Gulf. The Forces' director-general of public affairs was ordered to assist with the development of a media pool of four national journalists aboard the ships.[8] The Canadian military clearly saw the impending conflict as a golden opportunity to build popular support for the Forces. "This opportunity to maximize media coverage and encourage popular support for the Canadian Forces must be actively encouraged when viewed in a macro sense vis-à-vis the future of the Canadian navy in particular and the Canadian Forces in general."[9]

To that end, the news media would be accommodated as much as possible given operational considerations. The pre-deployment phase of public affairs activities was deemed crucial. The news media was directed toward the eighteen- and twenty-year-old ships' upgraded weapons and sensors at every opportunity, and to as many human interest stories as possible. The aim was to reinforce the "boy next door" sentiments of the public so audiences became personally involved in support for Canadian sailors and aircrew.[10]

By November 1990, public opinion polls led military planners to conclude that their strategy was working. The general public and the news media had a keen interest in the Forces' operations, planning, and combat preparations. Between 64 and 69 per cent of Canadians approved of the government's decision to become involved in the blockade. The communications strategy was revised to enhance public understanding of and support for Canada's role by nurturing and capitalizing on extant public interest. The military aimed for "maximum disclosure of information consistent with maintaining the operational security of Canada's forces and those of other allied nations participating in the Gulf operations."[11] In its after-action report on its public affairs planning, the Canadian military stated it knew that the news media would play an influential role in that communications strategy because they would be the key conveyors of information about, and interpreters of, the war's events to the Canadian public.[12] Military public affairs planners made every effort to inform Canadians proactively.

They sought to take command not only of the news media's agenda but of virtually every sector of society, including its democratically elected institutions. The messages the military wanted portrayed to Canadians included: that Canada's mission was to deter Iraqi aggression in Kuwait and enforce UN sanctions; that Canadian ships and aircraft were fully capable of conducting their missions; that morale was high and personnel were confident; that Canadians would operate under Canadian command and control; and, finally, that the Canadian Forces were participating with appropriate legislative and diplomatic approvals in addition to operational considerations.[13] Those messages were to be conveyed to nine target audiences (seven external audiences and two internal audiences) that military communications planners had identified.

The first external audience targeted was the general Canadian public, in communication thrusts via news releases, public briefings, the news media, debates in the House of Commons, and in replies to ministerial questions and inquiries. The second target was the news media, stimulated through background briefings, news releases, query responses, and operational theatre visits. The third audience was elected officials, who would be reached via briefings, questions in the House of Commons, committee presentations, and various elected officials' visits to operational theatres. The fourth target audience was Canadian academics, whom the military planned to reach through background and technical briefings. The fifth audience was defence analysts, who would also be reached through technical and background briefings. The sixth audience was ethnic Canadians, who would be informed through media reports and public briefings. The seventh external audience was international publics that would be reached through foreign missions, briefings, and assistance to international journalists.[14]

The first internal public identified was Canadian Forces members, who would be informed through internal information programs disseminated by base newspapers, video releases, and briefings. The second internal public was Canadian Forces members' dependents, who would be reached through command briefings, family support centres, internal information programs, and base newspapers.[15] Although the internal publics are an important constituency from a Canadian Forces point of view and worthy of study, this chapter will focus on the external publics the Forces identified. The common thread throughout the military's attempts to shape public opinion of Canada's role in the Persian Gulf, with all but two exceptions, was the news media. The two external publics in which the news media were not identified to support the military mission were academics and defence analysts. Presumably, they did not need the news media for basic information and had a higher level of understanding of Canada's military role in the Persian Gulf than the general public, parliamentarians, and other government officials.

Given the Canadian news media's high level of interest in the Canadian Forces Middle East (CANFORME) operations, on 9 November 1990 the Forces developed a news media policy based on operational security requirements:

a. Within the scope of operational security, media will be accorded every possible assistance in the preparation and filing of their reports; b. Censorship will not be invoked by DND or by CANFORCOMME. The imposition of censorship can only be derived from censorship policy of the Canadian government. Therefore, it is paramount that a good working relationship with the news media be established to ensure they understand the necessity to voluntarily comply with in-theatre security screening guidelines. Accordingly, media covering the roles, operations and activities of the Canadian Forces Middle East should be prepared to submit their copy for security screening only; c. There will be no suggestion that media expunge critical commentary from their reports unless there is an impact on security of operations; d. Before they are provided access to in-theatre operations, all media are to be provided unclassified briefings about Canadian Forces operations and activities in the Persian Gulf, security considerations and requirements, and what is expected of them while they are visiting CANFORME units; e. Media embarked in HMC ships may use ships' communications resources, when appropriate and available. The Canadian Forces will provide protective clothing and equipment to media representatives when they are embarked in HMC ships; f. All interviews with news media representatives will be "on the record'; g. Journalists will be requested to dateline their articles and reports generically, such as ". . . with the Canadian Forces in Bahrain/Qatar/Persian Gulf." No specific locations will be used when filing stories; h. Media representatives will be assisted by on-site public affairs officers; j. Diplomatic clearances, visa and inoculations will be the responsibility of the media members; and, k. Media who are not prepared to work within these guidelines will not be provided access to CANFORME operations, activities and units.[16]

The only negative news reports that emerged from August to December from the deployment involved sailors' morale problems aboard the three ships and questions about their ability to carry out sustained operations.[17] One month later, the Canadian Forces developed a further communications plan for the rotation of three more ships to the Gulf—HMCS *Huron* and HMCS *Restigouche* from the West Coast and HMCS *Preserver* from the East Coast—to sustain Canada's commitments. It aimed to convey the messages that the rotation was the most cost-effective way to maintain operational readiness; it allowed trained personnel to relieve personnel serving since August; the ships' state of readiness was good; and the new personnel were confident they could do the job of the crews they were replacing.[18] To accommodate the news media covering the departure of HMCS *Huron* from Esquimalt, BC, the naval public affairs office was charged with handling all requests for media interviews with members of the ship's company. No direction was given at that time to withhold the names of members of the ship's company.[19]

In early January 1991, it appeared that Canada's military effort in the Persian Gulf might be escalating. On January 2, Canadian Chief of Defence Staff (CDS) Gen. John de Chastelain met with key staff to discuss a public affairs policy that envisioned the Canadian military's transition to war. The 9 November 1990 communications plan would remain in effect with the aim of enhancing public understanding and support of the Canadian military's Persian Gulf role. The key elements regarding the news media were: that their activities be conducted within the constraints of operational security; there be no censorship; and that media members must accept the November 9 guidelines to be accredited.[20] Events in the Persian Gulf, Washington, Ottawa, and around the world began to unfold rapidly after 12 January 1991, when Congress granted US president George Bush the authority to wage war.

By January 14, the Canadian Forces had developed a new media plan for the war. It called for the organization of a Canadian news media pool that would be assembled, deployed, and escorted by the public affairs office, with careful control of its access to air operations headquarters.[21] Canadian senior operations offices would hold regular unclassified briefings on the Canadian Forces operations and activities for journalists at Bahrain and Qatar. But Canadian journalists would be largely on their own if they wished to cover the Joint Allied Information Bureau in Dhahran, Saudi Arabia, where the British and Americans were organizing journalists into pools to cover the forward land battle expected in Kuwait. The joint information bureau was located at the International Hotel. The Canadians similarly would be on their own in Riyadh, Saudi Arabia, the location of the main American, British, and Saudi headquarters. There, senior US and British senior officers would brief journalists at the Hyatt Regency Hotel.[22] As an indication of the priority the Canadian Forces placed on the control of messages it wanted Canadians to receive, on January 15, CDS de Chastelain ordered that only approved spokesmen in Ottawa could comment on Canada's anticipated mission and roles in the Persian Gulf hostilities. The ostensible aim was ensuring consistency with government policy.[23]

The next day, January 16, Prime Minister Brian Mulroney rose in the House of Commons shortly and announced that Canada had joined with other UN members in driving Saddam Hussein's troops from Kuwait by force. To do so, Mulroney's cabinet gave de Chastelain full authority for Canadian CF-18s to fly combat missions in the Gulf. Even as the prime minister spoke, the fighter bombers had begun to conduct sweep and escort missions over Kuwait and Iraq, protecting Canadian and allied ships and personnel in the Gulf.[24] Their first role was combat air patrol (CAP) missions to protect coalition warships against Iraqi Exocet missiles. The CF-18s eventually flew 770 CAP sorties.[25]

Ten of the twenty-four CF-18s and about 160 personnel of the 700 who participated in the war came from 416 Tactical Fighter Squadron at CFB Cold Lake, Alberta. The rest came from Lahr, Germany, and Bagotville, Quebec. Retired Canadian Forces Brig. Gen. Ed McGillivray, commander of CFB Cold Lake in 1991, recalls that the news media were never particularly interested in his people before the outbreak of the Gulf War. "When Iraq was attacked, all hell broke loose at Cold Lake. All of a sudden, we had media parked outside the base. Every media in Canada was there, every news agency, TV, radio, even to the point where they had satellite trucks."[26]

Initially, McGillivray took it upon himself to tell the news media how the 416 Tactical Fighter Squadron fit Canada's contributions to the coalition war effort. The news media wanted more: they wanted access to relatives of the pilots to humanize their stories beyond squadron numbers.

Like many journalists across Canada, they wanted names and faces put to the pilots' families, who could share their thoughts and feelings about their loved ones' involvement in the war.[27]

Marion Kendall, the wife of Cold Lake pilot Maj. Dave Kendall, agreed to become the unofficial spokeswoman for all the pilots' families for the duration of the war. Kendall talked openly about how difficult it was for her children and other families who had never faced the spectre of war before. McGillivray relates: "She provided, shall we say, good news clips and they followed her, and they interviewed her all the time throughout the war to get her reaction as to how the war was going. Anytime they wanted a news clip, they'd give her a call and, generally, they'd get one."[28]

Like Americans who revelled in their hometown heroes,[29] newspapers across Canada were awash in "boy next door" stories that provided hundreds of local angles for journalists, which bonded Canadians to their military men and women. The Canadians were identified in stories and pictures by name and hometowns as pilots waiting to fly on missions and as medics mentally preparing for the grim potential of combat casualties.[30] Such identification is a standard North American journalistic practice, to engage readers and viewers. In most instances, journalists provide sufficient identification of "persons, organizations, places, objects and even the event itself for the reader to orient himself immediately."[31] Canadian regiments usually are identified by their official hometown or towns.[32]

Meanwhile, thousands of other Canadians across the country made headline news in the wake of Prime Minister Mulroney's announcement. Anti-war protestors responded to the news almost immediately. In Toronto, crowds blocked traffic on busy streets, chanting "Get troops out of Iraq" as they headed toward the Progressive Conservative Party headquarters on Richmond Street.[33] Outside the US consulate flags were burned. At city hall, 1,500 people demonstrated for hours. Upward of 500 demonstrators rallied in Halifax.[34] In Ottawa, security was tightened following poisoning threats at two water treatment plants and at regional water storage tanks.[35] About 200 demonstrators formed a human chain blocking the entrances to the external affairs department not far from the official residence of the prime minister at 24 Sussex Drive.[36] Across Canada, police, government officials, and religious groups readied themselves in case of terrorist acts in reprisal for military actions in the Gulf. Security was increased at Canadian airports and at Ontario's three nuclear power stations.[37]

In Halifax, RCMP stepped up airport security, as did the Halifax Port Authority.[38] In Quebec, the public securities minister boosted security at oil refineries, hydroelectric plants, and vital industrial plants, while local police forces, the provincial police, the RCMP, and the Canadian Security Intelligence Service (CSIS) prepared a list of names of "persons of interest."[39] In Ontario, security at border crossings, Pearson International Airport, and Ontario Hydro was intensified, while the RCMP consulted with CSIS over threats to Canadian security.[40] In Vancouver, seventy-five demonstrators set fire to Canadian, United Nations, American, and Petro-Canada flags.[41] All the above made national headlines.

Despite the abundance of news related to the unfolding war, all was not well within the ranks of Canada's news media. Unrest began to grow early in the campaign about "censorship guidelines" forced on their colleagues in the Persian Gulf. Defence minister William McKnight set out the guidelines in a letter to the Canadian Press. The *Globe and Mail* reported on January 19 that military censors would review stories by journalists on Canadian ships to determine whether they could inadvertently jeopardize operations or the "security of Canadian or other allied forces."[42] These were the 9 November 1990 guidelines developed months earlier by the military's public affairs planners.

News of these restrictions sparked debate over the practicalities of such restrictions and limits on the public's right to know. University of Toronto history professor Paul Rutherford argued that censorship of Canadian journalists wouldn't work because America's Cable News Network (CNN) had shown US warplanes taking off from Qatar for missions against Baghdad, effectively contravening the non-disclosure of mission points of origin other than simply land-based or carrier-based.[43] It was reported that the Canadian guidelines mirrored US Department of Defense guidelines that prohibited the details of military operations, size, location, or movement of intelligence activities or assessments of enemy camouflage. Prominent Canadian military historian Jack Granatstein argued that Second World War censorship forbidding the release of strategy, tactics, and military movements represented reasonable limits on what could and couldn't be reported in the news media. "Under no circumstances should the public's right to know jeopardize the life of one serviceman," Granatstein said.[44]

Freedom of press reporting from the Persian Gulf also was discussed briefly in the House of Commons. Prime Minister Mulroney was asked directly if the tradition of press freedom would co-exist with war zone security. Mulroney replied that the journalists had full freedom, subject to military authorities' requirements.[45] When asked on whose authority—because the Canadian Association of Journalists had complained that the Canadians were subject not only to Canadian military guidelines but to US military censorship—defence minister McKnight took responsibility for setting out the Canadian guidelines but stated he had no ability to guarantee Canadians access to other countries' military authorities.[46]

On the next day, 21 January 1991, news broke about a body bag found on the lawn of a sailor's home in Esquimalt and harassing phone calls to service personnel's families on the West Coast.[47] The news ripped through the Canadian Forces in other parts of Canada like wildfire. Matching and follow-up reports across Canada—wherever possible with quotes and comments from local military personnel giving the story local angles—fanned the flames. It didn't matter whether local military commanders indicated such harassment was not replicated at their bases. The story was reported anyway.[48] One news article written from Ottawa exaggerated the report of one body bag to multiple bags left on the doorsteps of several military families, although it said the reports were unconfirmed. The story included graphic quotes of one harassing phone call saying: "I have family in Iraq and if something happens to them I will come and get you."[49] Another said: "You are murderers."[50] The only military source for the story was a Canadian Forces colonel who did not state on what authority he could base his comments.

Making the threats universal, Forces commanders in Ottawa confirmed reports of "isolated incidents" of harassment, although there were no specific details, including the base where the reported harassment took place. Lt. Gen. David Huddleston told a parliamentary committee that he could only assume the offensive incidents were related to the war. "The less we discuss this matter the better; every country has its cranks and the more we talk about offensive activities like that, the more cranks get the idea to repeat them."[51]

On January 25, the CF-18s flew their first four sweep-and-escort sorties. In the sweep role, one or two pairs of jets flew ahead of coalition heavy bombers aiming to engage enemy fighters. In the escort role, three pairs of CF-18s rode shotgun on the bombers, ahead of, beside, and behind them. Details of those missions were dutifully reported in the Canadians news media in great detail, courtesy of American wire services. Accompanying graphics included separation distances between individual airplanes flying in four-ship formations in the sweep role and the separations between CF-18s and heavy bombers when flying in the escort role.[52] Across Canada and in the war zone, journalists localized Canadian pilots' involvement in the war effort as best they could. From Kentville, Nova Scotia, a journalist identified Reg Forsythe as the father of Stephen Forsythe, who was photographed by the Canadian Press in Qatar and whose picture accompanied a local story. His family in Nova Scotia had seen Stephen on television numerous times.[53] In Qatar, Capt. Doug Carter, of Prince Albert, Saskatchewan, and Maj. Russ Cooper, of Hamilton, Ontario, were identified by a *Toronto Star* reporter in a story saying the pilots were "psyched up" for the war.[54]

When Canadian pilots embarked on the first flights escorting bombers, Captains Arnie Tate, of Orono, Ontario, and Jeff Tait, of Richmond, BC, were reported in the *Toronto Star* as saying they would go back and do it again.[55] A follow-up story the next day localized that account even further, tracking down Capt. Arnie Tate's father-in-law Gus McNeil in Orono, where Tate lived with his wife, Lisa.[56] Lt. Col. Don Matthews, who was commanding officer of 439 Tactical Fighter Squadron, led the four CF-18s on their first sweep-and-escort mission. A *Toronto Star* photographer took Matthews' picture after the first mission in Doha, Qatar. The information below the picture indicated Matthews was raising his hands in jubilation upon return.[57] That was wrong.

> Standard procedure is for the pilot, once you've come to a full stop, is to get your hands out of the cockpit. You hold them up high so they're visible to the ground crew. That is the signal for the ground crew to go under the airplane and safe up your missiles. They don't want to be under the airplane if the pilot has his hands in the cockpit. Unfortunate-

ly, it was reported in a lot of newspapers and a lot of pictures that the colonel raises arms in victory after first mission into Iraq. Actually, the colonel was raising his arms so that the ground crew would trust him not to drop a bomb on their heads.[58]

Several days later, a follow-up news report in Montreal on January 28 indicated that Canadian Forces officials in Qatar had asked the media to break the convention of identifying service personnel by their hometowns. It said the servicemen had asked for that restriction, fearing harassment of their families. At that time, the main concern was harassing telephone calls. In the same report, the body bag incident was downgraded to a garbage bag made to resemble a body bag. The article reported that the Calgary parents of a Canadian pilot had received crank telephone calls.[59]

The same day it was reported from Qatar that Canadian pilots' wives in Germany had been evacuated from their homes as a result of a bomb threat that later proved to be false. There was no threat made. At that point, it was said that the Canadian pilots were turning their backs on the news media, possibly fearing harassment of their families.[60] Also, the issue of harassment of the Forces' families had taken on a life of its own. Even as the prime minister and his cabinet attempted to boost the Forces' morale with high-profile visits in February 1991, a reference to the harassing phone calls was reported from Ottawa as fact in the *Globe and Mail*.[61] The unattributed reference included an extended time frame. It stated as fact that on February 5, naval personnel in Esquimalt had been receiving threatening or nuisance phone calls not on an isolated basis but systematically since the outbreak of hostilities on January 16.[62]

The Canadian Forces commanders in the Gulf reportedly took matters into their own hands. They took the family harassment issue a step further by advising CF-18 pilots to refrain from giving their names and hometowns to journalists. The information was only voluntary: servicemen and women were free to give their hometowns if they wished. They provided some details of the harassment, including that families in Canada were being harassed by crank telephone calls. Being identified by name was described as "not a very bright thing to do."[63] The restriction was said to be the result of anonymous harassing telephone calls being made to military families and an incident in which a garbage bag was made to look like a body bag used to ship home servicemen's remains.[64]

Ignoring for a moment that references to hometowns may have been put on hold as a voluntary policy, a qualitative sampling of newspaper headlines reveals a larger story of operational censorship. The news media was denied basic information about the Canadians' operations in the Gulf. Military commanders would not even disclose the number of airplanes taking part in missions or if escort runs had been carried out or aborted, or even how withholding such details would reduce the risks.[65] The media was becoming frustrated with the amount of information—or lack thereof—that they were receiving from the Canadian Forces. "Shh . . . there's a war on," read one Calgary headline, and "Canadian journalists say they are frustrated by censorship," read another in Vancouver.[66] The overall sense of irritation was palpable: "Getting details of what Canadian soldiers, sailors and flyers are doing in the Gulf war is almost impossible. The Canadian military basically limits its answers to: Soldiering. Sailoring. Flying."[67] Most journalists in Riyadh who had not managed to get into the American-military-arranged news pools simply were stuck in their hotels, although those prepared to rent vehicles and lie at US army checkpoints could get close to the allied ground forces if they wished.[68] The Canadian journalists in Qatar covering the CF-18s found themselves largely stuck in hotels "waiting for phone calls from press officers to say they can come on the base for carefully arranged interviews."[69]

The Canadians were not alone in this development. Doubts were emerging in the United States about the completeness of information Americans were receiving about the bombing campaign. Although the video images of a guided missile repeatedly shown on television striking its target over and over again were flashy, the Center for Defense Information in Washington said it was suspect. Describing the video as obviously the "best of the best" in the US military's catalogue, one analyst said that 100 per cent of the missiles launched could not be striking their targets dead centre.[70]

In Canada, one week into the bombing campaign, frustrated Liberal opposition MPs complained their only source about the campaign was American television. Concerns were raised publicly that even the government, including the minister of national defence, was getting its war information from television.[71] Journalists laughed cynically over the lack of information they received from military briefers. When they asked where Canadian jet fighters had flown escort missions, they were told the mission took place "over a Kuwaiti-Iraqi land mass."[72] The Canadian military couldn't provide any detailed information because it had no control over allied intelligence data and couldn't release allied data.[73] By February 20, the Canadian Forces' public affairs personnel had had more than a month to study restrictive news media guidelines developed by the American and British militaries. As result, the Canadian military developed a new set of written guidelines combining those developed for the Canadian navy and by the American and British militaries for the Canadian news media briefings in Bahrain and Qatar. The guidelines were ostensibly "to provide the greatest permissible freedom and access while at the same time protecting the safety and security of Canadian and other allied forces. The Canadian Forces wish to be as open and candid as possible. However, operational security will and must take precedence."[74]

In the guidelines developed by the Canadian Forces, the following subjects could not be reported:

> a. For military units, specific numerical information on troop strength, aircraft, weapons systems, on-hand equipment or supplies (e.g. radars, missiles, trucks, water), including amounts of ammunition or fuel moved by support units or on hand in combat units. Unit size may be described in general terms such as "company size," "squadron," or "naval task group." Number or amount of equipment and supplies may be described in general terms such as "large," "small," or "many"; b. Any information that reveals details of future plans, operations or strikes, including postponed or cancelled operations; c. Information, photography and imagery that would reveal the specific location of military forces or show the level of security at military installations or encampments or information on defensive equipment capabilities.[75]

One day later, on February 21, the new guidelines were put to the test after the Canadian government ordered CF-18 crews in Qatar to begin dropping bombs and firing rockets on the Iraqi military. A *Globe and Mail* correspondent in Riyadh was denied access to the CF-18 pilots for interviews. The best he could do was quote, by name, a CF-18 pilot reached by telephone in a recruiting office in Hamilton, Ontario. The pilot, who was friends with the Canadians in Qatar, had an inkling of what the Canadians would be doing in their new role but couldn't divulge it. He could only say that the pilots felt good to be taking on the new combat role, because they had felt like poor cousins flying escort to other coalition warplanes.[76] Five days later, the journalist who remained in Riyadh still could not obtain any information whatsoever other than that the Canadians had dropped iron bombs on military targets. Some reporters in Qatar were shown CF-18 bomb loads before four jets took off, but that was the extent of their access.[77]

A qualitative review of selected English language newspapers' war coverage revealed that the journalists best able to report on the war were based either at Qatar or Bahrain. In Qatar, the journalists independently assessed the CF-18s' activities without military briefings. While they weren't learning specific details about the missions, they learned the frequency and number of jets in the air by watching and counting. Over time, they began to know the pilots' names.[78] With the historical benefit of having both the military's media guidelines from 1990 and 1991 and the news coverage that followed, the best that can be said is that the guidelines were applied inconsistently. When two CF-18 pilots attacked an Iraqi patrol boat believed to be armed with Exocet missiles, they were identified by name. Some news reports contained the exact locations of the enemy encountered, the armaments used, and the weapons and defensive capabilities of the CF-18s—all specifically prohibited by the guidelines. One pilot named was Dave Kendall, the husband of Marion Kendall, who had taken on the high-profile role as spokeswoman for the CF-18s crew members' spouses at CFB Cold Lake.[79] The pilots' names were repeatedly published in follow-up stories. Depending on the newspapers read, the pilots either were reprimanded for firing on the Iraqi ship[80] or commended for firing on it.[81]

The voluntary prohibition put on the use of service personnel's names and hometowns was not always invoked for non-combat personnel. Many women were identified by name and hometowns in one feature story on what it was like to work in a male-dominated environment in Qatar.[82] Some of the very women who should have most worried about navy service personnel's spouses being harassed didn't seem to care about the issue. In a Canadian Press news story datelined Esquimalt, several sailors' wives were identified by name, as were their husbands, after they travelled to Esquimalt to be with their spouses before the HMCS *Huron* departed for the Gulf.[83] When the Canadian CF-18 pilots' combat role in the Persian Gulf was changed from flying sweep-and-escort missions to an offensive ground attack role on 21 February 1991, pilots were identified by name in pictures and the body of one Halifax newspaper.[84]

One also possibly can develop a sense of the media restrictions' inconsistent results after the CF-18s' role was changed to bombing missions. A *Globe and Mail* correspondent in Riyadh reported that military officials in Qatar refused to make pilots available to talk about their new role.[85] His difficulty in obtaining information was highlighted in a report several days later that said Canada had joined America, Britain, and France in imposing a total news blackout on air operations to avoid jeopardizing land war offensives that had begun in Kuwait.[86] While the *Globe*'s correspondent struggled for information about the Canadian air operations, the *Toronto Star*'s correspondent in Bahrain, aided by the Canadian Press, identified pilots who took part in the first bombing run by name, hometowns, targets, and flight durations.[87] The *Chronicle-Herald* in Halifax shows that a Canadian Press correspondent in Qatar was briefed by military officials who, despite the news blackout, identified the lead pilot by name and his Owen Sound, Ontario, hometown.[88]

Covering the air war from Riyadh, Saudi Arabia, when the Canadians were based in Doha, Qatar, put the *Globe* correspondent at a disadvantage. His report could only be as complete as the information he received. While the *Star*'s correspondent was in Manama, Bahrain, his editors may well have been able to incorporate the Canadian Press report into his work in a way that the *Globe* editors could not. All that can reasonably be concluded is that the readers of all three news sources would have differing perspectives on that day's events, while those who read both the *Toronto*

Star and the *Globe and Mail* could be forgiven for being a little confused. The question is: Why?

That confusion likely started from a problem identified in the Canadian Forces' after-action report on public affairs activities in the Gulf War. There were two coalition media centres in the Gulf. American, British, and Saudi Arabian officials had joint headquarters and a joint information bureau in Riyadh, while another was established in Dhahran for journalists attempting to cover the land forces on the Saudi-Kuwait/Iraqi frontier. Given the single-entry visa available to the news media in the Gulf, journalists could not move from one country to the next, restricting their ability to report. Where they arrived at the beginning of the war was where they had to remain for its duration.[89] Access to information is everything to journalists. Without information they have nothing to base their work on. Geography coupled with restrictive military information policies made war correspondents' work difficult at best and nearly impossible at worst.

On February 20, defence minister William McKnight announced that Canada would switch to a more offensive role: Close Air Support (CAS) sorties or bombing missions. They eventually flew fifty-six CAS sorties.[90] The only problem after the announcement was retrofitting the CF-18s for the bombing campaign and training for the new role. Matthews explained:

> We went through a period there where I was told that I was going to have to bomb. OK, no big deal. We have bombs. We know how to do that. The only thing was we spent all of our careers preparing to fight in Norway, the plains of Northern Germany or the rolling hills of southern Germany. We were very, very good, one of the best NATO contingents for dropping bombs from low level, from a low-level attack.
>
> In the Gulf, we were going to be asked to drop our bombs, to roll in at 30,000 feet in a six-degree dive, or drop them from level flight at 35,000 feet. We'd never done that, never trained for it, had no concept. The only guys that had even thought about it were the fighter weapons instructors and they did that on their Top Gun course. So, I was told in total confidence, in total secrecy, that this was going to

happen. I said, "OK, we can handle this. What we'll do is we'll fly some training missions here in Qatar just so that we know how to point ourselves in a six-degree dive and drop the bombs without killing ourselves or friendly troops." We managed to get a few people trained with eight bombs for high-level delivery before the actual first day of bombing.[91]

Just four days passed between the announcement that the Canadians would begin a bombing role and their first missions. All the while, Matthews said the Canadians continued to fly sweep-and-escort missions and combat patrol missions. "I mean we had jets flying twenty-four hours a day. We had a minimum of two F-18s airborne throughout all combat. We flew night; we flew day; we flew escort; we flew combat air patrol; and then, during the land offence—which was only about three days—we flew bombing missions." The Canadian news media never was told what the bombing targets were or any other details about the Canadians in combat. For the first time since the war began on January 17, Canadian military officials in Bahrain suspended its media briefings.[92] Nonetheless, Matthews says the main focus of their bombing missions was the so-called "Highway of Death."

After US ground troops flooded into Kuwait, annihilating Iraqi troops in their path, Iraq announced it was withdrawing its forces from Kuwait but refused to acknowledge UN sanctions. Iraqi tanks, armoured vehicles, trucks, and troops by the thousands fled the allied onslaught. In doing so, they formed huge queues on the road north from Kuwait to the southern Iraqi city of Basra. High above them, the allied forces launched a devastating bombing campaign on the fleeing troops, killing thousands.[93] Matthews recalled Canada's involvement on the final days' bombing missions: "I think we dropped 100 tons of bombs in about three days, but, you know, as it turned out, the weather was terrible and all of the smoke from the oil well fires. We ended up dropping most of them from level flight at 30,000 feet on convoys that were five kilometres long. It was carpet bombing."[94]

The Canadian military's assessment of its news media policy after the war identified three issues: journalists' pools; providing journalists with military personnel's hometown information; and the release of operational information. Regarding pools, the Canadian military had no influence over issues negotiated before the war by the media in London and Washington. Canadian journalists in theatre could not negotiate their way into them. One solution was that Canadian pool membership should be negotiated before future outbreaks of hostilities.[95]

Secondly, the after-action report said the release of operational information to the news media was problematic because public affairs officers operated under two conflicting imperatives: a political imperative of openness and operational security. In hindsight, the report acknowledged that the Canadian Forces were more reluctant to divulge operational information than their allies. The British eagerly made available information on air-mission targets and released videos as proof. Canadian headquarters forbade giving out similar information, but public affairs officers in the field could not explain why the British could release such information and they could not.

Also, the news media in Qatar could readily obtain operational information simply by looking out their windows and observing CF-18s taking off and landing. Over time, the news media became familiar with CF-18 armaments, their numbers, and whether their missions were combat air patrol, sweep and escort, or close air support. The Canadian Forces only had one Boeing CC-137 air refuelling tanker, which the media could see whether it was flying or not. The after-action report said: "It was therefore ludicrous to not confirm such details, but to do so often conflicted with direction from higher headquarters. Recommendation: We should standardize with our allies who have had more operational experience than we have and adopt their more liberal release of info policies."[96]

The third lessons-learned issue was the release of military personnel's hometown information. Without being specific, the report said it proved to be hazardous, causing "a few instances of harassment of family members in Canada that resulted in an unwillingness of some members to be interviewed at all."[97] The difficulty was that the Forces had provided such information readily before hostilities began and the news media could not understand why such information was withheld after hostilities began—until after the harassment received publicity.[98]

For example, several days after the body bag story broke, it was reported from Ottawa that Canadian Forces women had been ordered to wear civilian clothes in unidentified parts of Canada to avoid abuse. At the same Ottawa briefing where that development was announced, the deputy chief of defence staff, Lt. Gen. David Huddleston, confirmed that harassing phone calls had been made to the wives of husbands serving in the Gulf, who were told their husbands had been killed.[99]

On the same day, it was reported in Toronto that military police were probing threats made to military families in Victoria. The language shift from the original story was subtle, but the story said the military would not confirm that body bags had been left on the doorsteps of some military family homes, nor how many threats had been made, against whom, or where.[100] There is a substantial difference between military police having no physical evidence that harassment had taken place and a statement that they would not confirm incidents. The implication was that the military had information it would not divulge. The other detail of note was that body bags were left on doorsteps, not on lawns. Although numerous news reports perpetuated the story of harassment of military family members, what was not widely disseminated through the media was information in a follow-up *Globe and Mail* story indicating that civilian police in Victoria and civilian and military police in Esquimalt had not received any physical evidence about the alleged harassment.[101]

The news reports and the military's after-action report on the harassment never offered proof that the most egregious incidents, the alleged dumping of a body bag on the lawn of a naval home in Esquimalt and harassing telephone calls to wives, ever happened. The military's recommended procedure for dealing with such incidents was to make the military police aware of them. The police found no evidence to support the allegations.[102] A complete search of Department of National Defence records from August 1990 to 31 January 1991, for military police records involving the alleged dumping of a body bag or a threat analysis, found nothing.[103]

A search of the origins for the 1991 *Vancouver Sun* story about harassment of naval spouses from Esquimalt ran dry in Victoria, BC. None of the wives were quoted either by name in the story or in any of the numerous follow-up news reports. The 1991 source about the body bag being an actual type used by the military was a sub-lieutenant who was not part of the Canadian Forces public affairs structure. All attempts to reach him through the Canadian military or public resources—beginning with the CFB Esquimalt public affairs officer at the time who knew him—failed.[104]

Paul Seguna was the public affairs officer at CFB Esquimalt who was quoted in *Globe and Mail* and *Toronto Star* stories about the harassment.[105] In the *Globe* story, Seguna said there had been roughly a dozen complaints and in the *Star* story about six.[106] Both military and civilian police were reported to be investigating the incidents, asking families who had received threatening messages to turn them over to police as evidence. Seguna was quoted at the time saying women had received calls from people claiming to be senior military officials, stating their husbands had been killed in action, even though their ship, HMCS *Huron*, was not even going to the Gulf. Astonishingly, without facts to back it up, Seguna told the *Globe*, although he was not quoted directly, about allegations that one wife found a crude imitation of a body bag on her front lawn.[107] Families were told to keep evidence and turn it over to police, but Victoria and Esquimalt police received no such evidence.[108]

To the best of Seguna's recollection, he first heard about the incidents not from military family members but from a CHEK 6 television news report in Victoria. A search of the television station's archives revealed no evidence that such a story was ever aired.[109] Nonetheless, Seguna felt duty bound to meet military spouses at the military Family Resource Centre in Esquimalt. He told them that, having let the cat out of the bag to the news media about the alleged harassment, they must deal with the media and should verify facts. "In essence, we made it clear, you know, that once you've opened the door you just can't shut it."[110]

Brig. Gen. McGillivray, commander of CFB Cold Lake in 1991, knew there were war protests taking place in Canada. But there was or were no incident or incidents of a body bag or body bags thrown on the lawns of air force personnel in Cold Lake.[111] The only other place the CF-18s fighting in the Gulf came from was Baden-Soellingen, Germany. Lt. Col. Matthews, who flew in the war, was commanding officer of 439 Tactical Fighter Squadron based in Baden-Soellingen. Although armed guards stood around the military homes in Germany and on the base's school buses, there was no concern about attacks in retribution on fighter pilots' family members. His wife remained in Germany while he was flying missions in the Gulf, and she was in constant contact with military families in both Canada and Germany. The biggest concern among the families was in Canada and not in Germany, a striking observation in that pilots' wives in Germany were once evacuated from their homes in a false bomb-threat incident.

> She thought the Canadian perspective was a little bit overblown. I mean, she actually had armed guards at her front door and everybody in Canada was much, much more afraid than she was overseas. She was taking care of the families in Germany while we were off fighting. They were calling from Canada and they were just terribly concerned. My wife was saying: "Well, you know, I'm here and I've got an armed infantryman in my yard and I'm not nearly as concerned about all this as you appear to be back in Toronto."[112]

Given the far-ranging effect on Canada's democratic institutions years later of an urban myth, the body bags, its origins are worth pursuing. The *Times Colonist* in Victoria, on 2 January 1991, reported on the Greater Victoria peace organization's plans to protest the departure of HMCS *Huron* for Halifax. Its crew was slated to relieve the crew of the HMCS *Athabaskan* in February. The two last sentences at the bottom of the story suggest that the myth may have its origins in a protest that took place 31 December 1990, outside the gates of CFB Esquimalt.

> Meanwhile, members of the Greater Victoria Disarmament Group, some dressed in homemade body bags "linked hands for peace" at the Canteen Road entrance to CFB Esquimalt on Monday. The body bag dress was to dramatize the possibility members of the Persian Gulf force will come home in body bags—something that does not need to happen if sanctions and mediation continue instead of war, the group argues.[113]

The departure of 280 servicemen aboard the *Huron* for Halifax via the Panama Canal was big news for the *Times Colonist*, which dispatched a reporter and a photographer to spend three days aboard the supply ship HMCS *Provider* accompanying the *Huron* on its first leg to Long Beach, California. They planned to spend one night on the *Huron* writing stories about and taking pictures of the local men and women headed for the Gulf via Halifax. On 4 January 1991, the newspaper published the names and ranks of all 280 crew.[114] The first news story that reported that harassing phone calls made to military families was published in the *Times Colonist* on January 16. It contained a body bag reference. A military wife whose husband was on the HMCS *Huron* said: "Some of the wives have had phone calls saying their husbands will be the next ones in those body bags," she said. "Others are just vulgar calls, the 'if you're lonely just call me,' calls," she said.[115] One spokesman claimed harassing calls telling women their husbands were dead had come from a man identifying himself as a Canadian Forces lieutenant colonel. He spoke during a rally of military wives and girlfriends in front of the legislature in Victoria to support their spouses.[116]

Following the UN-sanctioned attack on Iraq, security was tightened at CFB Esquimalt. The base information officer, Lieutenant Seguna, declined to comment to the *Times Colonist* about the security measures or whether they were in response to a terrorist threat.[117] The tension was raw. The same day, military personnel were evacuated from HMC Dockyard following a bomb threat that turned out to be a hoax.[118]

The next story about harassment appeared in the *Times Colonist* on January 19. It was focused primarily not on military family members but on Victoria's peace activists, who claimed they were being harassed with calls for harassing military wives and throwing garbage on ships in Vancouver. Toward the end of that story, the harassment of wives was said to take the form of people claiming to be insurance agents attempting to make appointments with women whose husbands were aboard a ship.[119] An insurance official with London Life Insurance reported that bona fide insurance agents required both spouses to be present for an interview, but such calls could be made by accident to such a solitary military spouse. The way to avoid that, the insurance company official said, would be to circulate the list of HMCS *Huron*'s crew members among insurance companies and agents indicating their families were off-limits.[120] Two days later on January 21, the *Vancouver Sun* wrote about a navy wife who had an actual military body bag on her lawn and harassing phone calls.

The *Times Colonist* followed up on the *Vancouver Sun* story six days later. On January 27, it quoted base information officer Lt. Seguna saying the military wives were reluctant to make complaints to military police. Whereas Seguna previously had told the *Globe and Mail* there had been roughly a dozen complaints and the *Toronto Star* about six, when asked again how many complaints there were, he would only say: "Several—I don't want to give a fixed number."[121] Seguna said, for all he knew, all the harassment could have been the work of one person. "One person can create a lot of havoc, which is why we need these women to get the reports into the police."[122] By then, readers would have found it difficult to separate fact from fiction. The story reported: "Families of men on HMCS *Huron* were the focus of national media attention after some women reported being phoned by a man purporting to be a senior officer telling them their husband was dead, or of having body bags strewn on their lawns."[123] One of the spouses—April-Ann Hamilton, wife of Leading Seaman Harold Hamilton—was identified by name. She did not confirm the body bag story. What Hamilton did, however, was put her finger on the nature of the problem. She said second- and third-hand reports of the harassment were made public before police could properly investigate them, and the rumours started flying.[124]

The military wives formed a media committee to shed positive light on their experiences, but it was too late. The nation's news media weren't getting their information from them anymore. They were feeding on themselves, cutting and pasting various versions of the story's most appalling angle into their own reports. Some of the *Times Colonist* story was focused how some of the harassment incidents had been overblown. But second-hand accounts of phone calls saying that husbands would be coming home in body bags on January 16 had become body bags strewn on lawns by January 27. In years to come, two things happened whenever Canadian CF-18s were called upon to take up a combat role. First, the Gulf War lessons-learned report recommending that the Canadian Forces should learn from more operationally experienced allies and adopt more liberal policies regarding the release of operational information to the news media were either forgotten or ignored. Second, the half-remembered images of body bags strewn on the lawns of naval family members in Esquimalt took on mythical proportions.

Murray Edelman writes: "The word 'myth' signifies a belief held in common by a large group of people that gives events and actions a particular meaning; it is typically socially cued rather than empirically based."¹²⁵ Myths simplify a complex world and promote conformity to a pattern of thought and behaviour.¹²⁶ With profound consequences for Canada's democratic institutions, that socially cued body bag myth became burned into the memories of Canadian Forces members, some of whom assumed higher command years later. The 1991 myth rose like a Phoenix when Canadian CF-18s soared into combat in the skies over Serbia and Kosovo in 1999.

7

Like an Overnight International Courier

On the evening of 24 March 1999, the day NATO's Operation Allied Force bombing campaign began, CTV's Joy Malbon was in London, England, where she had worked in the television network's London bureau since 1997. Malbon was telephoned by her news director in Toronto and was told to travel immediately to the US Air Force base in Aviano, Italy, to cover the Canadian military's first participation in an aerial bombing campaign in Europe since 1945. Then a seventeen-year veteran of the Canadian news business, Malbon was no stranger to the Canadian Forces. She had covered their deployment to assist with the Manitoba flood disaster in 1997 and attended the war correspondent course put on by the Forces at the Princess Patricia's Canadian Light Infantry Battle School at Camp Wainwright, Alberta, in May of that year. Well versed in working on the fly, Malbon called her cameraman and headed straight to the airport for a flight to the Italian port city of Trieste, on the extreme north of the Adriatic Sea.

> We flew commercially to Trieste where we rented a car for the drive to the Aviano air force base. We basically followed our nose through the signs and when we got there nothing had been set up. I recall it being very late or early in the morning, maybe three in the morning, something like that. There was a huge field across from the American air force base in Aviano where ABC and a few others were setting up their satellite dishes. What I recall is, my first impression, is

actually seeing a Stealth fighter fly overhead. I'd never seen such a thing.[1]

There is a lot of Canadian journalism history that preceded Malbon's arrival in Aviano. It has been recognized that since the Crimean War, journalists covering wars shape public opinion and the policies of governments and their militaries.[2] It is a profound understatement to say that when the Kosovo air war broke out in March 1999, much had changed in the news media since William Maxwell Aitken became Canada's "Eyewitness" to the First World War under the authority of the Canadian War Records Office in London.[3] From 1914 to 1919, newspapers were the only widely available news media. Even during the Chanak affair in 1922, the licensing of commercial radio broadcasting had only just begun, and it would be a year before radio stations were operating in every Canadian province but Prince Edward Island and Nova Scotia.[4] By 19 August 1942, both print and radio reporters were on the beaches at Dieppe, when hundreds of Canadians were slaughtered in a failed raid on the German-held French coast during the Second World War.[5]

Television had only begun to become commercially available in Canada in the early 1950s when Canadians soldiers were sent to the Korean War "police action."[6] The year 1982 marked a milestone for the news media when the *Canadian Charter of Rights and Freedoms* ensconced freedom of the press and other media of communication as a fundamental freedom in the Canadian Constitution.[7] By the beginning of the 1991 Persian Gulf War, the modern Fourth Estate[8] had enormous communications tools at its disposal, including satellite telecommunications enabling live television broadcasts of the American bombing of Baghdad. When the war in Kosovo broke out in 1999, the Internet, computerized email, and cellular telephones had all been added to the news media's resources, although the iPhone had not yet been invented. All three elements of the Canadian Forces—the air force, the navy, and the army—had come to know at different points in time that, like it or not, they would have to deal with the news media on operations. Six modern examples will illustrate.

First, during the 1991 Gulf War, the Canadian Forces learned that significant public support for the war effort was generated by news media coverage, which was extensive. Journalists from the CTV and Baton television networks and the CKAC radio station, and print journalists with the *Toronto Sun*, the *Toronto Star*, the *Free Press*, *Reader's Digest*, *Le Soleil*, Associated Press, Reuters, and the *Financial Times*, were in Bahrain. Journalists from the CBC, CTV, The Journal, CHCH, and Radio Canada television stations; Broadcast News, CBC, CJMS and KKAC radio journalists; and print journalists from Canadian Press, the *Toronto Sun*, the *Toronto Star*, *Maclean's*, Southam, the *Province* (Vancouver), and *Journal de Quebec* were in Qatar.[9]

Television pool journalists from the CBC and Radio Canada and print journalists from the *Toronto Star*, the *Free Press* and the *Province* (Vancouver) were aboard Canadian ships. Television journalists from the CBC, Radio Canada, The Journal, and CTV, and one CBC radio journalist and print journalists from the *Toronto Sun* and *Maclean's* were in Dhahran, Saudi Arabia, while journalists from CBC radio network and print journalists with Southam, the *Globe and Mail*, *Maclean's*, and *Le Soleil* were in Riyadh, Saudi Arabia. That commitment by the various Canadian news media outlets to cover the Gulf War did not come cheaply. Not only can war journalism be dangerous from time to time, it is expensive. It involves international travel and often inflated living and travelling costs. In 1991, Gulf War pool journalists aboard the Canadian ships alone estimated their costs at $50,000 each.[10]

The Canadian Forces learned during the Gulf War that ten full-time public affairs officers were insufficient to meet the news media's demands and they needed augmentation by reservists.[11] As mentioned above, in Chapter 6, they learned that restrictive Canadian media policies that prevented the release of target information and accompanying video which illustrated that point were inconsistent with what their more experienced allies were doing. One section in the after-action report's appendix also dealt with the identification and hometowns of military personnel causing a few instances of harassment of family members back in Canada.[12] An appendix to the public affairs action report said: "We should standardize with our allies who have had more operational experience than we have and adopt their more liberal release of info policies."[13]

Second, in 1997, the navy published *Adjusting Course: A Naval Strategy for Canada*, in which it said the lessons of the 1991 Gulf War and the Canadian Forces disaster in Somalia were clear. It said in part: "military forces will be called upon to respond to a greater range of situations based upon a broader conception of security, and the commanders of those forces must anticipate and plan for intense media coverage in future military operations as an integral element of operational strategy."[14]

Third, in March 1997, the Canadian army's lessons-learned centre devoted an entire edition of *Dispatches*, its internal briefing document, to the proposition that the media can have a significant impact on military operations and the politics of the Canadian Forces. It cited changes in defence ministers, resignations of senior officers, and the disbandment of the Canadian Airborne Regiment as examples of the news media's power to focus the Canadian public's attention on military issues. The power of the news media, it said, "comes from its ability to select *what* is reported and *how* it will be reported."[15] As a result, it said the importance of public affairs preparedness could not be overstated. It added:

> To be effective, media relations must be planned for and practiced. It cannot be an after-thought or something to be addressed once in the area of operations. Unfortunately, soldiers who spend so much of their careers planning for operations and anticipating courses of action often get caught off guard by the media because they did not anticipate media interest in their operation nor were they prepared to deal with this interest. Ignoring the media will not make them go away, it guarantees that "our" side will not be heard.[16]

Fourth, the Canadian army had taken concrete, proactive steps to raise the bar on the quality of military journalism by offering a war correspondent course at the Princess Patricia's Canadian Light Infantry battle school in Camp Wainwright, Alberta, in 1995 and again in 1997. The concentrated five-day courses were offered to seventeen working journalists in 1995 and in 1997 to ten working journalists, twelve journalism students, and three others with an interest in the course contents. The course contents included convoy discipline, mine recognition and dealing with minefields, live-fire weapons recognition, negotiating belligerent checkpoints, combat first aid, combat-related stress, and field craft that included eating, sleeping, and living in a war zone.[17]

Fifth, the most powerful indication that the Canadian army planned to take command of the news media's presence during operational missions emerged in army planning documents in 1998. They show that the army viewed public affairs to be a command prerogative that should not be left in the hands of media specialists alone. The goal was to project an image of the army as progressive, sustainable, and combat-capable. The plan stated:

> Public affairs is an important tool that a commander must understand and know to use in support of the operational mission. For many years we have taken the reactive approach to public affairs and have been often outmaneuvered in national or international issues. Successful commanders will often take the proactive approach to ensure the right message is provided to the media.[18]

Sixth, also in 1998, Canadian Forces adopted public affairs (PA) guidelines for operations, effective January 30, known as DAOD 2008, that required the Forces to integrate public affairs policy and direction into "all aspects of military doctrine, as appropriate, to ensure that PA is fully integrated into CF military planning, decision making, standard operating procedures, and operations."[19] Included in DAOD 2008 were guidelines in the event of escalating military tension or war that required the deputy chief of defence staff to fully integrate public affairs into military doctrine and the director general of public affairs to draft and implement a national public affairs plan.[20] Within the guidelines, it clearly recognized the key priority of any Forces operation was to achieve its mission, but, at the same time, it recognized there would be heightened media and public interest. The challenge for the Forces was to inform Canadians of the national and operation dimensions "in a manner that is accurate, complete, timely and respectful of the principles of openness, transparency and operational security."[21]

It is clear, however, that the document recognized that the requirements for openness and transparency and operational security could be conflicting imperatives. By operational security it meant "the principle of safeguarding the integrity of a military operation or activity, and/or the safety of the CF members and other personnel involved in the military operation or activity."[22]

In short, there was a lot of journalism and policy context history for the public affairs activities that could have shaped what took place in Aviano, Italy, and in Ottawa in the months leading up to the outbreak of war on 24 March 1999, and afterward.

Malbon could not file her own televised report on the first night they arrived because they had to wait for CNN and ABC, with which CTV had contracts, to set up their satellite dishes. Instead, her Toronto desk had her file a report by cellular phone that could be incorporated with video images the network had received from an American network.

> They basically told me the pictures they had. I believe they had shots of the Stealth fighter. We were taking pictures as well, but we couldn't send anything just yet. We ended up giving those pictures to ABC once they got their stuff up and running early in the morning. Toronto would get it as well because they share pictures on feeds.[23]

Though she filed a report on Aviano, Malbon really wanted Canadian CF-18s on camera and to interview some of the pilots, even if only in general terms.

> We wanted to speak to the Canadian pilots because, as I recall, this was the first time that Canadians were actually carrying bombs and that was a huge deal in Canada. We wanted to talk to them about that, we wanted to talk to them about their role. I mean, the target was Yugoslavia, everybody knew that. We didn't need to know specifically what the targets were but my role was to get to the Canadians. Other people were doing big-picture stories about the war, the bombing, there were all sorts of technical briefings in London, in Canada, in the US about what was going on

in Washington. My role was specifically to get to the Canadians and find out what we're doing there.[24]

Unfortunately, all the journalists who arrived en masse in Aviano were kept in the field more than three kilometres from the action, which was on the tarmacs and in the hangars on the north side of the base. The field was on the south side of the base across the main road from the administration building. The journalists weren't getting past the American military's heavily armed security checkpoint. All Malbon wanted to do was speak to some Canadians—anyone. "We were told the Canadian in charge, Dwight Davies, would come to speak with us. I remember that because another Canadian journalist from London had arrived, as well, and that's what she heard, too. He was going to speak to us at four in the morning. So, we waited, and we waited and he never showed."[25]

Malbon wasn't alone in her frustration. For several days, the only news for journalists involved in covering the worsening crisis in Kosovo was bad news. Hours before the bombing campaign began, the Yugoslavian government seized many western television news outlets' equipment, including a transmission facility operated by the European Broadcasting Union, used by ABC, CBS, NBC, and CNN. Some western reporters in Kosovo were threatened at gunpoint and fled.[26] Others were accused of being spies or having double assignments in the region, including Anthony Lloyd. Lloyd was a foreign correspondent for the *Times* (London) and a former lieutenant in the British Army's Royal Green Jackets who fought in the 1991 Gulf War.[27] After the first night of bombing, some journalists staying at the Pristina Grand Hotel had their equipment broken by police. Two were arrested, one was beaten, a television crew was shot at, and another's Land Rover was stolen by soldiers. Some journalists were dragged out of their hotel rooms at gunpoint and had their visas cancelled. While some reporters left the country voluntarily, others were ordered out.[28] The CBC's Céline Galipeau was expelled to Macedonia, while the *Toronto Star*'s Olivia Ward escaped angry Serbs by fleeing into Hungary just before the second wave of NATO bombs hit.[29]

Meanwhile, in Ottawa, opposition MPs received the same information about the war as was being provided to the news media. They complained throughout the war, as Official Opposition Leader Preston Manning stated in the House of Commons: "Mr. Speaker, to date the government has done little or nothing to involve the House in developing Canada's commitments in Yugoslavia. Most members of the House get more information from television and newspapers than they do from the government on this subject."[30]

Outside the House, the opposition had two other potential sources of official information on the military activities. One was the House of Commons Standing Committee on National Defence and Veteran's Affairs (SCONDVA), which met twenty-six times from March 25 through June 8. Opposition MPs quickly learned that they would only receive bare bones information about military information for operational security reasons from defence minister Art Eggleton or the deputy chief of defence staff, Lt. Gen. Raymond Henault. When questioned about it, Eggleton explained in SCONDVA:

> It's a very serious situation. We want to make sure that we're not divulging information that gives comfort to the enemy side or that can in any way jeopardize the safety and security of our Canadian Forces personnel. I'm sure the honorable member wouldn't want us to do anything that would jeopardize their safety and security.[31]

When frustrated SCONDVA members complained about the lack of information they were receiving, Eggleton suggested that they attend the technical briefings being provided to the national news media every afternoon: "You might recognize General Henault, because he is on television every day at one o'clock giving technical briefings, together with staff, as to what is happening."[32]

The first of those technical briefings happened at National Defence Headquarters March 24, on the first day of NATO air strikes against Yugoslavia. Lt. Cmdr. Jeff Agnew, the J5 PA or joint operations public affairs officer, co-ordinated the daily technical briefings. NATO drove the overall public affairs approach for the Kosovo operation and held daily press briefings at its headquarters in Brussels after the bombing campaign started. The Canadian Forces followed suit. Agnew, the lead public affairs officer, monitored the televised briefings in Brussels every day during the war and press briefings at the US Pentagon to become familiar with issues that were being raised by European and American journalists. Given that he was already familiar with the issues raised by reporters at NATO headquarters and in Washington, he briefed Henault and his staff on what was said by NATO and American commanders, the questions put to them by reporters, and their responses. After those briefings, Canadian commanders attended the technical briefings, which usually began at 1:00 p.m.[33]

On March 24, day one of the bombing campaign, Lt. Gen. Henault addressed the news media along with Air Staff Lt. Col. Yvan Houle, a former CF-18 flying instructor. The Air Staff position was created in 1997 to oversee production and training for air personnel. The first several days' briefings set the tone that would persist until the war ended. Most briefings focused on the NATO operations, with limited time spent on the Canadians. For example, Henault and Houle told the media that 130 Canadian military personnel and six CF-18s in were Aviano. All were extensively trained and fully interoperable with their NATO counterparts. Houle, a CF-18 pilot, discussed the CF-18's weapons systems, including its infrared targeting pod and laser designator, "an advanced night-time capability that only a handful of countries bring to this theatre."[34] Advanced nighttime capability was not the truth, but the reporters were in no position to challenge Henault or Houle and hold them accountable—the primary role of journalists in democracies—because none of the reporters in Aviano was able to learn about the pilots' previous training for night missions or their lack of night vision. The truth was that the Canadian pilots operating out of Aviano were flying as blind as bats without night-vision goggles and, well into the mission, were nearly killed doing it.

Henault and Houle said they couldn't discuss details of the Canadians' first mission, such as whether all the Canadian aircraft had returned. "Again, the aircraft are involved in operations and therefore for operational security reasons, we couldn't divulge it even if we knew," Henault said, explaining that the CF-18s would carry out the full range of missions, including close air support.[35] When one journalist asked about targets, they responded that they didn't know. Another asked a pointed question about the CF-18s refuelling at night. "You're coming out of your first combat mission in history, in your history, and the first thing you have to do after you get safely out is to tank at night from a tanker. Is that like the real high risk, high heartbeat?" Houle replied: "Yeah, refuelling is a tight operation. It requires training and proficiency but if the aircraft is not damaged, that should be a rather routine operation."[36] Nothing more was asked or said about air-to-air refuelling or advanced nighttime capability.

Henault was asked if Canadians higher in rank than Col. Davies were in Europe. "Not in this particular portion of the operation, no," he replied.[37] That was not the truth. The truth was that Brig. Gen. James Cox was in Mons, in NATO's Supreme Headquarters Allied Powers in Europe (SHAPE), sitting in the same war room with Gen. Wesley Clark, who ran the war.[38] Henault was asked if the journalists in Aviano could talk to the Canadian pilots. CTV's Craig Oliver put the question directly: "Can you make it possible in the post-attack scenario for reporters in Aviano to talk to the Canadian fliers? What happens too often is the Americans open things up. We can go in and talk to American pilots but we can't talk to our own Canadians."[39] Henault replied: "That's a very good point. We'll take that; our public affairs folks are here, and we'll do what we can to provide access to our pilots and the members of the contingent that are there." In response to Henault, Oliver replied: "Don't make that mistake again. It's infuriating, and it happens too often." Henault said: "Understood."[40]

In Mons, Gen. Clark monitored the American news media's coverage of the bombing campaign. On the first night of the campaign he watched NBC by satellite and became disturbed that anchor Tom Brokaw identified the NATO coalition's attack as "American-led air strikes." Clark involved Allied aircraft to pre-empt criticism in Washington that NATO allies were not carrying their fair share of the burden. He had public affairs staff call NBC to correct the report. The network promptly changed the way the strikes were identified.[41] Later, Clark wrote that, from the start of the campaign, he sought to shape the information released about the air strikes. A high level of secrecy initially was meant to maintain surprise and operational security. During the first NATO press conference he attended in Brussels, on March 25, the day after the bombing campaign began, he was asked by a *New York Times* reporter why he couldn't identify the targets NATO had struck, since the Serbs already knew what had been attacked. Clark explained that such an operation was scrutinized by many nations that might share information. While refusing to comment on the contributions or performance of individual alliance members, he confirmed information released by the British that a Dutch CF-18 and US jets had shot down Serbian planes.[42] Within a few days he realized the political need to be more open to build popular American support for sustained operations.[43] To that end, he appeared at NATO press conferences four more times before the bombing campaign ended.

On the second day of bombing, March 25, the first news reports from wire services of Canadian participation in the NATO bombing appeared in major Canadian daily newspapers. The sources, in most cases, were defence minister Art Eggleton, Henault, or Capt. Dave Muralt, the Canadian Forces public affairs officer in Aviano. But there were no details about what the CF-18s had done. Most reports were lengthy but contained just one or two sentences reporting that four jets participated in the action and had returned home safely. Most references to the CF-18s appeared in the middle or at the end of the stories. Many Southam newspapers ran virtually the same wire service story, datelined Belgrade, because they all used the same wire service.[44] A few newspapers noted that the CF-18s had been in Italy since the previous June and everyone in Aviano was happy the pilots had returned safely. Canadian Press's John Ward in Ottawa wrote the original story on the CF-18s quoting Muralt, who was reached by telephone in Aviano. Some newspapers had their own journalists rewrite Ward's story quoting Muralt.[45]

Many newspapers also ran a sidebar—a short, less prominent story accompanying the main news story—about the history of the CF-18s, their role in the 1991 Gulf War, and the precision-guided bombs that were acquired for them two years previously. Some identified Ward as the author, some did not. Only one newspaper, the *Ottawa Citizen*, tied the CF-18s to CFB Bagotville, reporting tension and pride among the base members.[46] Many carried an accompanying picture of a CF-18 taking off from Aviano during the daytime that was identified as a Canadian fighter plane. Some carried a correction the next day identifying the jet as a Spanish CF-18, some did not. Since television could report on same-day activities at night, the CBC reported Henault's remarks during the March 25 press briefing that Canada now was back in "the club" with the employment of smart bombs.[47]

By then, Henault had obtained more information about the first night's operations. He told the journalists that four CF-18s had participated in the alliance effort. which struck forty targets and had safely returned. The military's policy, he said, would reflect Clark's wishes by giving Canadians as much information as possible without jeopardizing the safety of the missions.[48] Clark's wishes were exactly the opposite. At the beginning of the bombing campaign, he tried to limit the amount of information released to the media to retain as much surprise and operational security as possible.[49] Henault said that Davies would be the designated spokesman for the Canadians in Aviano. "At the moment, we're trying to limit exposure to the pilots for the time being and again, it's for operational security reasons, but ultimately, you will have access to them."[50]

Houle noted that the CF-18s reported some activity from the Yugoslav radar systems, which did not hinder the mission. When asked whether the Canadians had been targeted, were fired upon, or fired in return, Henault said that no aircraft were fired upon, that Yugoslav radar painted the Canadians, and three Yugoslav fighters were brought down. Henault was pressed about Canadian involvement. He said: "They were not involved in that operation."[51] That was not the truth. The truth was that Canadians led that operation and Dutch aircraft shot down the Yugoslav MiG-29 heading toward them. The fourth pilot in formation that night had been fired at with a surface-to-air missile that forced him to take evasive manoeuvres.

When he was asked if there had been any military assessment of the domestic risk to military personnel and their families, Henault replied: "Absolutely. In fact, our director-general of intelligence is at the moment trying to determine if there is any domestic risk. We have to be concerned about that in that we do know that there are many folks in Canada who are not necessarily supportive of the operations that we're doing."[52] There had been demonstrations against the air campaign in Toronto, Ottawa, and other cities, hence they were being cautious about releasing details such as pilots' names because "we don't want any risk of family harassment or something of that nature, which, again, is part of that domestic risk we face."[53]

Meanwhile, Malbon struggled for access to the Canadians in Aviano. Because she could not set foot on the base with the heavily armed Americans guarding the entrance, she could only reach them by cell phone. With the help of Muralt, Malbon got on to the base the next day, but she couldn't get access either to the Canadian pilots or the ground crews.

"They offered up a Spanish pilot, but they got antsy because we were near the Stealth. The next boatload of journalists wasn't given access to that site."[54] The Canadian military was reluctant to provide even the barest bones of information the journalists needed to construct a news report. They wouldn't tell the journalists what the CF-18s were bombing, they wouldn't let the pilots be photographed, and they wouldn't give them any of the pilots' names. "It was explained to me there was a fear of terrorists and some wacko slowing video down and attacking families. So, OK, I bought it."[55] However, Malbon's news desk in Toronto could see that the Spanish and Portuguese pilots were talking openly to reporters.

> We were still waiting on a request to interview Canadian pilots and the Toronto desk was telling me: "Wait a second, the Spanish pilots are speaking, so were the Portuguese, why aren't we seeing our Canadian pilots? Canada was involved in this war and Canadians want to know what we're doing over there."[56]

The *Times* of London also shows that some foreign journalists were far more successful at obtaining information than the Canadians. The *Times* identified countries that had struck targets three days into the bombing campaign and named NATO pilots. After a Dutch F-16 pilot shot down a Serb MiG that threatened the Canadians on the first night of bombing, the *Times* ran a picture of a Dutch serviceman painting a MiG symbol on the F-16 of pilot Jon Abma, who shot down the Serb plane. American F-15 fighters were also identified as the jets that shot down two Serb MiG29s in the United Nations no-fly zone over Bosnia.[57]

Desperate for footage of any kind, Malbon approached the Americans because it was their base.

> I don't remember exactly who it was, but what they did is, they'd met us in a jeep at the main road and they took us into the base. They took a lot of us, myself and a few other foreign journalists, and they put us in a big kind of bunker, shelter, whatever, and we had to wait. But I started speaking to this one American guy who took me and my cameraman

in a jeep over to the camp where the Canadians were. He drove close by and we said: "Look, we just want to take a few shots on the base, whatever's restricted is fine, you know, wide shots are OK, non-identifiables." We saw a Canadian flag flying there so we asked him to stop. We had to slyly kind of take pictures but the American guy kind of understood our problem and just let us take them, so at least I could say this is where the Canadians are on the American base because we were getting absolutely no access.[58]

Meanwhile, more of Canada's most prominent journalists were on their way to Aviano, including CBC television's Middle East correspondent Neil Macdonald. A twenty-seven-year veteran of the news business, he was in Jerusalem when the bombing started. Macdonald was called by the CBC in Toronto and told to make his way to Aviano because CBC correspondent Céline Galipeau—who had been trying to travel to Pristina—had been expelled. Macdonald recalled: "It was evident we were not going to be able to get a Yugoslavian visa for some time. They wanted coverage. Canadian fighters were flying out of Aviano and they thought it seemed logical to put a reporter in there for a while."[59]

Once Macdonald reached Aviano, his experience was the same as Malbon's. "The Canadians were being so unco-operative that it was virtually useless being there. They were telling us precisely nothing, basically."[60] What frustrated Canadian journalists in Aviano was that their American, British, and Spanish counterparts had tremendous access to their military personnel. Macdonald said:

> I did one story sort of rounding up what went on elsewhere in the world and stitching in a bit of stuff from Aviano, but a reporter from the BBC got on a British AWACS and reporters there from other countries were getting quite good access. Long after the Spanish and the Americans had started allowing journalists not only to interview pilots, but identify them, we couldn't. It got to the point where I went in to Pordenone which is a town nearby and bought a pair of

high-powered binoculars, so I could at least count the number of Canadian jets going out of the base.⁶¹

Colonel Davies began speaking to the media, but he provided them little useful information. Malbon said:

> I do remember Dwight Davies calling us on to the base. We were all excited thinking: "Oh, finally we're going to get something." There was Neil Macdonald, myself, and some other radio reporters and print reporters from Canada. This was just Canadians talking to the Canadian official in charge. He wouldn't let us put him on camera and I remember watching Neil get very frustrated because he's asking things that Canadians want to know. "What are the Canadian pilots' roles here? What targets? Are we hitting our targets? Are we missing them? Are we part of, from what we're hearing, civilians and buses being blown up? Was it a Canadian bomb?" He was asking all these things and he was getting: "No comment. No comment. No comment. No comment." He kind of got a little frustrated there at the time and it just seemed like a total waste of time.⁶²

Back in Canada, public affairs officers at 4 and 3 Wings struggled to develop a media plan while Ottawa tried to develop a coherent media plan for Canada and Aviano. Five days before bombing campaign began, it was an "open secret" in Alberta that CF-18s from Cold Lake would replace the Bagotville jets. However, Ottawa wouldn't let the public affairs officers comment on the deployment because of "political hurdles."⁶³

One day after the bombing campaign started, the 4 Wing public affairs officer received persistent telephone calls from the *Edmonton Journal*, the *Edmonton Sun*, CTV National out of Edmonton, CKSA Lloydminster, ITV News Edmonton, CFRN Edmonton, QR77 in Calgary, CBC radio from Edmonton and Calgary, and A Channel Television in Calgary and Edmonton for interviews about the deployment. That officer was locked in a battle with the wing commander to buck Ottawa and confirm the information."I'm still fighting this battle and trying to convince the WComd

[Wing Commander] that we should do it."⁶⁴ Unable to interview the military, the journalists talked to local residents in nearby Cold Lake.

In Ottawa, on March 26, the joint operations public affairs officer, Lt. Cmdr. Agnew, issued a directive that illustrated the difficulties in developing a coherent media policy for the aerial bombing campaign. It showed that the Canadians had no plan for handling media requests for access to combatants in Aviano. Two different strategies were developed, one for pilots in Canada and one for overseas.

> Peacetime rules apply in Canada. More restrictive rules apply in theatre. No pilot interviews authorized until authorized by NDHQ. Pilot interviews authorized in Canada. Do not talk about future ops [operations] but you may, within op sec [operational security] talk about missions that have been done in the past. Ottawa will brief daily at 1300 [1 p.m.] but may curtail these if nothing new happens and we would just issue a statement.⁶⁵

The 1:00 p.m. daily news briefings in Ottawa continued like clockwork, with the defence minister attending from time to time. Eggleton gave the assurances that the Canadians could maintain their combat posture, artfully providing answers devoid of any information that could reveal the nature of the challenges the Canadians caused by the Forces' peacetime weapons inventories. For example, one astute journalist asked Eggleton directly: "What is the stockpile of these laser-guided bombs that Canada is using? Do we have a large enough inventory to keep up with this run of bombings for any length of time?" Eggleton replied:

> Well, it depends on how long the attacks go on. But we can replenish what we have there and we'll do so to ensure that we can continue to be part of the mission. In other words, our planes will not be sitting idly by because we have run out of ammunition. It's our intention to be able to continue with the functions that we've been asked to carry out. Thank you.⁶⁶

Journalists' lack of access to aircrews on the ground in Aviano ensured that Canadians would not learn the truth about the shortage of bombs, that they were buying the dregs of American bomb stocks with their government-issued credit cards.[67] They would not learn about the heroic lengths to which those crews went to keep the CF-18s from sitting idle because they were running out of ordnance. They would not learn about the ground crews' struggles with bad backs or sore feet. It wasn't just Eggleton who avoided revealing the air force's critical deficiencies. On March 26, Henault was asked by a journalist about an air force association claim that half of Canada's CF-18s were grounded due to a lack of pilots. Henault replied:

> I think that is an unfortunate statement because we have our CF-18 aircraft fully manned and certainly the operational squadrons are manned such that they can conduct operations like this one very, very successfully. In fact, the six aircraft that are in Aviano have been extended to the September time frame, as you may know, and we've already been assured by the air force that they can continue rotating aircraft and ground crew into Aviano and their maintenance folks, as well. And they can sustain operations in Aviano as long as we ask them to.[68]

That was not the truth. The truth was that the dearth of targeting pods in Canada was stretching pilot training to the limit.[69] Two days after the bombing campaign began, CF-18s from Cold Lake left Canada for Italy. Two of them were likely to participate in the bombing campaign, which was an obvious news story. After a final debriefing, Capt. Travis Brassington, one of the two pilots who was about to depart for actual combat duty, not only had to say goodbye to his wife and children—knowing soon he would put his life on the line—but he had to deal with the news media, too.

> When we left, I remember coming out the door from 441 and the cameras were all there and they were kind of in everyone's face. My kids were really little at the time, like my youngest was just a year old and my oldest was a little over

> two years old. They didn't really know what was going on. It was just dad going away again but it was uncomfortable because it was pretty emotional, actually. I remember being fairly choked up and kind of glad that I had a visor to slide down and cover my face 'cause we were, we were kind of heading into the unknown.[70]

Just before takeoff at 8:30 a.m., *Edmonton Journal* photographer Chris Schwarz took a picture on the tarmac of Brassington in the cockpit of his CF-18 with the canopy open giving a thumbs-up sign. Brassington's face was half hidden by his visor and the cutline information accompanying the picture transmitted to Southam newspapers across Canada carried the warning: "Please note: Military personnel would not allow the pilot to be identified for security reasons."[71] The picture ran the next day in the *Edmonton Journal*, the *Calgary Herald*, the *Ottawa Citizen*, and the *National Post* (Toronto). The accompanying stories focused on the anguish of unidentified family members watching their loved ones fly off to war.[72]

All things considered, Brassington was thankful for his family's sake that his name was not published. He was deployed with a Sea King helicopter squadron during the 1991 Gulf War and remembered pilots' families receiving harassing phone calls. Because the Kosovo conflict was long over, Brassington said he was comfortable years later explaining:

> As far as somebody knowing there was me over there, what I was doing was no problem. What we were concerned with, I guess, was sympathizers tracking down the Brassington name—which is [the] only one listed in the phone book in Cold Lake—and phoning and threatening families or harassing families. We'd seen it happen before with what we'd experienced with the Gulf War—some of the names of the guys had gotten out and phone calls would be made to the home. I know when I worked at a Sea King squadron we had quite a few phone calls come in during the Gulf War. I wasn't really interested in dragging my family into this and the system wasn't going to allow it and that was fine.[73]

That day, March 27, when Brassington's unidentified picture was published, Henault told journalists that the information received about the CF-18 missions out of Aviano was restricted for operational reasons. It began with Henault telling journalists that four CF-18s had departed for missions that night and that their missions were aborted due to poor weather. The journalists were also shown pictures of the Navasat Heliport and Satellite Origin Depot, the Batanika airfield close to Belgrade, and a SAM-6 storage facility that were typical of the kinds of large military facilities NATO warplanes—not specifically Canadian warplanes—would target. One journalist calculated that Canadians had flown twelve missions to date, seven of which had been aborted. He also asked if that was the ratio that had been expected. Henault refused to provide any comparative information. "I can tell you that on these types of operations, there are absolutely no score cards kept. It's not at all like a baseball game. These are uncertainties that we have to face as we go through operations of this nature."[74]

But one journalist did his own analysis. *Toronto Star* Ottawa correspondent William Walker had a story published that same day, March 27, which said two of the four CF-18s the previous evening had not dropped their bombs because they could not positively identify "single large military targets. . . . That means three of the first eight bombing missions conducted by Canada's fighter jets in Operation Echo were unable to hit their targets in the rugged Yugoslav terrain with laser-guided bombs." The headline read: "Canadian pilots miss military targets."[75]

Because of that article, Davies chose to curtail giving the media even basic information about the CF-18s' missions, such as the numbers of pilots who had dropped bombs; how many had hit their targets; how many had not dropped their bombs because they could not identify their targets for whatever reason—including poor visibility; and how many had returned to Aviano without dropping their bombs. A *Toronto Star* reporter, Rosie DiManno, first reported on Davies' decision on March 30, quoting Davies, who said: "My young aviators are reading articles in the press that say Canadian pilots can't hit a huge military complex with precision-guided munitions. That demonstrates to me an appalling lack of concern for the guys flying these missions."[76] Davies was referring, in DiManno's copy, to more than one article and, evidently, was not pressed for more information about the pilots who allegedly were affected by negative coverage.

Back in Canada, the news media compared the access of their journalists to the Canadian pilots to the policies of the American military, which, they claimed, was not only allowing print and broadcast interviews but the identification of pilots as well. The question was put directly to Henault on March 28 as to why Canadians couldn't have similar access. He responded:

> I would say to that, that we have a very small fighter pilot community in Canada and it's very easy to identify where that particular pilot may have come from. I think you are only too aware of the number of bases that we have or the wings that we have that conduct fighter operations. American pilots giving interviews is a little less of a compromise. It is difficult with a 220 million population to identify more categorically where a pilot may come from and from where he's operating. That's really the reason behind which we're still maintaining some operational security in that respect.[77]

The Canadian journalists' increasing frustrations at not gaining access to the Canadian personnel in Aviano was relayed to their colleagues in the Ottawa press corps. The latter pressed air force commanders and the military's top brass for access to the CF-18 pilots. CTV's Jim Munson, for example, led off the media's questions during the March 31 daily technical briefing by asking Jurkowski about access to the pilots in Aviano. Jurkowski maintained the Forces were not allowing journalists access to the pilots at that time for reasons of security.

> As you know, we have a very small fighter pilot community that fly out of only limited numbers of locations and because of mission security and security for themselves who could be very easily identified, and for their families, we have for the moment not allowed journalist interviews with fighter pilots. We are balancing these factors and when the balance is right, and we will try and do this as quickly as

possible, you will certainly have access to the pilots. When that is going to be I can't say for certain.[78]

One week into the bombing campaign, internal briefing notes show the chief of the air staff and his deputy wanted to know the rationale for the restrictive public affairs communications policy for Operation Echo.[79] Behind the scenes, the highest-ranking air force officials were deeply concerned about the lack of media access to pilots in Aviano. It had also been discussed in meetings with Eggleton, Baril, and Henault, who had consulted with Davies in Aviano and the 3 Wing and 4 Wing commanders. A March 31 briefing note is the second indication that the top brass in Ottawa had no plan for news media requests for access to pilots and ground crew in Aviano. Lt. (Navy) John Coppard, the director of air force public affairs, told the chief of air staff: "J5 PA has indicated the DCDS [Deputy Chief of Defence Staff] will provide guidance to CAS [Chief of Air Staff] as soon as a policy has been decided upon."[80] The specific concern was that "the pilots in the missions over Kosovo are not being given any opportunity to speak to the media, security considerations notwithstanding."[81] It added: "The matter of increasing the exposure of pilots to the media is a high political and military priority."[82]

After much consultation, Henault cleared ground crews in Aviano to speak to the news media. As for pilots, several options were considered, the preferred one being interviews with pilots and ground crew by telephone on a no-name basis. The background briefing document continued: "There have also been suggestions that televised interviews with pilots be conducted, but only showing the back of their heads. This approach has been used by our UK allies. All options are in accordance with SACEUR policy."[83] No prior plan envisioned allowing Canadian news media access to the pilots in Aviano, because the Canadians were following the NATO public affairs plan, not developing their own. Lt. Cmdr. Agnew explained: "Once you accept it was a NATO operation, we were the Canadian tail."[84] The sole orchestrated plan for the news media was the daily press briefings at National Defence Headquarters.

Another Canadian journalist representing a major news agency arrived in Aviano about four days after the bombing campaign began. He was shocked to learn that journalists in Ottawa could only talk to a

Canadian pilot by speaker phone while they stood at the gate outside the base. He had convinced his organization that he would have a competitive advantage by spending the money to go to Aviano.

> I pushed to go there because that's where the bombing was happening from. We wanted to be close to it so that we could basically be in the neighbourhood in case something bad happened to a Canadian pilot. We would get the information first and we would get it in a timely manner. I mean Canadian military assets are fighting a war. They're dropping bombs. We should be there covering it. It's really that simple.[85]

He discovered, however, that he could reach the base only courtesy of the Americans, who only let journalists in for short periods twice a day. "They had little events for us. They'd take us around in pools to show us planes that we could photograph and the odd American pilot that we could speak to and that was it."[86] After the Ottawa teleconference took place, he said:

> I got a phone call telling me that one of my colleagues in Ottawa had went [sic] to this press conference and got a first-hand account of what it was like to drop a bomb. They put this guy up as sort of like a gimmee. They threw him out to do that. They offered him up to me the next day, one on one, but it had already been out, right? I mean it had been in our paper. Every other media outlet had done it so there was no value to it the day after. I told them basically to stuff it. You guys are wasting my time. I basically ignored the Canadian participation from that point on because it wasn't relevant. There were other countries doing more and there were more interesting stories than how many bombs Canadian planes are dropping on any given day.[87]

Instead, that journalist took a ferry from Italy to Albania and covered the refugee crisis for several weeks, discovering first-hand how dangerous war reporting can be.

We went to the front lines of the Albanian-Kosovo border and I think it was a South American cameraman that got shot in the head—killed by a sniper—a few days earlier. We couldn't really approach too closely because there were snipers several hundred metres away and they could have killed us. A couple of days before that an American pilot dropped a bomb by mistake on the wrong side of the border and nearly wiped out a bunch of journalists and aid workers that were heading out to the same field that I was in. When the border opened, we were able to go into Kosovo. I went in with the German army and we saw atrocities and destruction and interviewed people who'd lived through the occupation. Basically, it was [sic] nothing to do with the Canadian government.[88]

After a week, the lack of media access to pilots and aircrews in Aviano was becoming intolerable, especially since the British and Americans had increased the media's access to pilots both abroad and at home. CTV's news desk in Toronto told Malbon that, given the lack of access, she should travel with her cameraman to Brussels, where NATO's civilian spokesman Jamie Shea was briefing journalists on the campaign's progress. She left Aviano for Belgium. Meanwhile in Ottawa, the lack of information about Canada's involvement in the campaign led Munson to tell viewers on March 31: "The daily briefings make the bombing runs sound like an overnight international courier delivery."[89]

8

A Blanket of Secrecy

The first live interview that a journalist conducted with a pilot in Aviano came a week into the bombing campaign on April 2. The CBC's Neil Macdonald was able to interview a pilot on the condition that his face was not shown. It wasn't the best story Macdonald ever had done.

> He said precious little. He had all the insignia taken off his uniform. We weren't allowed to shoot his face so, as he was speaking, we shot him sort of clasping and unclasping his hands. It's a visual gimmick, I mean you've got to shoot something, the guy's talking. We had to agree that we wouldn't identify him. I wasn't too crazy about that really. I don't like doing that.[1]

Macdonald explained why:

> The CBC really frowns on hidden or silhouetted interviews as they are called. If somebody's talking, the public, the viewer has a right to see who it is. God knows who they're putting out in front of the camera, you know. I'm sure the military's very honest but there are organizations that are less than honest in their public dealings with the media. We like to see faces. We like to see the people we're talking to, but we had no choice. We were there; it was a condition for the interview. It came very late, I mean we had to do it very

quickly—sort of in a field, as I recall—this fellow came out in a jumpsuit without any insignia on it and they presented him and said: "OK, go ahead." He wasn't, you know, the best talker in the world, I mean the guy's a pilot, he's got a job to do. I don't expect them to be orators, but it was precious little.[2]

Macdonald was looking for information about the kinds of missions Canadians were flying, what kind of opposition they were encountering, and whether they were hitting their targets. Instead, the pilot talked about the nervousness of flying into combat, seeing a Dutch warplane shoot down a MiG on the first night's mission, and his belief that when he took out targets, it was buildings or jets that were neutralized, not people.[3]

Also, on April 2, journalists attending the daily technical briefing in Ottawa finally talked to a pilot in Aviano on a speaker phone for ten minutes. He was asked in both English and French by CTV and Radio-Canada if he would identify himself, and both times he refused. When asked whether he was sensitive to news reports that the pilots had missed targets and if that was affecting morale, he replied that weather affected some missions. "That does not change the morale at all on the pilots and, no, they don't follow what's going on or the way it's reported in the news media."[4] The interviews turned to the pilot's feelings about being in battle and how it differed from his training. He talked about the first time he entered enemy territory and was targeted by an enemy MiG that was shot down by a Dutch warplane. When asked about his thoughts regarding the people on the receiving end of his ordnance, he replied, "As pilots, we deal with pain. I have to stop an airplane from flying. I have to destroy a building. The human factor is never ever in my mind at that point in time. I think it's the same thing for a lot of pilots."[5]

That story, or parts of it, appeared in nearly every major Canadian daily newspaper the next day.[6] Agnew, the joint operations public affairs officer, was relieved. "Once we organized that one story, they [the Ottawa journalists] were happy. They were quite comfortable with one story and that interview took the pressure off. Once it's over, it's over. It's yesterday's news."[7]

The unidentified Canadian pilot who participated in the April 2 Ottawa-Aviano teleconference interview was Lt. Col. Sylvain Faucher, commanding officer of 425 Tactical Fighter Squadron. Faucher explained that he could have said more but the information was classified, especially that the CF-18s were playing a lead role in the bombing campaign.

> I think the journalists were trying to conclude that the role that we would play in such a conflict would be secondary in nature, that we'd be camping somewhere very far from the action and we wouldn't be doing much. Let me tell you on the first night Canada was far from being at the end, in a secondary role. As a matter of fact, the Canadian airplanes were the first to cross the enemy lines on that night. We couldn't talk about it then and I'll be honest with you, I'm not even sure if I can talk about it now. But Canada was right there in the front lines.[8]

Other journalists in Aviano also were allowed to talk to Faucher by telephone. The *Globe and Mail*'s Moscow bureau chief, Geoffrey York, was one of them. An elder statesman of Canadian journalism who had covered wars in Somalia, Chechnya, Afghanistan, Iraq, the Philippines, and the Palestinian territories, York said:

> When the Kosovo war broke out, our London correspondent was the first on the scene in Macedonia covering the exodus of refugees from Kosovo. I suggested that I could also help cover the war since Moscow is not far away. I proposed to my foreign editor that I could perhaps go to Aviano to cover the Canadian aircrews involved in the NATO bombing campaign. Since Canada was participating in a war, I thought it made sense to investigate Canada's role in the war and let our readers know what Canada was doing. My editor agreed, and I flew from Moscow to Italy. Then I rented a car to get to a town near the Aviano air base. We were allowed to enter the base, but we were restricted to a big empty building just inside one of the entrances of the

base. The building was a very short distance from the entrance gate, as I recall. At this building, everyone simply waited for a briefing or interviews. There was very little access to anything. We were totally frustrated and we weren't being given any interviews—in fact hardly any information at all. My recollection is that we had one briefing on the first day—late in the afternoon—by Col. Dwight Davies. On the second day, I think, we were put into a bus and taken to the runway to watch some planes landing, but we weren't allowed to talk to anyone. After much complaining by the Canadian journalists, we were finally allowed a telephone interview with one Canadian pilot. And that was the full extent of our entire access in those two or three days.[9]

During the April 4 technical media briefing, primarily about Canada's decision to accept some 5,000 Albanian refugees, the Canadian Forces again put an unidentified CF-18 pilot in Aviano on the speaker phone for journalists to interview. Munson asked the pilot to walk the journalists through one of his missions. The pilot replied: "I'm not sure if I want to do that one more time because..." before he was interrupted by Munson, who asked incredulously: "You're the same pilot?"[10] The journalists in Ottawa asked about the refugees, the frustrations of dealing with the weather, the hours they were working, and how political decisions affected the campaign. The pilot replied that the pilots were focused only on their missions, were putting in sixteen-, eighteen- and twenty-hour days, and the weather was frustrating. As for politics, the pilot said he did not follow them either, but carried out the missions to the best of his ability. Ground crew were standing by, but none of the journalists posed questions to them. No major daily newspaper or television network used any of the pilot's material from that interview.

Two days later in Washington, a Pentagon spokesman faced the first of several grillings over collateral damage, the unintended destruction of a building, admittedly by an American warplane. On April 6, reporters asked about an apartment complex that had been hit the night before. They were told candidly that cloud cover may have interfered with a laser-guided bomb and caused it to fall short of its target. That was part of the risk of combat operations, said Kenneth H. Bacon, the US defense department's assistant secretary of defense (public affairs). "We have said from the very beginning that we will work hard to hold civilian casualties to a minimum, and we are not targeting civilians.... There are risks to every combat operation, and those risks cannot be—they can be minimized, but not avoided."[11]

In Ottawa that day, Eggleton and Henault were also grilled over the accidental killing of civilians. One reporter asked point blank: "And my question to you is: How can you say this war is not against the people of Yugoslavia when our bombs are killing innocent people?"[12] Eggleton's reply took the high moral ground:

> It is regrettable that civilians are hurt or killed. We've always known that that was likely to happen, but certainly our targets are military targets. Our effort is to minimize whatever damage to non-military facilities are and that'll continue to be the effort. However, with an intensified air campaign, there are higher risks in terms of civilians. But I must say that while we're doing that to try to stop what has been going on, meanwhile, there are people being lined up and shot against the wall, sometimes in their own home, in Kosovo, and being shot. That is the kind of thing we want to bring to an end.[13]

When asked whether Canadian bombs had killed any soldiers or civilians, Eggleton replied: "No, wouldn't know. There have been, certainly, weapons released by Canadians on many occasions and we continue to fly the sorties with those weapons, but again every effort is made to target military facilities."[14]

Totally frustrated with the lack of access to the Canadian Forces in Aviano, two journalists did what some journalists do in such situations: they wrote about it, in articles that were published on April 8. Rosie DiManno of the *Toronto Star* and Geoffrey York of the *Globe and Mail* both documented their inability to learn more about the Canadian war effort. DiManno toured the Aviano air base with a group of journalists tightly controlled by military escorts. From about 100 metres away, DiManno could see a dozen Canadian airplane mechanics stripped down to their undershirts working on the CF-18s. It took six of them to lift a missile on their shoulder, carrying it like a casket. But that was as close as the escorts would let her get. The agenda for Canadian journalists on the American air base that day was Americans and their warplanes.[15]

York devoted an article to the Canadian Forces keeping their aircrews under wraps. A "blanket of secrecy" had dropped over the Canadians in Aviano. Canadians were dropping bombs on the former Yugoslavia, that much he knew, but that was all he knew. When reporters were allowed to talk to one pilot, they couldn't divulge his name, rank, or hometown. Nor would the pilot discuss his targets. York asked a military public affairs officer why there was such secrecy, but he refused to be quoted. "Apparently even the reason for the secrecy is considered a secret. 'As far as we're concerned, it's a dead issue,' the officer said. 'I'm not talking about it anymore.' He then asked that his name be kept secret and that his comment be kept off the record."[16] York wrote that secrecy had been the hallmark of the Canadian Forces since the 1991 Persian Gulf War, when Canadians bombed retreating Iraqis but refused to say what they hit or what damaged they caused. He claimed the Canadian Forces had studied the book *Hotel Warriors*, which described how American journalists were shuttled from their hotels and "media pools" during the 1991 war, which was like the system being used in Aviano.[17] York explained that this process was wrong in principle.

> Canadians, including the readers of my newspaper, have a fundamental right to know the activities of their government and their military, since Canadian taxpayers are financing those military activities and since Canadian voters have a right to elect or defeat a government on the basis of a full understanding of its activities. If Canadians are denied basic information about the activities of their government (including its military), then how can they judge whether their tax dollars have been properly spent and whether their government has been held accountable for its actions? How can they judge whether their government has acted fairly

and deserves re-election? This is just a fundamental rule of democracy.

Secrecy often leads to more secrecy, and then to corruption and abuses. Ordinary Canadians need the media to be a watchdog over the activities of their government and their military. If a government is concealing information, our readers need to be informed of this, so that they can decide whether to vote for that government in the next election. This is what democracy is all about. And when a military is involved in the taking of human lives—in this case the possible killing of Yugoslavian soldiers and civilians—it is all the more important that Canadians be fully informed of the basic facts, so that they can decide whether they want to re-elect such a government. As a matter of democracy and morality, Canadians have a right to know the full facts when their government is involved in causing the death of people, regardless of whether it's a war or not. Killing people is not automatically a moral act and a democratic act just because a war is going on. Even when a war is happening, voters have a right to debate whether their government is waging war in a fair and just manner—or whether it is waging war in an excessive and abusive way. This is why the Canadian military should have been releasing more information about the targets that they were attacking. In some ways the basic argument seems pretty obvious: If the Canadian government is authorizing its military to kill people, Canadian taxpayers and voters have a right to know the extent of that killing.[18]

These were exactly the kinds of hard questions the defence minister was dodging in Ottawa, saying he didn't know whether Canadians had killed any civilians or military personnel. York, like the other journalists who travelled to Aviano, never obtained any of that information. He left Aviano and travelled to Skopje, Macedonia, where he reported on the unfolding refugee crisis caused by hundreds of thousands of Kosovar Albanians fleeing ethnic cleansing.

At the Ottawa technical press briefing on April 14, reporters asked Henault about requests from Gen. Clark for more aircraft to escalate the bombing campaign. One reporter asked if Canada had sufficient precision-guided munitions (PGM) kits to outfit more CF-18s should they be sent to Italy. In reality, Canada outfitted twelve CF-18s with FLIR pods, some borrowed from allies. No more pods were available for six more CF-18s that were being considered for the operation. Henault evaded the question: "The PGM kits we have right now are sufficient for the operational tempo that we're currently envisaging and, yes, I would say that we're capable doing the mission as we have now defined it."[19] Henault also said that Canada was mixing precision-guided munitions with non-precision bombs, leading one reporter to ask if that was because Canada was running short of smart-bomb kits. Henault replied: "No, not at all. In fact this is all very much part of the air campaign and part of the deliberate campaign that has been progressing over the last three weeks now into its fourth week."[20] He added: "No, we are not short of ammunition. In fact, we are in the process at the moment of replenishing our stocks and we have more than enough stocks at the moment to satisfy operational rates as we know them." The truth was that Canada was, indeed, running out of bombs, and those available increasingly were the dregs of American stocks. No stories were published about the Canadians' bomb issues. Such information might not have been helpful to an enemy, but it certainly would have embarrassed the Canadian government.

During the April 14 briefing, Henault also was asked whether Canada had enough qualified pilots to meet a NATO request for more CF-18s. The reporter calculated Canada had some forty pilots and twelve jets in Aviano. Henault replied that the air force thought the operation was sustainable and that they would be in Aviano for a period of six months. The truth was that the dearth of FLIR pods in Canada was causing a crisis in qualifying pilots. Still, Henault said, "I would say that we're certainly capable of another rotation. So, we can go for a period probably six to eight, perhaps twelve months at the current rates, putting people back into theatre as required."[21] Several days later, during the April 17 technical briefing, Henault repeated his calm assurances, saying that beyond the thirty-five to forty pilots deployed to Aviano eighty more were combat ready in Canada.[22] The truth was that had the bombing campaign lasted more than another two months, the gaps in the CF-18 wings' training would have manifested themselves.

On April 15, the *Maple Leaf*, a weekly tabloid-style paper published by the Department of National Defence and the Canadian Forces, provided a detailed story about the first Canadian mission on March 24 (when Canadian pilots led the coalition strike package into Serbia). Although the author was unidentified, the article titled "My First Combat Mission" provided every bit of dramatic detail that Canadian journalists in Aviano had longed to obtain from one of the CF-18 pilots. It discussed details on the takeoff of four CF-18s; how they were tracked by fire-control radar as they entered Serbian airspace; that an enemy surface-to-air missile (SAM) was launched; that the Dutch destroyed a MiG fighter closing in on the Canadians; that their target was a military base; that the pilot struck his target; and that he returned to Italy at 900 kilometres per hour while his wingman was tracked by SAM radar.[23]

More than a month after the fact, the "best-before" date of that story had long passed. Just four Canadian newspapers bothered to pick up a wire story by the Canadian Press based on the *Maple Leaf* article.[24] Its unidentified author was Lt. Col. Faucher, who had no grand designs such as helping the Canadian public understand the experiences of CF-18 pilots. Indeed, he had no intention of publishing his account. Faucher explained: "Initially, I wrote it for me. Then somehow through discussion, public affairs got a hold of that and decided to share it with a bigger audience."[25]

It wasn't just Canadian journalists who were frustrated over a no names policy for military personnel in Aviano; American journalists complained as well. During a press briefing at the Pentagon on April 16, they protested being unable to identify individual crewmen by name and hometown. Said one journalist: "If we want to talk to someone who's from Long Island and identify them as such as we've done through every military engagement I can remember, why are we arbitrarily saying you can't do that now?"[26]

US Maj. Gen. Charles F. Wald, vice director for strategic plans and policy for the joint staff, admitted some Americans were identified on television in the first nights, but since then could be identified only by their first names. "I was there and know these folks. . . . When I was there, we did not want our names on TV at that particular time in the middle of an operation."²⁷ Seconds later, the assistant secretary of defence for public affairs, Kenneth Bacon, explained that SACEUR Gen. Clark had the policy put in place for security reasons.

> Certainly, we have pilots who are flying at risk every single night. And to the extent that those pilots run the risk for being shot down and might be shot down, as one was, I think the commander, I think the wing commander and I think the pilots would all prefer that they not have information out about their names and their hometowns and where their families might live. It is a choice that has been made by the military commanders, and it's a choice that obviously could be open to question, but so far is a choice that's prevailed for the life of this operation.²⁸

That line of questioning was dropped. An explanation for why that argument might have been accepted may be found in the transcripts of an earlier briefing on April 2 about the capture of three US soldiers by Serbs in Macedonia on March 31. When journalists asked to be briefed on the soldiers, Bacon said that the Serbs were letting the captives call their families. But their phone lines were choked by journalists trying to interview them, making it hard for the soldiers to get through. Wald asked the press not to interfere with those attempts. "So, I ask you to maybe back off a little in your calls so that important calls can get through if they're allowed by the Serbs, and we hope they are. It would be every encouraging if they did allow them to communicate with their families."²⁹ In other words, it was the American news media itself that constituted a potential threat, badgering soldiers' families while simultaneously denying soldiers the opportunity to talk to their loved ones.

During the April 17 technical briefing in Ottawa, defence minister Eggleton told journalists that Canada was adding six more CF-18 aircraft to the campaign, bringing to eighteen the number of Canadian jet fighters in Aviano. When asked if those aircraft had any assignment or would be carrying the same kind of weapons as the other twelve, Eggleton replied that the CF-18s already had a role, but the new ones could provide other functions, such as flying escort missions, making them "multi-purpose combat capable."³⁰ He avoided any response to the question about the weapons they would carry. At the next day's technical briefing, a journalist followed up that line of questioning, asking if the six CF-18s going to Aviano would have precision-guided munitions kits. Jurkowski replied: "They won't be carrying any weapons, if that's what you are asking."³¹

The reporter responded that this was not what had been asked and put the question directly: "Will they have the FLIR pods?" Jurkowski replied: "They will have the full capability when they arrive. They will be put into the same pot as the other aircraft, so that they will be fully capable of receiving any PGM-related [precision guided munitions] equipment." The thrust and parry continued. The journalist said: "I guess what I'm asking is, we're going to have eighteen aircraft over there. Will we be able to field eighteen capable aircraft at once or are we moving kit around between aircraft? Jurkowski replied: "We will be able to field eighteen aircraft to do whatever is required, multi-role." The journalist thanked Jurkowski for his responses.³²

The truth is the first casualty in war, but war journalists habitually are identified as the propagandists and myth makers.³³ That often is the case.³⁴ But like Eggleton and Henault, Jurkowski avoided telling the journalists the truth about Canada's participation in the Kosovo air war by telling only partial truths. For example, the new CF-18s could receive PGM-related equipment, but the truth was that no more FLIR pods were to be had. The truth was that the additional CF-18s were not used like PGM-capable jets; they were put in a separate area and were cannibalized for parts, because a lack of strategic lift stretched the supply lines to Aviano to their limit. Moreover, Canadian military brass were more than comfortable in not telling the whole truth. Baril told the CBC quite candidly about Kosovo: "There is a great difference between not releasing information and telling the truth. We're telling the truth, we are just not releasing some information."³⁵

Years later, Baril, by then retired, explained his thinking about what the news media should be told about the Canadians' participation in the Kosovo air war. The military had a democratic duty to inform to the news media about the war, but the question was how much, given security constraints.

> Security is based on some very well-known principles in the sharing of information. If information is coming to us from another country, there are restrictions attached to it. Anything coming from the US, for example, is extremely sensitive because of their rules and regulations that they shared with us. If we don't respect it, that's the last time we're going to hear from them on the issue. Anything coming from Europe will have strings attached to it as far as security is concerned.[36]

Regarding the information given to Canadians via the news media, Baril said:

> The information has to be general purpose information, in as much as you can give to the press; I mean to the people of Canada. You know much of the very detailed information, but you certainly don't want to tell the capability of your airplane publicly. You just don't show your hand to the enemy that way. We were very careful never to tell what packages our airplanes were part of or anything like this. This is not only our Canadian view but that was the NATO view. Everybody was rather careful when telling what was going on.[37]

Captain Dave Muralt, the Canadian Forces public affairs officer in Aviano, sent Faucher's article to the *Maple Leaf*. He also bore the brunt of many journalists' outrage over the lack of access to the pilots and ground crew.

Toronto Sun reporter Joe Warmington, arrived in Aviano in mid-April from Macedonia, where he had travelled to write on the Kosovar refugee crisis. Muralt was able to get Warmington on the base to talk to the Canadians. Warmington talked to one pilot for an article published April 17 about the pressure to avoid collateral damage and how he thought of his targets as buildings, not people. Though the pilot wouldn't have objected to being identified, he had to abide by the anonymity conditions. That anonymity, Warmington said, robbed the article of its life and his readers of any opportunity to identify with the piece in the way that using names and hometowns does.

> The whole reason to go to the scene is to localize it, you know. Here's our guys; here's our gals; here's what they're doing well; here's what they're doing wrong; and here's the equipment they're working with. But the Canadians had a theory that somehow identifying them would leave their families vulnerable back here. I thought it was appalling but I didn't really know how to go around it.[38]

Malbon, meanwhile, said the trip to Belgium was a second exercise in frustration because, while NATO spokesman Jamie Shea provided detailed briefings about the bombing campaign, no details were emerging about the Canadians' role. A review of the transcripts of the Brussels press briefings for the entire war revealed that the word Canada was used just three times in seventy-eight days.[39] The most information that Shea revealed about the Canadians' involvement was one sentence one week into the campaign when he discussed NATO's resolve, noting: "Canada has just announced that, for instance, six CF-18s are on their way to augment the Canadian contribution already there."[40] As a result, Malbon said that her network determined it would be best if she returned to London.

> They kind of said: "You know what? You're not getting much out of there, so there's no sense CTV spending all this money to keep you there [in Belgium]. We can get just as good stuff from the feeds. Because you're not getting information on the Canadians, we're going to send you home." The next morning they changed their mind. Our vice-president of news told us he wanted us to stay and keep pushing and pushing to try and get more access to the Canadians, so we stayed.[41]

The costs of her trip on her fourth week on the road were high, very high. "Think about it: Flying us there, hotels, cars, food, and the satellite feeds. We were feeding from ABC sometimes, CNN sometimes, sometimes some of the freelance people in Europe. I don't know what they were charging but these mobile trucks were pretty costly."[42] The timing of her return to Aviano was fortunate because a Canadian Forces reserve public affairs officer Naval Lieutenant John Larsen from Calgary, had arrived to replace Muralt. Larsen had transferred from naval operations, as a diver, to public affairs early in his career. He had completed seven years in the regular force public affairs branch, including a stint in Bosnia, before transferring to the reserves and being asked if he'd go to Aviano. Larsen arrived in Aviano with strong thoughts about his role. Larsen was one of the "two fellows" in the car with Malbon who Muralt said was trying to get her on the base.

> It wasn't until John Larsen came that he tried, he really did try, to kind of free up, try to get Dwight Davies and the other officials to allow us more access, because they wanted the publicity, too. They wanted Canadians to know: "Look what we're doing over here. This is important stuff. Look what we're doing."[43]

He had spent a lot of his time in Ottawa working to convince his senior public affairs bosses to work as facilitators, while still ensuring operational security. Larsen considered himself an enabler who helped the media obtain the information they needed from the most authoritative source. "One of my central tenets is, if I was truly successful in my job, I would never be quoted once but I'd have all the operators quoted to facilitate that."[44] He went to Aviano fully aware that the military's media policy was restrictive. "That's the exact message I went over with, that the only two people who have authority to speak directly to the news media are the commanding officer and the public affairs officer."[45]

> When I arrived in Aviano—and this is not a state secret by any means—by and large, the Canadian media were outside the gate. Many of them had already left. They had been out there since the beginning of operations with essentially zero exposure to the operation, the pilots, or anybody else. That was a bit of a source of personal frustration to myself because, as a junior officer, I have no choice but to abide by policies that have been sent down. But I believe that media relations transcend just going out and doing interviews. I

think one of the things that was incumbent upon me as a public affairs officer in the field was to say: "If you've got journalists standing out there in the mud for days on end, you've got to communicate with them." Maybe it doesn't mean they can get an interview. Maybe it doesn't mean they can get an interview the way they want one, but you've got to have a discourse with them. You've got to get them to understand why you're doing what you're doing. I don't mean to imply that they have to agree with that, in fact many of them never did agree, but a relationship needs to be built.[46]

Larsen continued:

So, when we first got there, several of these people had already pulled their pegs, Joy Malbon being one of them. We immediately hit the phones and said: "Could you come back? There is an important story to be told here." They said—with no fault to them because it's certainly legitimate—they said: "Well, we were there and we saw nobody and we heard nothing." So, one of the things that we began talking about very early on was: Can we not start to tell our story in a way that still accords to the letter of the law as dictated, which is pilot safety will not be jeopardized and identification will not be made? The rationale was that they didn't want to jeopardize the safety of the pilots and they didn't want them identified. So, we felt that we could begin a process of getting these guys some exposure without doing that and we did that. We did interviews without the names and we did interviews with the back of their heads, right? So, it was initially crafted no interviews with aircrews. It was quickly changed to, "You can interview aircrew, you just can't identify them."[47]

Malbon did two brief stories for her national network with Larsen's help. The first aired on April 18, quoting an unidentified pilot saying that dropping bombs did not rest easily on his mind. At that point there were twelve

CF-18s in Aviano with six more on the way.[48] Malbon did a second piece that aired April 24 for which she could interview a Canadian pilot, a padre, and a ground crew member, on the condition they not be identified. She said that before the camera was rolling, the pilot told her a very moving, emotional story about what it was like being in combat. But that's not what he said when the camera started rolling. Malbon explained:

> You had to abide by the rules or you wouldn't get any Canadians, but from what I remember, this pilot, he was a young pilot from Alberta. His family was absolutely terrified for him. Again, when it's not on tape—for television—it doesn't exist. But he told me that, yeah, he felt lousy about dropping bombs, but he's Canadian, he's a soldier, his country told him this is what he has to do, so he's doing it. He talked about missing his family. He talked about his mom and her fears about him over there. Before we interviewed this particular pilot, a plane had been shot down and there were all these rumors circulating because there was no information coming out. There were rumors, at one point, that it was a Canadian pilot that was shot down. So, can you imagine his mother sitting at home in Alberta getting information on the television saying a pilot's been shot down? CNN's reporting that they think it may be Canadian because of the markings. Can you imagine what she was going through?[49]

In Malbon's story, the pilot said much less than what he did off the record. What he said was:

> You can't sit back on the sidelines and say: "Somebody else take care of that." You know, it's a terrible injustice but, you know, we don't want to get our hands dirty. We had a couple of times where we'd come back and sat down and sat across the table from each other and, "Hey, do you realize what we just did? We just dropped bombs on a target." And then you think about it after. But during the mission, you're not thinking about that, you're concentrating on what it is

> you're doing. And you have to do that, otherwise the guys who are shooting back at you have the advantage.[50]

When Malbon interviewed the pilot, the camera shot him in the foreground, with his back to the camera. She found it less than ideal, because her story lacked basic information, such as a name and a face, that makes television stories credible.

> For television, it's everything. Television is visual; you want someone's face. You want someone's name. You want to find out who they are. When you have blacked-out faces on TV, especially on TV—not so much for print or radio—it just looks suspicious. It looks like the person's lying or it's not true. It adds doubt to the story. But we did the best we could. I know the desk was happy with the story because we were so desperate to hear from the Canadians. You've got to imagine back in Canada the desk wants to know what are our boys doing over there, what are they up to, what are they thinking, what are they feeling?[51]

Larsen saw time and again that the stories the journalists generated in person and over the telephone were not the ones they really wanted. The journalists had to lean toward softer, human interest stories, due to the lack of operational information. As Larsen explains:

> Let me put it this way: The questions that they asked did not necessarily mean those were the stories they wrote. The questions they asked we often couldn't comment on and so they couldn't generate stories out of them. What they wanted to know was: "How many planes are you putting in the air? What is your ammunition? What targets are you going in after?" They were the standard high-tempo military operations questions that for logical security reasons you really can't address. Those were the questions that we were asked most often. The stories that they picked up on most often were: "What are the pilots thinking? What are the pi-

8.1. CTV's Joy Malbon interviews an unnamed CF-18 pilot who has his back to the camera to protect his identity for unspecified security reasons. Photo courtesy of CTV News.

lots doing? What is the life of a fighter pilot? We haven't gone to combat in fighter aircraft for ten years and we haven't launched an operation of this magnitude since Korea, so how does that affect the people there? What's the mentality?" It often sort of swerved between the hard news stories right into that human angle.[52]

In between Malbon's two stories, Joe Warmington wrote a second story for the *Toronto Sun*. For the first time, Warmington discussed one shortcoming of the aging CF-18s, which were computer-challenged compared to those flown by the US Air Force. One unnamed pilot compared the CF-18s' on-board computers to an early 1980s Commodore 64 computer, as opposed to a Pentium-powered model.[53] Warmington's story, published

April 18, revealed just the tip of the iceberg of the technological challenges the aircrews had to overcome, but was also the first like it to appear.[54]

Years later, Warmington explained that he didn't go to Italy looking to portray the Canadian Forces in a negative way. In fact, he hadn't planned on going to Italy at all; the trip was an afterthought. Warmington's rationale for convincing his editors to send him and a photographer to Europe was to cover the Kosovar refugee crisis.

> You know I work for the *Toronto Sun*. It's not a network, or, it's not even a paper of record, really. It's a strong local tabloid, so we're not out there covering a war every time it happens. I'm not a Joy Malbon. I know Joy. I worked with her in the Soo.[55] She's big time. But sometimes these big-time faces, you know, they almost become the story because of who they are and what they represent. I'm kind of a small-time reporter who usually focuses mainly on people. I don't generally get into the major politics.[56]

Warmington's first stop was Skopje, Macedonia, where he wrote his refugee stories. Then, he and his photographer flew to Venice and drove to Aviano on the strength of assurances from an Ottawa contact that he would be able to get on to the base. "When we got there, a guy from the Canadian group came out and said: 'No, you can't do that,' and left. He kind of blew us off at first and steered us toward Wesley Clark and the press conferences, which we certainly weren't really interested in." [57] Warmington's Ottawa connection eventually paid off and he was allowed on to the base to talk to the Canadians.

> I made a call back to Ottawa and got some people on the phone. I guess they phoned around and we did get around those guys. We got in what they call the loop and we went right up to the CF-18s and we touched them. We took pictures, talked to the crew and this kind of thing, but the part that we were not happy with, and we had to live with, was the fact we couldn't name the pilot. We had to agree that we

> wouldn't use any names to get in there. We had to take pictures of a silhouette and stuff like that, so it wasn't perfect.⁵⁸

As for Warmington's second story on the CF-18s' computers, he stumbled upon it while sightseeing in the historic town of Pordenone, a fifteen-minute drive from Aviano.

> We ran into a couple of Canadian pilots and a driver that were on a very short leave I guess, maybe a twenty-four-hour leave or a twelve-hour leave or something like that. They just wanted to go for a walk away from the base. That's where I got that story from. I thought well that's a good story, you know. What happened, when I wrote that story, that whole Ottawa gang just pooh-poohed it the next day. That was the end of it, but you know what? It turned out to be true. There was lots and lots of stuff after that that came forward. That story was ahead of its time.⁵⁹

Warmington was right about top military officials in Ottawa denying there was anything to his story. Jurkowski told Warmington's Ottawa colleague there "are no structural problems of any sort, and the systems are very, very capable of sustained operations of the kind we are involved in at the moment."⁶⁰ At the daily technical briefing, Jurkowski also continued his gavotte with journalists attempting to obtain accurate information about the CF-18s' precision-guided munitions. He was asked directly: "OK, but has Canada enough equipment that all eighteen could go up in the air on the same day at the same time with precision-guided missiles?"⁶¹ Jurkowski replied: "Typically, that may or may not happen. You may end up with some doing combat . . . combat air patrol. I'm not going to get into numbers of how many pods or weapons we have. I'd rather not address that."⁶² Of course, he could not. To tell the truth, at that point, would have exposed the house of cards on which the air force's combat capabilities were built. Further, it was simply not possible to put all eighteen CF-18s in the bombing campaign at one time. There were not enough FLIR pods, and six of the planes were being used as parts bins. The only more dishonest answer would have been "Yes."

Back in Aviano, Larsen had Forces' videographers shoot film discreetly showing the Canadian operation. He tried to supply that film to television networks in Canada via satellite, so they could use it to build their own stories. Larsen says:

> I don't for a minute blame the media for not doing more. I mean, if you come down with a television camera and all you can get are the backs of somebody's heads, you're only going to be down there once or twice to do the key stories. After that you're going to take stock footage. When the media visitation really dropped off markedly, what we did was we relied on creating our own B roll and sending that over by satellite and then having media and, this of course was TV media, electronic media, build their own stories from what we were sending them.[63] It wasn't what journalists would like. We didn't show them anything in the air. We showed pilots going through the briefings but we had to be careful the maps were removed. We had visuals and pilots taking off and what not. It was quasi-professional, certainly good enough to work on the national networks.[64]

Larsen continued to have difficulty with the American military's security guarding the Aviano air base's main entrance. The security personnel, as opposed to public affairs officers, cared not one iota about Larsen's need to give the Canadian news media film his military photographer shot. One day, he had film shot for CTV and tried to get it to an Anik satellite uplink. "There was a truck waiting and the media were waiting in Canada but there was a security dude there who would not let us through. We ended up throwing the tape over the fence."[65]

Malbon remembers that incident precisely because she was on the receiving end of that toss. "I remember there was some footage of a Canadian pilot that the combat video people took. The truck was waiting, we were phoning, and they actually threw the tape over the fence to me so I could feed it back to Toronto."[66] The good news was that her network had some film to work with. The bad news was that it wasn't really what they wanted.

> We always have problems with that because it's not our footage. It's someone else's footage. We prefer to shoot our own. But we were pretty desperate, so we took it and sent it to Toronto and they were happy with it. Again, you have to explain to people that it's not CTV footage, it's military footage. Military footage isn't necessarily going to show you what you want to see.[67]

In Washington, meanwhile, US Assistant Secretary of Defense for Public Affairs Bacon had taken up the Pentagon press corps' issue over improved access to American pilots in Aviano with Clark. As a result, on April 19 Bacon said that the journalists should be able to talk to the pilots at their discretion. He added: "There's nothing in the Constitution that says a pilot has to talk to the press, but should they want to talk to the press, they'll be free to do that. We are going to, however, adhere to the rule that they talk by first name only and not identify where they're from. This is to protect both them and their family's privacy."[68] There were no questions from the news media, and the subject was not revisited during the Pentagon press briefings for the duration of the war. Judging from the transcripts of the briefings at NATO headquarters in Belgium while Clark attended on March 25, April 1, and April 13, the issue of access to pilots was brought up only in the Washington and Ottawa press briefings, but not for the record by the international news media in Brussels.[69]

9

Friction and Iron Will

Along with the fact that combat required pilots to kill came two other sets of problems. First, as commander of 425 Tactical Fighter Squadron, Lt. Col. Sylvain Faucher, said, some pilots arrived in theatre with an overly aggressive mindset. He had to move to settle that down in short order.

> Most of the fighter pilots that we had in the inventory at the time—we were at about forty some odd fighter pilots in theatre—you can imagine some of those guys were a few years' young in the job. Guys like me were many years' old in the job, but some of them—and I'll use the term some of them—showed up in theatre with a knife between their teeth, i.e. "We want to destroy things. We want to kill something. Let's go." I had to quiet that down fairly fast.[1]

Faucher and Lt. Col. Jim Donihee did so by putting an emphasis on keeping people on the ground safe.

> I'm thinking of the civilian population. Believe it or not—and it may come as a surprise—a lot of our own military personnel flying didn't know why we were there. And if people don't know why they're there and why they had to accomplish a mission or the mission they're given, you've got a problem. I used an audio-visual presentation to brief my folks. I used pictures of all the folks and all the—we call

them atrocities but they were fairly close to that—happening to the civilian population in Kosovo.

So, I used a bunch of slides that we used in Aviano the rotation before. I inserted in those the military flags we were using, whether it's the armourer, whether it's the admin folks, day-to-day training/operation issues or operation events. I think I put in a musical background with Alanis Morissette singing "Thank you." You could have heard a fly in the audience of about 200 because people looked at what happened there. They looked at that job you can do to help these people and they fairly quickly realized why we were there. As I was saying, guys were coming to theatre to, some of them were coming in theatre to shoot something and bomb something. I had to quiet that down fairly quickly and I think we were successful. The pilots who came back with their bombs because they couldn't identify their targets are pretty good examples of that.[2]

Second, although some pilots found ways to deal with the shortcomings of their search-and-rescue training by joking about it or their lack of night-vision capability, most found killing people no laughing matter. Deep inside, they all found ways to deal with the fact that they were dropping bombs that were maiming or killing people or that had the potential to do so. Some distanced themselves psychologically by thinking about targets as inanimate objects. Faucher said:

> You think nothing. I'm not killing anyone. It's because of the nature of our job, it's highly technological. I'm looking at a screen and I have to put a dot on a certain shape on the screen and that's my mission that night. I don't have in mind the personal issue, the human factor issue and the consequences. My job is to do this and I think most of the pilots that's how they treat it. Their job is to ensure a bomb that reaches the time of flight in seconds and that the bomb makes it to the designated point they've studied for the last hour or two or three.[3]

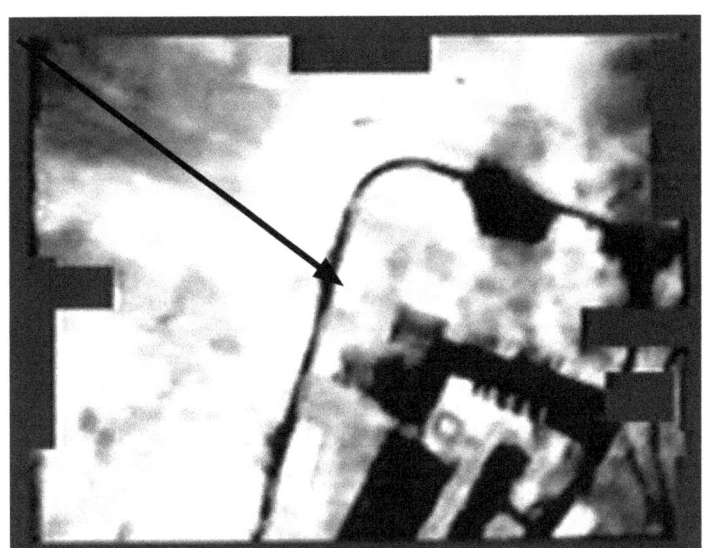

9.1. CF-18 cockpit targeting imagery—ammo storage. Photo courtesy of the Department of National Defence.

9.2. CF-18 cockpit targeting imagery—radio relay. Photo courtesy of the Department of National Defence.

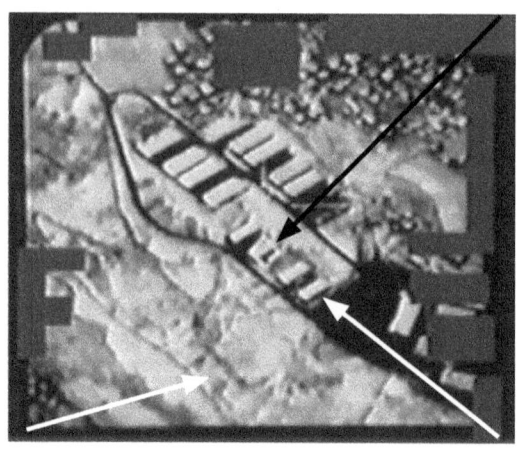

9.3. CF-18 cockpit targeting imagery— army barracks. Photo courtesy of the Department of National Defence.

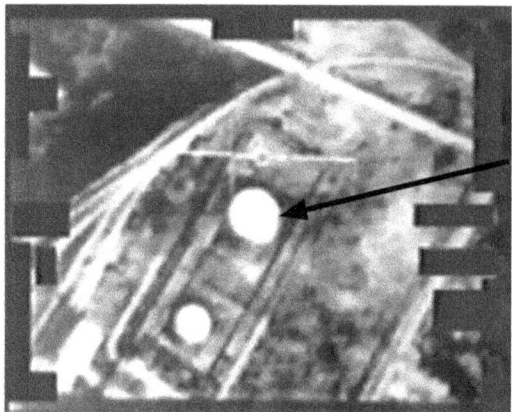

9.4. CF-18 cockpit targeting imagery— industrial site. Photo courtesy of the Department of National Defence.

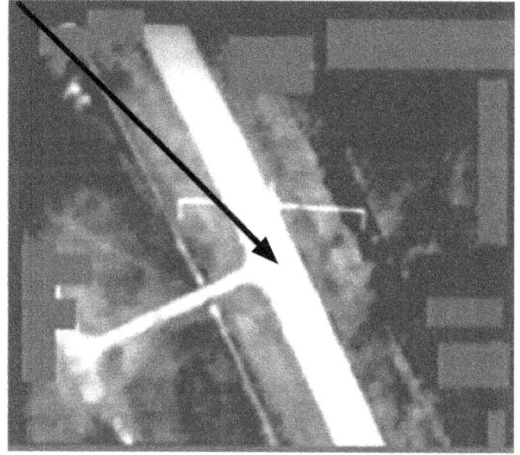

9.5. CF-18 cockpit targeting imagery— airfield runway Photo courtesy of the Department of National Defence..

A Cold Lake pilot said:

> Nobody really dwells on the fact you're shooting missiles at people or you're dropping bombs on people. That's kind of something that's in your hind brain, but it's not something you'd concentrate on. For us, we're taking out airplanes, we're taking out facilities and we're taking out vehicles. The fact that there's people in these things is secondary really for us. Most of what we were tasked to take out was buildings, munitions facilities, armoured vehicles, things like that. It was always assumed to be a vehicle, a building, something that we were tasked to take out. At the same time, though, there were certain targets you knew that there were people in those targets, and that's something you put in your hind brain and you just did your job.[4]

A Bagotville pilot disconnected himself from the possibility that people might be working in the bomb dumps and the buildings he was bombing.

> As a pilot, you have a good idea that there's nobody sitting there. You've gotta believe that there's not 100 workers in that building or, even if it's one single building, even if you're at night, that there's no night janitor working or anyone doing any kind of work there. I had a lot of ammo dumps and things like that, which should be nobody there. It was not bad that way, but, no, it's not the greatest feeling. It's not something you dream of hoping to kill people in your lifetime, unless you're the type of guy that wants to just do that. You do it because you're told to do it and it's your job, right? If you don't want to do it, you're in the wrong business.[5]

Others thought about the humanitarian purposes of their mission. One pilot said he found moral comfort in one particular aspect of the American news media's coverage of the war.

> I had some reservations initially about the whole thing just because it was not a unified global approach, i.e. there wasn't a United Nations resolution. It was strictly a NATO decision to go and use force to try and end hostilities. I kind of thought about that back and forth for quite a long time and I remember specifically watching CNN one day. The German foreign minister, and I don't remember his name, was on CNN. He said something that made it very clear and morally correct for me to go. It just kind of clicked into place that the war or Allied Force—the NATO action to stop the war in Kosovo—was a war against old European nationalism and hate and lack of understanding of other religions and people's beliefs. It was that versus the spirit of unification that was going on in Europe at the time and compassion and understanding and co-operation. When I looked at it like that, it became very clear to me that this was the right thing to do. I was eager to go because my moral dilemma had been resolved by him expressing it all like that. It made clear sense to me and because I was a tactical leader on the squadron, I wanted to be there leading the guys into combat.[6]

Beyond that, this pilot was more than willing to kill Milosevic and his followers.

> All of us are trained to understand and respect the Law of Conflict and whether or not Canada declared war, we were flying combat operations so any target that was military was relevant. For me, it easy to accept because even though I thought: "Hey, I'm going to be killing people here, I'm killing those people for a reason. I do not want to see a nationalistic dictator—whose population is working for him to repress other races and religions—succeed in this day and age. I'm willing to kill him and the people working for him to try and promote a unified and co-operating Europe or world."[7]

> have a big army breakfast, go up the hill and sleep for five or six hours. Then if you weren't flying a mission that day, you could go to the gym, go play a few holes of golf or go to the beach. You know you'd be sitting on a beach in Italy watching half-naked women running around and eating seafood salad. It was just unbelievable. I'd sit there and think: 'How can I be doing this during the day and, you know, going to war at night?'[11]

One Cold Lake pilot arrived in early April to discover no room at the inn where the other Cold Lake pilots were staying, and a relentless work schedule.

> They'd rented an apartment downtown by the old town of Vicenza and they had two of us living there, hot bunking. He'd sleep there in the night, I'd sleep there during the day, share a fridge, share a car and we'd drive back and forth from work. It was twelve hours on, twelve hours off for really the first month or six weeks. It was relentless, no time off, and I was night shift the whole time. Basically I didn't see a lot of daylight other than just before coming into work and sleeping during the day. It was pretty stressful; I ended up losing about twenty pounds during the first six weeks. It felt like we were eating a lot, but times we were so busy we didn't realize we were hungry, right? Under the stress your hunger seems to be somewhat muted. I went in about 210 pounds. I was probably down to 188 by the end. And again, it was simply the stress, the pace.[12]

One Bagotville Major said there was no telling how pilots who had trained for years in Canada would react under the stress of combat. Some handled it well, some didn't.

> Until you physically get involved in a live mission, that's when you see if somebody's going to do the job or somebody won't. We saw the whole spectrum of people starting

on day one. Some were doing a superb job; we saw other pilots take a few missions to get used to it. Some pilots had to be returned to Canada for further training. A lot of it is dealing with stress and that's probably a big part of [it], dealing with the stress, dealing with the fact, yes, you could be shot down, be a POW, and be thinking about the wife and the kids, and mom and dad.[13]

The major difference in the performance of Canadian pilots during the bombing campaign was the result of more than just stress; it was the outcome of an extremely sensitive issue that doesn't appear in any of the publicly available after-action reports on the air war. According to retired Col. Jim Donihee, the Canadian air force's war-fighting capabilities in Kosovo—individual combat capabilities—were directly affected by erosion in the flying and combat training of the CF-18 pilots since the end of the Cold War.[14] Spending had been in a downward spiral since the end of the Cold War, but that trend was accelerated by the Chrétien government in 1994.[15] Hence, the pilots' combat capabilities generally were residual capabilities from bygone eras.

In 1990, Col. John David, director of flight safety at National Defence Headquarters in Ottawa, explained that CF-18 pilots flew 240 hours developing their flying and combat skills every year.[16] After the demise of the Soviet Union, pressure to cut those flying hours mounted. The issue was money, pure and simple. The cost of flying a Hornet was said to be about $1,070 an hour.[17] David Jurkowski said that pilot skills were directly related to the number of hours they flew. The more pilots fly, the better they get.[18] A two-year study of jet fighter programs in twelve NATO nations backed Jurkowski's claim. "Flying time seems to be the bottom line. If you don't spend the money on flying time, you're going to be spending more money to buy new airplanes or going to funerals."[19]

Over the years leading up to the Kosovo war, shrinking defence budgets caused the average number of pilot flying hours in the CF-18 to drop from 240 annually to 210, then to 180 hours.[20] As Donihee explained:

> A lot of the senior people on the squadrons were folks who had grown up in that era of the 240 hours or the 210 on

9.6. Two United States Navy EA6Bs take off while a CF-18 waits on the tarmac. EA6Bs flew a Suppression of Enemy Air Defences SEAD) cover mission for Canadians when they bombed a Serbian MiG-28 air base at Batajnica northwest of Belgrade. Photo courtesy of the Department of National Defence.

> the CF-18 and so the experience levels were quite high. But some of them, the very junior folks, had just come through the training mill and were trying to reach the capability levels of some of the folks that had a much deeper well of training and background to fall upon. We also had very, very limited exposure to the precision-guided munitions.[21]

Some claim there isn't necessarily a straight line between the dollars being spent on national defence and pilot capability. "Hooker," 441 Squadron's weapons and tactics officer during Kosovo, was one of them.

> There might be a straight-line relationship between dollars available and pilot flying hours, and that really is for the senior leadership to decide. The point I make was there isn't

necessarily a straight line or linear relationship between dollars available and capability on the line. The reason that I say that is because when the service is placed under pressure, financial pressure, often times we find some way to work smarter and more efficient ways to train to try to make up the difference. I think as a community we have gotten much better in terms of the way we train our guys with the hours we have available than perhaps we did ten or twelve years ago when there was more time.[22]

He said that the average of 180 flying hours per year is just that, an average.

Some pilots fly more and some pilots fly less. The issue is that it was generally the pilots with the least experience who did the least amount of flying. The fact of the matter is that there are different levels of qualification of fighter pilots. There are guys who are our new guys or relatively unqualified in the airplane and there are older guys who are more experienced and who have a lot of qualifications in the airplane. As you would expect, the experienced guys train the inexperienced guys. Because some people have experience and because they have qualifications and because they are needed to train other guys, often times they may get a little more than their allocated 180 hours. Your experienced guy might get 205–210 hours while your inexperienced guy, who really would actually need the flying time, would only get 170, well, 160 hours possibly. So that's an issue.[23]

Flying in combat is much different from flying during training or on exercise. As "Hooker" put it, "At the end of the day, it was just that much more difficult when you're in a combat zone. Finding yourself in a situation where you're getting shot at tends to reduce your grey matter a little bit."[24]

Lt. Col. (retired) "Billie" Flynn explained how putting pilots into combat in those circumstances manifested itself during the air war.

> This is a sensitive subject for some people to talk about—how people performed—but I'm happy to chat about this. I would have still chatted about it candidly had I had a uniform on, because it's important for people to learn. Pilots got sent home, got kicked out of theatre. Some pilots spent their whole time on what we call probation and other pilots spent their whole time under supervision or spent a significant portion under supervision.[25]

Although at its peak Task Force Aviano had thirty-two pilots available for missions, over the course of the 78-day war, sixty-nine pilots were rotated through those thirty-two positions. Of those sixty-nine, five were on probation and another ten were under supervision. Someone under supervision is an unknown quantity, while someone on probation is known to be a liability. Flynn explained:

> Under supervision, I'm not sure how you're going to do. You're thought to be not as strong coming into combat. As a result, you flew with senior tactical leaders until you're established; you've proved your competency. A guy on probation is someone who has either made some mistakes or who has failed to demonstrate competency in the air in combat. They were put with a standards evaluation pilot and then they flew together from there. In one case, after ten missions it was determined this pilot couldn't handle this, couldn't handle combat, and he was sent home.
>
> It happens all the time that strong leaders have to take weaker, less experienced people with them. That's how you mentor and train in the fighter-pilot world. I was one of these guys who had weak pilots with me in my cadre of day pilots. I had some pretty strong aviators that were forced to take some pretty weak pilots along with them. When you have a weak guy, if he's dangerous, you're just not going to let him fly. You're going to send him off to a ground job. Well, when we got to that point in a couple of cases they were grounded and sent home.[26]

The problem was not having questionable pilots flying with more senior pilots, Flynn explained, but the number of the questionable pilots.

> You're talking about fifteen guys, which is almost one-quarter of the guys who are under supervision at any given time. It means that in every day and night shift, you're carrying a couple of weak guys. We consciously did not document any of this because, and I regret that now, we believed that in such a small community, everyone was a known quantity and that the commanding officers would be able to take care of this and decide what their futures would be. In the end, not all commanding officers had the same philosophy of how this should be done and, basically, it just got washed out, got forgotten. One guy who got sent home for fatigue, he could fly an airplane, but he should have just not gone into combat.[27]

Because the issue of pilots' training and their competency in battle was so sensitive, it was purposely never documented. Flynn said it was still a significant issue, despite assurances to parliamentarians by defence minister Art Eggleton that the Canadian Forces in Aviano were well trained. All the pilots were trained, but the minister's assurances were misleading. The real issue was combat performance, which was seriously compromised. Flynn said: "Remember, you're talking about the Minister of National Defence. He has no idea what the point end of a CF-18 looks like. He is not a credible source of our competency."[28]

Other problems involving the war-fighting skills of even the most competent of pilots developed as the war stretched from a few days to months. Pilots got tired. While the war effort was ramping up, pilots typically stayed in Aviano flying patrol missions over the Balkans for about three months before returning to Canada for one of two reasons. Flying—even in a relatively benign theatre—is stressful. Pilots simply needed a break. Second, flying a warplane like the twin-engine CF-18 into combat or potential combat is both a skill and an art.

The first of the 138 CF-18 Hornets acquired by the Canadian Forces arrived at CFB Cold Lake, Alberta, in 1982. As a flying platform, the CF-18

9.7. The CF-18s twin General Electric turbo-fan engines are put on afterburners for takeoff. Photo courtesy of the Department of National Defence.

was a technological marvel. Its twin General Electric turbo-fan engines propelled the warplane to almost twice the speed of sound.

It climbed 20,000 to 30,000 feet per minute with a maximum combat ceiling of about 50,000 feet. However, its superb performance places enormous physical stresses on its pilots. The lightning-quick turning and climbing ability that makes the CF-18 ideal for combat manoeuvres can exert nearly seven times the force of gravity on the pilots who fly it. That can cause them to black out or to experience vertigo and hallucinations. If they black out momentarily, they are trained to put absolute faith in their plane's instruments when they come to. At such rates of climb, the hairs in the pilots' inner ears can make them feel as if they are tumbling backward or doing a back-flip. The pilots also must operate their flying controls and weapons systems despite gravitational forces that make it feel like they are carrying nine kilograms of lead in each hand.[29]

Moreover, because they were flying only two kinds of missions—bombing and combat air patrols—their overall war-fighting skills were deteriorating. Capt. Neil McRury explained:

> In laymen's terms, if you're painting fences all day, you're going to get real good at painting, but you're not going to be as proficient doing carpentry. It's a finite art to fight in an aircraft. You need the knowledge of the aircraft, its weapon systems, the feel of it when it's doing certain manoeuvres and knowing when you can capitalize on your opponents' mistakes. That takes training. We actually had to come home and do some dog fighting to brush up on some skills.[30]

Over the 78-day war, whenever a cadre of pilots was rotated out of Kosovo, fully trained replacements were required. This need posed massive training problems. At the beginning of the war, there were about twelve pilots in Aviano. When the number of CF-18s doubled to twelve, the number of pilots rose to twenty-four. By the time the final six CF-18s were committed, the number of pilots was increased to thirty-two. Yet there were only about seventy-four combat-ready pilots in Canada's four tactical fighter squadrons. By the war's end, almost half of the combat squadron pilots in Canada were in Aviano, though one also could draw on a cadre of another twenty-five instructor squadron pilots.

Wings in Cold Lake and Bagotville oversaw training sufficient pilots to replace those rotated back to Canada every two months to rest, and to brush up on their training. However, the dearth of Forward Looking Infrared (FLIR) pods came back full circle to haunt them. There were just three FLIR pods in Canada to train thirty to forty pilots who could be rotated into Aviano. As Donihee explained:

> We were very short of spares, very short of people. We were funnelling all the very best people over there. At the same time, we were doing everything we could to support the people who were actually in theatre. 3 Wing in Bagotville was nipping at our heels because they needed equipment to start regenerating their pilots in case this went on for a

longer period of time so that they could be ready to go in behind us. Basically, you've got three mouths to feed with barely enough equipment to nourish one.[31]

Canada's purchase of just thirteen FLIR pods damaged the war effort. As "Hooker" said:

> There's no question about that. We have long said that having thirteen pods total is not the way forward. The good news is you put those pods you had at home on three or four airplanes and you fly those airplanes time and time and time again with different pilots in the airplane so they can get their training done. Ultimately that's just the way it got done. We were training up probably twenty or thirty guys to ready and had to do it with three or four pods. It was certainly made more difficult and more challenging by the fact that there was so few available, but it's what we had to do and it's what ultimately we did do.[32]

Donihee is far more critical of the training problems he was expected to solve:

> I mean we were flying all hours of the day and night in order to make the very most use you could of two or three serviceable pods that you might have. Every pod became absolutely critical to your ability to train the pilots to go over and meet the rotations. A lot of these folks had virtually no experience on the pods whatsoever and so it was quite critical that we give them some exposure or some refresher using the pods before they went back overseas. I mean the lineups to get your hands on the training equipment were just unacceptable.[33]

The Canadian Forces' own lessons-learned assessment of the dire situation it faced stated:

Over a short period of time from twenty-four March 1999 to 11 May 1999, the TFA grew from 130 to 250 to 300 personnel. It grew to twelve and then eighteen CF-18s, and increased operational tempo from four to sixteen sorties per day. This surge impacted on 3 and 4 Wing's ability to train for new and additional taskings, conduct national surveillance and complete domestic operations. The bombing campaign ended on June 24, 1999, before the shortfalls in the CF-18 Wings could fully manifest themselves. However, the CF came close to being challenged in the ability to maintain a training pipeline while still fulfilling national, domestic and Alliance commitments.[34]

In other words, the Canadian air force had its back to the wall from training and operational perspectives and came perilously close to suffering from the shortcomings. However, the destruction Canada and the NATO allies wreaked on the Yugoslav military was catastrophic. Although weather affected pilots' ability to acquire their targets on fifty-four of the seventy days, the Allies still pounded the Serbs' air defence network, military barracks, ammunition production and storage facilities, and command centres and airfields, leaving them in smoking ruins. NATO warplanes dropped or launched some 20,000 missiles and bombs, 99.6 per cent of which hit their targets.[35] They destroyed 100 airplanes, hit four army brigades on the ground, nine main airfields, most of the surface-to-air missile sites, bridges, communications facilities, mortars, artillery, tanks, and armoured personnel carriers.[36]

Post-mortem evaluations of NATO's bombing campaign reveal that its tactics at the outset of the war were deeply flawed. Because the NATO goal was coercive, to force Milosevic back to the negotiating table, insufficient resources were marshalled to achieve a decisive military victory. The 350 warplanes that launched Operation Allied Force were only about one-third of the number that was eventually necessary to win the war.[37] The role that the United States played in the air war is telling. America's NATO allies contributed just over one-third, 327 planes in total, of the war effort. Canada and the European allies dropped just 20 per cent of all bombs and 20 per cent of the precision-guided bombs.[38]

One of the greatest military thinkers in history, Carl von Clausewitz, identified the things that could go wrong in war as "friction." He wrote:

> Everything in war is very simple, but the simplest thing is difficult. The difficulties accumulate and end by producing a kind of friction that is inconceivable unless one has experienced war. . . . Countless minor incidents—the kind that you can never foresee—combine to lower the general level of performance, so that one always falls short of the intended goal. Iron will-power can overcome this friction, it pulverizes every obstacle, but of course it wears down the machine as well. . . . The proud spirit's firm will dominates the art of war as an obelisk dominates the town square on which all roads converge.[39]

The Canadian mission in Kosovo was plagued by friction from start to finish. Transportation to and from accommodations, shortfalls in equipment, the lack of radios and deficiencies in those that existed, the lack of night-vision goggles, along with heat, rain, exhaustion, injury, stress, and pilot performance represented just the tip of it. The iron will and proud spirit of the Canadian Forces dominated and kept the mission moving forward.

10

On Body Bags and the News Media

Brig. Gen. David Jurkowski stood behind the podium at the National Defence Headquarters' daily technical briefing in Ottawa on April 20, the day after the Pentagon announced its press policy of identifying pilots by their first name only and withholding hometown information. He revealed why the Canadian Forces would not provide what the news media so desperately wanted: interviews, pictures, and TV footage with the faces, names, and hometowns of the Canadian airmen and women involved in Operation Allied Force. It was day twenty-eight of the aerial bombing campaign, and a journalist again had asked Jurkowski whether he could produce a pilot who had flown on combat air patrol missions to provide his perspective on them. As Jurkowski said, the Forces' policy was to guard the privacy of pilots and their families. But, for the first time, he explained why its policy was so restrictive. Jurkowski said it stemmed from lessons learned about revealing pilots' names during the 1991 Persian Gulf War.

> We had learned some lessons during the Gulf War and some of those lessons relate to threats back to families back at home—telephone calls, harassing telephone calls, body bags on the lawns of wives and kiddies back home in Canada and of individuals who were found to be operating in the Gulf. We learned those lessons and until there is a proper moment to be more open with our pilots and ground crew, to a certain degree we're going to maintain this policy.[1]

In fact, the lessons learned from the 1991 Persian Gulf War were just the opposite, that the Canadian Forces should learn from their Allies and adopt a more liberal public affairs policy about releasing operational information to the news media. The person who wrote the public affairs portion of the 1991 Lessons Learned report, the senior staff public relations officer, Lt. Cmdr Jeff Agnew, knew that. He reviewed the 1991 Lessons Learned report before Kosovo but argues that it wasn't his place to challenge Jurkowski. "Public affairs is a command responsibility. I'm just a public affairs officer. Yes, I want to be as open as possible, but our job is to assist the commanders. As public affairs officers, our first priority is security."[2]

After Jurkowski's explanation, the journalists did not pursue the issue of pilot identification further then, or for the next several days. On April 22 and 23, just how little the Canadian Forces intended to reveal about its pilots' participation in the bombing campaign was underlined. On April 22 the American military released a video of what it said was a Canadian CF-18 hitting a target with a laser-guided bomb two days prior. The journalists wanted to know why they had to see such videos courtesy of the Pentagon. Jurkowski explained that Canadians hadn't dropped bombs on April 20 due to cloud cover. Since other nations were flying F/A-18s, as was Canada, the warplane likely was misidentified as Canadian, but questions were being asked to determine if the misidentification was an honest mistake.[3]

Jurkowski repeated the argument about why Canadians were reluctant to release their own cockpit videos, why any videos that were shown were identified only as NATO videos, and why Canadians were being told little about the air force's participation in the bombing campaign.

> You know our policy, I've stated it before, that we typically don't show our [sic] videos we have. We've shown NATO generic videos, but we don't single out any particular nation. That is our policy and the reason that we haven't been showing too many videos to start with is because of what I've said in past time, that we have a small family of pilots and a small family of Canadian Forces and we're not interested in

exposing any of our members of the Canadian Forces to any undue threats, concerns.[4]

Some journalists doubted that Jurkowski did not know whether the video they had seen was Canadian, despite his assurances. "That's pretty incredible," remarked one.[5] In fact, Jurkowski's inquiries later that day did reveal that the CF-18 had been misidentified as Canadian. Investigations were able to confirm that the Pentagon video was mislabelled because the Canadian CF-18s' recording format was very different from what was shown.[6] Both the CBC and CTV television networks aired stories that night that showed the video, quoting an American major general as saying: "This is an MUP Army barracks hit by a Canadian CF-18. Very tough target to hit. Potential for collateral direct hit."[7] They also said the CF-18 might have been misidentified, while Canadian officials were angry at the Americans for releasing the video. Similar stories woven into other stories ran in eight major daily newspapers the next day, with one tagline in the *Toronto Sun* mocking the Forces: "Memo to Pentagon from the Chief of Defence Staff: No praise please, we're Canucks."[8]

The next day, Jurkowski sparred verbally with a reporter who asked for clarification on the factors that decided how much people were told, how much is kept secret, and why the Americans had a different set of rules. Jurkowski said he wasn't sure that Americans had a different set of rules, while many facts, if exposed to the public, could have unintended consequences.

> When it comes to video, I think I mentioned a while back that there is certain data on the digital display indicator from which the video is taken that gives examples of altitudes, air speeds, therefore the delivery parameters, ranges, things like that that are not critical but you really don't need to let people know that sort of thing.[9]

Jurkowski repeated that information about which targets Canadians bombed might spark someone sensitive "to do something that we wouldn't necessarily want them to do. That's it basically. We are, we don't want to give an indication of, certainly from the Canadian side, of exactly what kind of targeting we're doing."¹⁰ Jurkowski's response, including that he preferred to err on the side of caution, didn't satisfy the reporter, who said:

> It seems that Canadians, in a sense, are being kept in the dark about just exactly what the Canadian pilots are bombing and shouldn't Canadians have a better idea of what's being hit by Canada, as opposed to saying: "Well, it's all part of NATO and we're all in on everything." There's an accountability question here that Canadians should be thinking about. You're saying: "Well, we don't want to spur somebody to do something that . . . ," but I mean one of the things that it might spur would be a certain type of debate within Canada about what it is Canadians are doing and that might be healthy.[11]

Jurkowski didn't budge from his position that the Forces were doing their best to be accountable, especially with people's lives at risk during combat, and in concert with the steps they took to ensure that they were bombing only military targets. The line of questioning was dropped as other reporters focused on the refugee crisis. Jurkowski may have been telling the truth when he pleaded ignorance about whether the Americans were playing by a different set of rules than the Canadians. The United States was following NATO rules, which allowed individual countries to decide how much information they disclosed to the media.[12]

One of the first items Jurkowski addressed during the May 6 technical briefing was the addition of a GBU-10 2,000-pound bomb to the inventory of bombs Canada used in the campaign. Slides showed the difference between the GBU-10 and the GBU-12 500-pound precision bombs and the Mark 82 500-pound non-precision bombs Canada also was using. Sanitized in the extreme, it made no mention of the reason for acquiring the GBU-10. Without journalists in Aviano who might have discovered the whole story, journalists in Ottawa could not know the 500-pound GBU-12s bombs failed to take out their targets, or the risks pilots took in delivering them. This allowed Jurkowski to put the best possible interpretation on the shortcomings of Canada's war stocks by illustrating the flexibility of the CF-18 and the ability to strike a wider variety of targets, which was true as far as it went but was far from the whole truth.[13]

Not until a few days after May 7, when a NATO warplane accidentally bombed the Chinese embassy in Belgrade, were the Canadian media's suspicions confirmed that some American and British journalists could learn more about the air campaign than they could. For example, the *New York Times* identified the errant aircraft as a US Air Force B-2 stealth bomber, which dropped satellite-guided bombs on the embassy, misidentified as the Serbs' federal procurement and supply directorate.[14] It is not clear from that front-page article where that information came from. The United States or its warplanes were never identified, but the *Times* could find that information in a less formal way. When reading press briefings in their entirety, specific nations were never identified with regard to targets. They were always identified as NATO warplanes. But the *Times*' journalists worked around that restriction even when resulting news reports portrayed the US Air Force in a bad light.

The May 15 briefings revealed that NATO warplanes had accidentally killed up to eighty civilians during an attack on a military command post in southern Kosovo. One journalist asked which country had done the bombing. Maj. Gen. Walter Jertz, the spokesman for NATO's Supreme Headquarters Allied Powers Europe, replied that specific countries were never identified, but he challenged journalists to find out which country's warplane it was. He said: "I already indicated to you that it was F-16s, so it is up to you to find out which country it was, and it is always up to the country to announce—if they want to announce it—if it was theirs or not."[15] The *New York Times* reported on the next day that four US F-16s had launched the attack that accidentally killed civilians.[16]

Canadian journalists believed that American journalists and others had superior access to NATO officials and their countries' pilots or ground crews. Still, an examination of the complete war coverage of the *New York Times* and the *Times* (London) from 24 March to 30 June 1999 offers no evidence that American and British journalists published human interest stories identifying individual service members. There were no hometown-hero stories. In fact, two weeks into the air war, the editors and executives from seven American news organizations protested by letter to US defence secretary William S. Cohen regarding the dearth of information:

"On many days, the state-controlled Yugoslav media has been more specific about NATO targets than the United States or NATO."[17] The editors understood the need to withhold information that jeopardized "on-going operations or endanger lives," but argued "the current restrictions go way beyond that need."[18]

In retrospect, Gen. Clark wrote that he realized very early in the bombing campaign that NATO must be more open with the news media, if only to counter the Serbs' superior communications capabilities, particularly regarding civilian casualties. The Serbs were on the ground and able to immediately exploit NATO accidents in the world's news media. They went to great lengths to portray the NATO strikes as targeting civilians. Thus, NATO commanders came under tremendous public pressure to avoid collateral damage. "The weight of public opinion was doing to us what the Serb air defence system had failed to do: Limit our strikes."[19] The lesson to be learned, he wrote, was that military commanders must address the news media because public support is necessary for sustained operations.[20]

Still, in the United States an absence of relevant and timely information about the war caused the media to lose interest in covering it over the long run. Stephen Hess, a research fellow at the Brookings Institution, discovered that the total number of minutes the three major American broadcast networks devoted to Kosovo showed a steady decline. At the end of April and the beginning of May, there was a total of some 215 minutes broadcast that week. It fell the next week to 63 minutes and finally, when Hess stopped keeping track in mid-May, to just 55 minutes in total.[21]

Meanwhile, the Canadian Forces did its best to keep the CF-18 pilots under the news media's radar. Maj. Stéphane Hébert, the deputy weapons and tactics officer for 433 Tactical Fighter Squadron in Aviano, remembers that he was ordered not to breathe a word about the fact that he and three other Bagotville pilots had volunteered to return to Canada with four jets that had reached serviceability fatigue with 300 combat hours' flying time on them. Hébert recalled:

> They didn't want any media to be aware jets were coming back with the pilots and the aircrew. That was done hush,

hush. Nobody was told. My wife was basically phoned like a couple hours before to say: "Hey, come here at this time." That was it, and so we landed and basically went home. They didn't want to have the whole media circus or whatever. The media were hungry for news and for information because of General Clark and the shift in the whole focus of the war. The decisions were made at a much higher level than I.[22]

Hébert recalled an Internet security threat to pilots that sparked a concern over pilots being identified in the Canadian news media. When the Bagotville pilots first went to Aviano in October 1998, they were encouraged to send pictures of themselves to local newspapers in Canada. One such picture somehow was published on an Internet website. They were identifying people saying: "These are the ones that are killing Serbs." The RCMP had to take it out, but we were told specifically about this website and to keep it quiet and advise our families that they should be on the lookout for anything suspicious.[23] Hébert said the word about the pilots' families needing to be suspicious of things around their homes manifested itself into a scare at CFB Bagotville that was relayed up the chain of command all the way to the commander in Aviano.

They almost sent me back because somebody had come to my house and had taken pictures of my dog. My neighbours saw him and a bunch of guys, when they tried to stop him, the guy just fled away. So, it looked really, really weird. My wife phoned the military police and the MPs made an investigation with the local police and the city to see if they had sent anybody to the house. After about a week, the city had told them, "Hey, there was nobody hired by us." Then they dug a bit deeper and they figured out that it was a sub-sub-contractor or something who was hired by the city to come and take a look at the meters for property tax or something. That was the end of it, but we were told, like I said, to be very, very conscious of the media and to make sure that we keep our names and faces quiet.[24]

Still, John Larsen continued his efforts to attract Canadian news media to Italy. He called the CBC with the promise of on-camera access to the pilots. Paul Workman, the CBC's Paris correspondent, was called in mid-May by his news desk in Toronto, saying that the military's rules were relaxed and that it was worth going to Aviano with the expectation of getting "a decent story."[25] Workman met up with a cameraman from London, flew to Italy, and drove to the American air base at Aviano. When they arrived, the Canadian public affairs officers were waiting for them with clearance to take them on base, but they discovered that the non-identification restrictions his colleague Neil Macdonald battled almost two months earlier had eased up only marginally. Whereas Macdonald could only film the back of a pilot's head and his hands, Workman's cameraman was able to show half of a pilot's face with his helmet's visor lifted halfway to his nose, revealing his lips. Workman explained his difficulty with that policy from the media's perspective:

> Obviously, a pilot who appears on television is only there for a few seconds—twenty, thirty seconds, maybe of a full report—so it isn't a long period but it can be dramatic. It seems to me that a picture of a pilot with his visor half-open adds more unnecessary drama to the scene than is necessary. These pilots, by and large, had just come back or were just going on missions and we were interested in what they had to tell us about their targets, the activity they saw, whether they had come under fire, their fears and the dangers they might have perceived and what they thought of the conflict. If they could answer those kinds of questions and it seemed to me when you can only see half their face it: a) yes, it adds to the drama, but b) it makes it much more difficult to accept what somebody is telling you.[26]

The one piece that Workman produced during that trip to Italy was the filming of two air force personnel: an unidentified pilot and Col. Dwight Davies. The unidentified pilot talked for twenty seconds about his first combat mission and about thinking about his family. Davies talked about receiving new, bigger bombs a week earlier, which illustrated how capable the CF-18s were.[27]

Davies' command ended on May 11. He flew immediately to Ottawa, where he appeared with Jurkowski at the May 14 technical briefing before the national press corps. During his presentation on the bombing campaign, Davies used charts and graphs in a slide show to illustrate how many sorties Canadians had flown, their number in Aviano compared to the overall NATO effort, and the targets. But with no numbers on the charts, the journalists could not quantify the Canadian contribution of eighteen CF-18s to the NATO total in any meaningful way. Davies explained: "I've deliberately left the numbers off of the side of the scale. You can, I guess, calibrate it, given that we've provided eighteen. That'll give you some idea."[28] When a journalist asked how many of Canada's bombs had hit their targets and how many had missed, Jurkowski jumped in, saying: "I don't want to get into the exact numbers of weapons we've actually released. I'm not prepared to discuss that, nor is the colonel."[29] None of that empty information was used in that night's television broadcasts or major daily newspapers the next day.

Two things that Davies did tell the media are worthy of note. During his slide presentation, he spoke glowingly about the Canadian Forces resupply system, claiming it was extremely effective for ammunition, parts, equipment, and personnel.[30] That was anything but the case. The supply system was stretched to its limits, draining morale because the troops couldn't get their mail, let alone decent boots and aircraft parts. The ground crews working with borrowed equipment were retooling the dregs of American guided munitions. Trained pilots were in such short supply due to the shortage of FLIR pods in Canada that the system was bordering on collapse.

11

Canada Missed a Good News Story

Ironically, in late May during the last days of the bombing campaign, it was Brig. Gen. David Jurkowski, who had becoming highly skilled at giving journalists ambiguous information, who spoke real news about the success of the Cold Lake and Bagotville pilots at one of the technical briefings. He talked about Canadian pilots leading half of the missions they had flown on and, of the successful strikes, sorties and missions, Canada had accomplished 10 per cent of them. Also, ironically, the information came from an American, not a Canadian, source. Jurkowski commented on it after the fact in a *Toronto Star* article on an advance team of 139 soldiers arriving in Skopje, Macedonia, to prepare for the arrival of a Canadian contingent sent to join NATO ground forces. In that story, a US embassy source told the *Star*'s reporter that the CF-18s were doing 10 per cent of the strike missions. Jurkowski said that on any given day, Canada comprised from 5 to 25 per cent of the strike force dropping weapons. He said: "We've been far more successful than the average Canadian is aware."[1]

The *Toronto Star* was the only news outlet in Canada to carry that story on that day. Two Canadian news outlets ran similar and more detailed stories on the air force's successes, the *Daily News* (Halifax) on June 17 and the *Ottawa Citizen* on June 21.[2] On June 26 just two newspapers carried stories with some detail about the success of the CF-18s, after the bombing campaign ended. Both the *Toronto Star* and the *Calgary Herald* ran the same Canadian Press wire story, buried in the back pages of their front sections.[3]

Had the journalists been given broader access, some of the pilots and ground crews would have been willing to talk to them. Bagotville pilot Maj. Alain Pelletier explained:

> I actually like to talk to the media because this way I could actually pass on my message and attempt to let the folks in Canada know how people are feeling, that behind this whole issue of the conflict there were actually people involved and that people have feelings. We're not war machines; we're trained professionals there to do a job that the government has decided that we would get on with. I think it would have been important for the aircrews to be able to pass on their experiences and their feelings.[4]

Even people like Pelletier were careful about what they said to the journalists in Aviano, because, like all military personnel, he followed orders.

> At one point, it was decided by the commander in charge of the whole force in Italy [Brig. Gen. Dwight Davies] that, for security reasons, we would not divulge the name of the pilots who would be actually talking to the media and that their face would not appear on the camera. Eventually—for a part of the time also in order to avoid compromising the security of the operations—pilots would not talk at all. All of the dealings with the media would be carried out by the public affairs officer that was in theatre at the time.[5]

Cpl. Patrick Savoie, responsible for the weapons inventory, said the order not to talk to the media was superfluous because he wouldn't talk to the media anyway. He didn't feel comfortable in the presence of journalists because, in the first instance, his work was all classified and, in the second, he just didn't like them hanging around.

> I did not want to talk to journalists. I don't want to take the risk of saying something that's going to get me in trouble. I did not want to have the question: "How many weapons

do we have here?" It looks so good to be able to report that you have X number of guided weapons. Our politicians were telling people: "We're over there because we have the latest in guided bombs and the latest in guided air-to-ground missiles." Well, they got told we had the latest, so they would come and go: "Can I see them?" and "How many do we have?" Well I can't tell you. And if you want a drink, have a few beers and relax, shoot the shit, you don't want to do it with a journalist around. You don't want to tattletale when you're having fun.[6]

CF-18 pilot "Chimp" wouldn't talk to the news media for an entirely different reason. He made no distinction between news outlets and generally thinks all journalists are the same: sloppy with their facts and biased in their reporting. He explained:

I avoid interviews. Anytime I read something that I know about, the reporting is full of inaccuracies and there's so many things that you read about in the papers that you're not an expert on. I also see a lot of bias. I see a country that's being fed many unflattering things about its military by its media.[7]

What irritates him most are news outlets that write stories at Christmas time about privates receiving food hampers from charities because they are destitute but ignore the motivations of soldiers working shoulder-to-shoulder with civilians working on disaster relief.

A couple of years ago when the Red River flooded, and the ice storms, where we had a corporal working next to a Hydro Ontario guy making triple time and the corporal's making his normal corporal's pay plus twelve bucks field allowance for the day. But he's doing this gladly because he's helping the Canadian public. We had forest fires that summer in Ontario and on and on and on. Then come Christmas time the media's into the privates getting their

Christmas food hampers because they didn't have enough money. That's shameful.[8]

Still other pilots would have been reluctant to talk to the media because they were concerned about reprisals against themselves from Serbs in Europe and against their families in Canada. Many pilots had heard the story about body bags thrown on the lawns of pilots in the Persian Gulf in 1991 to intimidate their families. Among them was Lt. Col. "Billie" Flynn, commander of 441 Tactical Fighter Squadron. Flynn explained:

> The press's [lack of] access to us was sold to us as being an element of self-protection. They were worried about Serb reprisals. Intelligence overseas said that we would be targeted. The other part is that our families might be targeted because there was a pretty strong aggressive Serb community. Remember all the demonstrations in Toronto and Ottawa? They didn't want the Serb community to come at our families and threaten them. That might be a gross overstatement of the threat, but that was the logic that was used. And that's why the press was not let near us. Remember from Gulf War One? They picked a couple of names from the cadre and the press followed them around and followed their wives and families. They were day-to-day press in Canada. During Gulf War One, people threw body bags on the lawns of Canadian airmen that were serving overseas. They didn't want body bags thrown on our front yards and terrorizing our families.[9]

In fact, just the opposite was true about the selected spouse. Marion Kendall, wife of Cold Lake pilot Maj. Dave Kendall, who was chosen by the Forces to be followed by the news media, suffered no incidents of harassment in 1991. Still, the myth about the body bags being thrown on pilots' lawns had grown to the point where it had taken on a life of its own. The deputy chief of defence staff during the Kosovo air war, Lt. Gen. Henault, later explained that he was not aware of any pilot harassment in 1991.

> I'm not personally aware of specific incidents and certainly I haven't seen any documentation either. Quite frankly, I was not involved in the Gulf War that directly because I was at the time the commander of Canadian Forces based in Portage La Prairie out in Manitoba and involved specifically in training people as opposed to providing combat forces. Any of that would have been the product of those who were directly involved in those campaigns or that campaign at the time.[10]

Meanwhile, Lt. (Navy) Larsen used every tool in his public affairs officer's kit to raise the profile of the air force in Aviano. He and his staff worked tirelessly against the clock meeting the internal communications needs of the Canadian Forces and generating material for the television outlets back in Canada.

> Everybody in the Canadian contingent put in extremely long hours. From my personal perspective it was made probably even more difficult because of the time change. As we're going to bed there, the news cycle for the evening news is just starting to ramp up in Canada because we're eight hours ahead. So, it's midnight in Aviano and it's four o'clock in Canada. Everyone's getting ready for the six o'clock news. Then they're getting ready to confirm new information for the ten o'clock news with [the CBC's Peter] Mansbridge. Then I would normally have my alarm set so that I would be able to take calls at around 5:30 [a.m.] so an eighteen-hour day would be average.[11]

Larsen and a colleague routinely filmed the Canadians' activities in Aviano and transmitted the images to Canadian television networks by satellite. In effect, he was producing secondary B-roll film in the hope it would be used by the networks.

> There were times when they'd say there was nothing on here that's really useful for them. They'd say what would work

for them is if they could get an interview, you know a double-ender with the commanding officer. A double-ender is where you record somebody, you get their face on camera and they're asked questions through a phone. You can satellite that entire recording back to Toronto and they can play it and Peter Mansbridge will ask the exact same questions and it will look as if it's a live feed. It's the same questions, it's the same response. It's totally ethical, the only difference is the time dimension and that you're not paying for a satellite truck to come right here and beam up at that exact time.

We'd set the CO up, put a headset on him and on the phone in his headset would be a producer from CBC. It would be four o'clock in the afternoon on our end it would be 8 o'clock in the morning in Toronto. We'd tape the stuff and we'd put some other images with that tape that we already had ready. We'd edit it together in two or three hours, we'd walk over and we'd have a pre-purchased satellite uplink time which ran at $1,000 a minute, right, and so we'd have a ten-minute up-feed time and up it would go. $10,000 later it would all be sent to Canada.[12]

Larsen used exactly the same technique if a television network wanted to do a story on escape and evasion for the pilots.

They would say: "I want to do a specific story on what kind of escape and evasion gear you wear when you fly. I want to do a story on that so I need visuals that support that." We'd say: "OK, we'll show you what we can. Maybe we can't show you this piece of gear or that piece of gear because it's secret, but we can show you all the other stuff." So, we would shoot that. We'd do an interview with the pilot, they would talk about it. Again, there was some parameters on what we could show and what we couldn't so, we'd show the back of the pilot and it would go up and it would be a story. In fact, it was a story on the national news.[13]

The television networks may have received stories they liked thanks to Larsen's skill, but the fact was that the military controlled the news media in this fashion and provided spoon-fed and sanitized stories. The issue is what the Canadian public was not being told, for example, that the CF-18 pilots' search-and-rescue radios were incompatible with their NATO allies' radios and that new systems were bought on the fly using Jurkowski's military credit card. Canadians were not told that the pilots had to put the newly acquired radios in their flight suit's pants pocket because of inadequate combat vests or that, if a pilot had to eject, in all probability his radio would be blown away and lost. One can only imagine the Canadian public's response had they been told the truth. Larsen said he never lied to the news media—there were just things he could and could not say.

> I don't pretend to know every single detail of flight operations but you'd have to be relatively thick to work in that environment and not pick up on some of these things. When I do media-relations training, I use Aviano as an example. I often get the question: "What if you know something and you've been told not to tell?" In a corporate setting, it's a little more difficult, but I often rely on Aviano as the perfect example of where media would say: "Well, John do you know this?" "Yes, I do." "Will you tell me?" "Well, no I won't." So, I say I never lie to the media, in that sense, because there are a great many things that you can't say for operational security. You just have to justify why you can't say it.[14]

In Ottawa, a Canadian Press reporter attended the daily press briefings at National Defence Headquarters (NDHQ). He said it was nearly impossible to write anything meaningful about the air war based on the information that was being provided.

> It got kind of difficult because there was very little information—very little meaningful information was being passed on. It was bare bones stuff. It was limited to: "OK, we launched X number of aircraft and they attacked targets and the targets were very vaguely specified—radio rebroad-

casting things, military barracks"—but there was no bomb damage assessment. There was no real assessment of what we'd done and there was very, very little available on any kind of hazards they might have encountered.[15]

The Ottawa reporters continued to push for greater access to the pilots, for more information and detail, but were consistently stymied by security considerations. "We kept pushing and we would constantly get: 'Well, for security reasons we can't give you that.'"[16] He had a long-standing interest in the Canadian Forces that spanned thirty-two years with the Canadian Press in Ottawa, Toronto, London, Edmonton, and New York City. He joined the parliamentary press gallery in 1988, was a member of the gallery during the 1991 Gulf War, and had been to Aviano in 1997.

He said that lack of information the military was providing was doubly frustrating for the half-dozen reporters like him in the national press gallery who were interested in the Canadian Forces and who went out of their way to become well informed about them. But only a half dozen journalists knowledgeable about the military aren't many when the size of the parliamentary press gallery is considered. The 1998–1999 *Canadian Parliamentary Guide* listed 359 journalists with Canadian news organizations or agencies.[17]

Apart from himself and the few reporters who were knowledgeable about the Forces, other journalists had just a passing interest.

> One of the problems with a lot of reporters is that they may be interested in the military, but they really don't know what's going on. I mean half of them can't even read rank insignia and couldn't tell you the difference between a master-corporal and a Polish admiral. Of course, when they start nosing around military stories, that drives the military nuts because the military has to start from scratch to explain what's happening.[18]

It is widely thought that 22 May 1999 marked a turning point in the war, not only for the bombing campaign's tactical success but for its axiological effects—Slobodan Milosevic's ability to control public opinion.[19] The effects of axiological air operation were predicted by air war scholars Peter Wijninga and Richard Szafranski in 1991 and confirmed by Paul Rexton Kan in 2004.[20] On that day, NATO's warplanes moved beyond the utility targeting of military assets and bombed the Serbian power grid, bringing the war home to the Serbian population.[21] It showed the Serbian population that Milosevic could no longer protect them or provide their basic needs. In Brussels, the May 22 press briefing for international journalists followed the same format as most other days, with NATO spokesman Jamie Shea leading off with the refugee situation in Albania and diplomatic initiatives, followed by a military update. Shea was deeply moved by reports that in Macedonia, 741 children were looking for parents, and 1,382 parents were looking for children.[22]

Militarily, Shea reported that NATO jets had flown 245 strike sorties and nine combat air patrol sorties. Some twelve Serb tanks were hit, along with eighteen armoured and other vehicles, nine artillery and mortar positions, and a Yugoslav barracks facility in Estok. The journalists were also told NATO warplanes had struck electrical power transformers and petroleum facilities at Drahovo and Smederovo, and that there was evidence the Serb military was extending minefields along the Albanian border to maintain its hold on Kosovo and prevent supplies from reaching armed ethnic Albanians.

During the follow-up questioning, *New York Times* journalist Michael Gordon asked for elaboration on the bombing of the Estok barracks facility, an allegedly unused prison that was hit nearby, and the potential for collateral damage, not about that evening's bombing success. The Serbs had released video of bodies and casualties from the prison bombing. Gordon wanted to know whether they were collateral damage. Before other reporters switched the line of questioning, Gordon was told the information NATO had was that the prison was unused and that the bodies were placed there by the Serbs and no one knew why.[23]

In Ottawa, turning point or not, the events of May 22 were marked by one of the briefest technical briefings held during the entire bombing campaign. The journalists were told the NATO planes had struck television and radio stations, radio relay stations, and electrical power stations. Two Canadian CF-18s had struck unidentified petroleum sites in Serbia and one mission was unsuccessfully engaged by anti-aircraft fire and missiles.

No mention was made of the strategic importance of the electrical station sites, and the press corps asked only three questions. The first called for speculation about a ceasefire; the second and third questions sought information about an advance reconnaissance party of Lord Strathcona's Horse (Royal Canadians) from CFB Edmonton going to Macedonia and how many there might be.[24]

Just what could and couldn't be released to the news media in the name of operational security is difficult to glean from the Canadian Forces public statements at the time. For example, by the end of May, the technical briefings had degenerated into meetings that few members of the news media bothered to attend and even fewer bothered to report on. The June 1 briefing indicates how the "operational security" reasons cited by the Canadian Press's Ward came into play. That day, one journalist tried to get a sense of what Canadians were doing in the bombing campaign by learning about the number of bombs dropped. He was stonewalled by Jurkowski on the grounds of security. The reporter wanted to know the cost of the weapons dropped to date and Jurkowski replied: "That could lead one to think about the number of weapons and by way of policy and security, we don't talk about the number of weapons employed."[25] The journalist pressed, wanting to know why the number of bombs was a security issue and arguing that Canadians had a right to know the cash value of munitions dropped. Jurkowski replied: "I don't have those numbers for you right now and for security reasons, I'm not going to address it any further."[26]

That line of questioning was dropped until the next day, when Henault was asked about the cost of bombs. Henault went on the offensive, saying: "We have been, I think, fairly open. In fact, very open throughout this whole process now at seventy-one days of giving you briefings daily so I think our process has been very open and transparent, probably in a way unprecedented in the past."[27] Having said that, Henault contradicted Jurkowski's argument about security by divulging that $20 million had been spent on Operation Echo and about 45 per cent of that was on bombs.[28] The journalists did not question the inconsistency—why that information was withheld for security reasons one day but was not a security issue the next.

What can also be noted is that whether the bombs' cost was a security issue or not, Henault's revelation was not big news. The cost figures that Henault revealed found their way into just one sentence of an opinion piece in the *Toronto Star* out of a total of three articles involving the CF-18s that ran in two Canadian newspapers the next day. The other two articles, variations of the same Canadian Press story that was carried by the *Toronto Star* and the *Gazette* (Montreal), focused on an engine maintenance error that could cost millions to repair. Just one sentence in both stories addressed the CF-18s' role in the campaign. One read: "Canada has contributed eighteen of its operational fleet of 100 CF-18s to NATO's Yugoslavia bombing campaign."[29] The other read: "There has been no special blade maintenance for the 18 CF-18s now based at Aviano, Italy, to participate in the NATO bombing of Kosovo."[30]

As the bombing campaign wore on, the technical briefings became shorter and shorter, providing less and less information about the CF-18s' operations. They had settled into a routine format that generally opened virtually the same way: "Welcome on Day 73 of the NATO air campaign."[31] On that day, June 4, Henault boiled down the previous night's combat air patrol and bombing missions to just three sentences in English, and two in French. The more detailed English version was: "In respect to our own Canadian air operations, Task Force Aviano flew ten of its assigned sixteen sorties yesterday including two combat air patrol tasks. Precision-guided munitions were used by our CF-18s to attack a petroleum storage site, a military radio relay station and a military airfield. The two combat air patrol missions were also flown without incident."[32] The nation's news media used nothing from the technical briefings that day or for the next week.

When the bombing campaign ceased on June 10, the war ended with massive media indifference. Television ignored the Canadian air force's role, as did all but one major English-speaking newspaper. The *Toronto Star* devoted a story to the appropriateness of Canada's participation in the bombing campaign and stated that the CF-18s had flown 682 sorties, 60 per cent of which were on bombing missions, and dropped more than $9 million worth of bombs.[33] Not until five days later on June 16, six days after the campaign ended, did stories appear that expressed the pilots' relief that the bombing campaign was over. The stories were identical, written from Ottawa by the Canadian Press's John Ward and published in three newspapers—the *Hamilton Spectator*, the *Daily News* (Halifax) and the *Times Colonist* (Victoria). Ward didn't actually talk to any pilots. Notwithstanding Public Affairs Officer Larsen's central tenet that if he was truly successful in his job he would never be quoted, it was he who talked to Ward by telephone from Aviano, saying that everyone in Aviano was grateful for the positive development. The Canadian public still had no details about the bombing campaign giving any sense of the dangers the pilots faced, the hardship the ground crew endured, or the challenges both overcame through innovation and inspiration. Ward could just recycle the only information he had: one unnamed pilot describing the blackness in front of him light up as a "Dutch fighter steered a missile into a Yugoslav MiG," taken from the story in the April 15 *Maple Leaf* about Lt. Col. Faucher's first mission.[34]

On June 16, the last technical briefing for the news media was held at NDHQ in Ottawa. Henault provided a comprehensive scorecard of what the Canadian air force had contributed to the bombing campaign. He augmented his address with slides and a welter of statistics showing the missions Canadians had flown. The Canadian pilots had performed superbly, he said, flying on 10 per cent of all NATO strike missions, leading half of those. He parsed their performance, showing that they had flown 2,547 hours over 678 sorties on 224 missions, and that 558 of the sorties had taken place on 167 air-to-ground bombing missions during which 361 precision-guided munitions were dropped. Even with Henault's statistics available on transcripts, it is difficult to follow his confusing narrative. CP's Ward was able to sift through Henault's numbers and discerned that about 25 per cent of the laser-guided bombs the Canadians dropped had missed their targets. Henault assured Ward that a 75 to 80 per cent rate of accuracy was consistent with that of NATO allies.[35]

It didn't matter much. Only one newspaper, the *Daily News* (Halifax) carried a brief story by Ward, who wrote of the Canadians' success.[36] In it, he pointed out that the Canadians had dropped 361 laser-guided bombs and 171 gravity bombs which hit 158 targets. The air force had not released assessments of the bomb strikes for security reasons. There was much else that could have been told but wasn't. Among some of the most egregious omissions were that CF-18 pilots had long pushed for night-vision goggles in the 1990s but were never provided them. As a result, the pilots had to fly in single-file formations at different altitudes at night to avoid crashing into each other, which also exposed the last jets in the formation to anti-aircraft fire and missiles. They also had to train their radars on their own jets in front of them, rather than enemy threats, to avoid collisions.[37]

The June 16 technical briefing was the last because, by then, NATO forces and the international news media, including Canadians, were on the ground in Kosovo providing the most up to date information on daily events. One of them, the CBC's Paul Workman, couldn't believe the difference in the access he was provided by members of the Lord Strathcona's Horse (Royal Canadians), who were providing reconnaissance support to the Canadian infantry battle group in the NATO peacekeeping force. Workman, working alone with his own television camera, was in Macedonia on the Kosovo border. He was trying to figure out how he was going to get into Kosovo when a convoy of seven of the Strathcona's Coyotes appeared out of nowhere and invited him to ride along with them. Workman explained:

> I'd been dealing with the public relations people for the infantry, and I had been asking them and asking them and asking them for permission to be able to travel into Kosovo with the forces. I had been given sort of an equivocal answer: "Maybe. We'll try to see what we can do. I doubt it. It's pretty difficult. We have to get permission from a lot of levels." The day that the NATO forces moved into Kosovo, the reconnaissance unit commanding officer, who I knew at that point, let me climb aboard. It was his personal decision to let me climb on board with my gear and travel into Kosovo and to let me spend, off and on, the next couple of weeks with them. It wasn't a problem at all to talk to them and identify them by name, rank, and regiment.[38]

That decision was made by Maj. Paul Fleury, who later became Lt Col. Fleury, commanding officer of the Strathcona's. Fleury met Workman by pure chance at the Frankfurt airport in late May. They flew together to Skopje, where they parted ways. From Skopje, Fleury went to train his reconnaissance squadron for integration with the British army's Fourth Armored Brigade preparing to enter Kosovo if the bombing campaign ended. As that cessation neared, Workman hired a local driver to take him to the Kosovo border. The driver refused to go any farther. It was pure serendipity that the Strathcona's arrived at the border on June 12 where Workman was trying to negotiate his way into Kosovo. Fleury invited Workman to climb aboard his Coyote armoured vehicle.

Thereafter, none of Workman's reports had anything to do with the air force in Aviano. In fact, only two interviews were conducted with pilots. On June 29, Capt. Jordan Kyrbyson was interviewed by host Valerie Pringle on CTV's Canada AM and identified on camera. Kyrbyson talked primarily about his thoughts on the bombing campaign, military lawyers vetting targets to avoid civilian casualties, and mission planning. He alluded to the primary job being strike missions in Serbia but gave no details of what that meant.[39] The CBC, meanwhile, obtained CF-18 cockpit video from the Department of National Defence for the first time. The tapes showed two bombs hitting a bridge, which collapsed. After the video was shown, reporter Eric Sorensen added that the Canadian Forces had admitted earlier to bombs missing targets 25 to 30 per cent of the time but did not take part in NATOs most infamous bombing mistakes that killed civilians. CF-18 pilot Lee Vogan was shown on camera, adding little to the report: "A lot of work went into reducing the collateral damage. There were a lot of weapons that weren't dropped because there was a risk of that."[40] There were no comparable newspaper articles.

Operation Echo's lessons-learned report did not analyze the success or failure of the Canadian Forces public affairs policy and practices during the Kosovo air campaign, unlike that of the 1991 Gulf War. The only evaluation of the military's public affairs policies during Operation Echo appeared in a 9 March 2000 NDHQ document. The Kosovo air campaign was addressed specifically for the ethical dilemmas it presented when considering the media and public's right to know versus operational security and care of personnel. Its language is cryptic; however, it avoids specifics and paints a self-serving picture of its public affairs practices.

> The subject of military security vs embarrassing information vs the public right to know will become a routine dilemma in future operations. The Kosovo campaign example of providing constant media briefings and the strategy reflecting candor, truth and disclosure to the extent possible

would appear to represent a strategy that fulfills our obligations of public disclosure and should serve to build public trust and confidence. Decisions to fully and promptly report any incident similar to the Chinese embassy bombing in Serbia are seen as consistent with defence ethical values. The questions of "What to report?" will always require a balancing of values, security issues and the ethic of care (morale) of our people.[41]

The balance the Canadian Forces struck between Canadians' right to know and security considerations meant that Jurkowski was right when he said that Canadian pilots were far more successful than Canadians knew. What Canadians could have known about the campaign was only what the news media could hear from the military brass. In Jurkowski's own words, that wasn't much. In retrospect, Jurkowski admitted that he never had any factual basis for telling the news media that body bags were found on pilots' lawns during the Gulf War. Jurkowski even considered it hearsay but used the myth nonetheless as reason for restricting the information provided to Canadians about the Kosovo air war. In Jurkowski's words:

> You know what? That was told to me, but I kept on asking: "Is that for sure?" My communications guys would say: "Yeah, that happened. I know." I was nervous about that, but I did deploy it publicly, so. In my mind, I had it as on an air force base and I often thought it was Cold Lake. I was trying to be really careful and make goddamn sure I said the right things in public. But I was pretty sure that I was told that it was in Cold Lake, that occurring.[42]

One of the most vigorous defenders of the Canadian Forces' media policies during the Kosovo air campaign was John Larsen who was promoted to Lt.-Commander and who received a commendation for his work. He actively tried to enhance the air force's image from Aviano. He rejects the suggestion that the air force's story was not told.

I can't accept the line, as a public affairs officer, that their story was never told—that's inaccurate. I've got videos, photos of our twelve planes flying back when it was over. That's part of a larger story we worked on. There are probably several newspaper clippings. We did interviews. Joy Malbon came down twice. She did interviews with the pilots about what they were doing, what their feelings were. As a media specialist I agree, that it was probably not told with the frequency and intensity that we wanted it told and that the story was certainly not told the way the vast majority of the media wanted it told; but the story was told.[43]

12

Homecomings

On 9 June 1999—day seventy-eight of the NATO bombing campaign—it was announced that NATO had signed an agreement with the Yugoslav military authorities to end hostilities, for the withdrawal of Serbian forces from Kosovo, and for the return of Kosovar refugees to their homes. United Nations Resolution 1244 (1999), adopted June 10, called for the immediate and verifiable end to the violence, the safe and free return of all refugees, and an international security presence endorsed and adopted by the United Nations.[1] Historians, political analysts, and diplomats, it is said, remain puzzled as to why Slobodan Milosevic agreed to a proposal brought forward by Russian envoy Viktor Chernomyrdin and Finnish president Martti Ahtisaari that ended the conflict on less favourable terms than the ones Milosevic had rejected in Rambouillet. Even worse, he was a war crime suspect, indicted by the Hague Tribunal, and ultimately ended his days in a cell undergoing trial.[2]

Although the ceasefire was agreed to ten days earlier, Lt. Col. "Billie" Flynn still was in Aviano on June 20 when Prime Minister Jean Chrétien and his wife, Aline, stopped there on a return flight to Canada from a G-8 meeting in Cologne, Germany. Defence minister Art Eggleton, Chrétien's aides, and a handful of MPs and top-ranking military personnel also were in Aviano during the prime minister's visit. Flynn told some key dignitaries that he thought it would be a good idea if a dozen pilots could conduct a CF-18 flypast over Parliament Hill during the upcoming Canada Day celebrations in Ottawa on July 1. Flynn explained:

I asked the prime minister's chief of staff whether he thought it was a good idea, then I asked Madame Chrétien if she thought it was a good idea and I asked a couple of MPs. By then everybody had already talked to the prime minister and then I asked the prime minister and he said: "What a great idea." About 10 minutes later, he [Chrétien] looked over to the chief of defence staff and said: "Hey, this guy [Flynn] said we could have twelve airplanes over Parliament Hill on the 1st of July, what a great idea. Make that happen." Well, to the chief of the defence staff [Gen. Maurice Baril] and his deputy [Lt. Gen. Raymond Henault] this was American showboating. They thought there was no reason for these guys to fly over Parliament Hill, it was total American bravado, as opposed to saying: "Wow. They just went into combat. All these Canadians who are proud of them would like to see them over Parliament Hill. What a great way to come home."[3]

The July 1 flypast did take place, but only after a dozen CF-18s and their pilots endured the gruelling return trip to Canada without American or French air-to-air refuelling tankers. They "island hopped," with all the risks of shutting down their engines and flying at low altitudes to accommodate Canada's lumbering C-130 Hercules air-to-air refuelling tankers. The CF-18s departed Aviano on June 27 in three sections of four. They flew over Scotland on their way to Keflavik, Iceland, where they spent the night. Two Hercules from 435 Squadron in Winnipeg, pre-positioned in Keflavik and Gander, were in the air the next day to fuel the CF-18s as they made their way to 4 Wing in Cold Lake and 3 Wing in Bagotville.[4] Six CF-18s remained in Aviano to support the NATO-led Stabilization Force operation until 23 December 2003.

On Canada Day, twelve CF-18s led by Flynn flew over the Peace Tower. The pilots who participated in the flypast and the follow-up activities have mixed opinions about the public relations exercise. One Bagotville pilot who flew seven missions explained:

> They said: "Come on guys, it's a way to thank you." It was not. It was just us being dogs and ponies there in front of people. We were a circus. We went to sign autographs, to please the crowd, which is fine. I know it's part of my job, but it was not "OK. We'll host you and thank you." It was like: "OK, we've got a schedule for you, the Museum of Aviation, the Museum of Civilization, you've got autographs to sign here, and autographs to sign there. Do this. Do that." It was strange.[5]

On the other hand, one Bagotville pilot who flew nine missions and had twenty missions cancelled due to inclement weather, thought the experience was terrific. He said:

> It was a thrill. I think that all the pilots were proud of what we had done over there. Everybody believed in the cause, that we had done a good job. Now it was time to show the flag. It was good to sign autograph for kids and adults, knowing that we had their support and that they were proud of us. After all, I mean, we put our lives on the line and I was happy to do it for my country, and Ottawa was a small token of their appreciation.[6]

But the twelve pilots involved in the flypast were a minority among the sixty-nine pilots involved in Kosovo. Most recalled there was no public recognition for their work, for how they had gelled as a combat team and how they had improvised and innovated on the fly to overcome a litany of equipment and supply deficiencies. There were no police-escorted welcome home processions up boulevards flanked by hundreds of trees bearing yellow ribbons and cheering crowds. For some Canadian Forces members who served in Aviano, the war ended long before June 10. During the normal course of rotations, many who flew and fought with distinction returned to Canada long before, with no fanfare.

One pilot, who was on the first bombing mission March 24, recalled his last days in Aviano before returning to Canada on April 20 after flying six missions.

> I remember Colonel Davies just screaming to try and get people sent home because he knew guys like myself had been there for a long time, probably getting tired, and needed to be sent home. I didn't want to get sent home. I wanted to stay there for as long as I could because this is what we're trained for, but we were tired. We flew home on the Canadian Forces airbus, as far as I remember. The airbus parked on the tarmac outside wing Ops, my girlfriend was waiting for me with a lot of the other wives and that was it. We went home.[7]

Some of the Canadian pilots who continued to fly combat air patrol missions for a few days after the bombing campaign ended had a similar experience. Capt. Travis Brassington's last combat mission was June 4, but he continued flying until June 13, three days after the war's end. While one pilot flew more missions (thirty-one), Brassington compiled some 135 hours in the air on twenty-seven missions. He remembers his Cold Lake homecoming compared to others he had seen.

> I remember during the Gulf War, there had been an incredible outpouring of support for the Canadian military. For us the "Hail the conquering hero" kind of thing—that didn't happen. I came home at 11 o'clock at night, to the airport. My driver who was supposed to pick up me and about four or five other guys was about an hour late. We loaded our stuff in to the back of the van, we drove home and he dropped me off at my house. That was my homecoming.[8]

Capt. Kirk Soroka was one of nine Canadians who flew twenty or more combat missions. After Soroka compiled eighty-six hours in combat—fifty-nine of which were at night on twenty missions—his return to Canada was inglorious. He also didn't participate in the Ottawa Canada Day flypast because he was medically repatriated on June 1, suffering from kidney problems due to chronic dehydration, the result of long hours spent in his CF-18's cockpit. He and another pilot landed in Edmonton around 11:00 p.m. "A corporal in a van met us. We got in the van and they drove us back. We got out of the van at our home and that was it. I remember looking up at the same night sky I had seen over Serbia and thought that was interesting. That was the end of our war."[9]

What the Canadians achieved flying the CF-18s out of Aviano through their iron will was remarkable. The Canadian commitment of eighteen CF-18s represented a little less than 2 per cent of the nearly 1,000 allied aircraft involved in Operation Allied Force. Nonetheless, the Canadians flew in nearly 10 per cent of the bombing missions, considered the most dangerous of all the missions flown. Bombing missions, combat air patrols, and other close air support missions amounted to more than 82 per cent of the Canadian air effort.[10] By the time a ceasefire was agreed to on 10 June1999, the Canadian Forces had rotated the task force's personnel three times. Over the course of the campaign, the CF-18 pilots flew 684 combat sorties in 224 missions and flew 2,577 hours.[11] They dropped 568 bombs representing nearly 500,000 pounds of high-explosive munitions. Of them, 171 were Mark 82 500-pound dumb bombs, 262 GBU-12 500-pound precision-guided bombs, and 128 GBU-10 2,000-pound precision-guided bombs.[12]

They had done their duty.

The Korean War has been called Canada's forgotten war that Canadians don't know much about or care about.[13] The Kosovo air war could be called Canada's non-existent war, because the Canadian government refused to call it a war and then let its warriors go unrecognized. Of the sixty-nine Canadian pilots who served in Aviano, twenty-two were recommended for Meritorious Service Medals. Just two, Col. Davies and Maj. Rob Parker, received them. Davies, promoted Brig. Gen. Davies, was awarded his for leadership during the task force buildup and during forty-eight-days of combat when the Canadians flew 370 sorties without mishap.[14] Parker, promoted Lt. Col. Parker, was awarded his medal for flying thirty-one combat missions, planning missions for more than forty aircraft at a time, and for his role in the training and qualification of Task Force Aviano personnel.[15] Some ground crew members were written up for medals but none was awarded.[16] Unlike in any of the other three wars to which the government consciously sent its armed forces, the Canadian government didn't acknowledge its warriors with a campaign medal and battle honours. By comparison, Second World War veterans were eligible to receive twelve medals, including the War Medal (1939–1945). Korean War Veterans received the Korea Medal. The 1991 Gulf War veterans received the Gulf and Kuwait Medal.[17]

Years after the Kosovo war ended, the ground crews and pilots say it wasn't the lack of public accolades that most grated on them, it was the absence of a war medal and battle honours. Some Canadian pilots initially received a NATO medal with a Kosovo bar and ribbon. Originally, the medal was to be awarded for twenty missions, but the allies wanted to reduce the criterion to ten missions. NATO finally decided the pilots could receive one if they flew a minimum of fifteen missions. Those who flew fourteen or less were out of luck. A NATO medal with the former Yugoslavia bar and ribbon was available to the pilots, the ground crews, the cooks, and other support personnel who served in Operation Allied Force for ninety days outside of Kosovo. But many who received them saw those NATO medals on their chest as an injustice. Both are considered peacekeeping medals, awarded to anyone who served with NATO in the former Yugoslavia. Some 10,000 have been issued since the mid-1990s. In terms of precedence, their medal ranks behind the Bosnia administrative peacekeeping medal.[18]

Soroka, who flew twenty combat missions, wasn't eligible for any medals when he left Aviano in June 1999 because his length of service in Operation Allied Force was not considered eligible for the Canadian Peacekeeping Service Medal. Soroka was sent back to Aviano in October 1999 and by November became eligible for the NATO former Yugoslavia Bar, with 160 days in theatre. He received his without ceremony in the orderly room. When the Kosovo medal criteria were decided upon, the pilots were allowed to trade the Yugoslavia medal for it. In 2003, Soroka said about that level of recognition:

> We're four years now. Four years that the Canadian government hasn't bothered to cut a campaign medal or a battle honour for us. This is just something that tears us apart. None of us joined to be rich men, we all joined for a higher calling. But you know, if a country doesn't recognize their warriors, wants to park them out in the woods somewhere, make us bleed in peace time and call us out when it's time,

you know. I tell the boys: "Bleed in peacetime or in war." I mean we bleed all the time. The big thing that tears me apart about that entire experience in Kosovo—not so much that I risked my life and my family's well-being and my kids growing up without a dad—what tears me apart the most is that, when we came back, we got no medals. Canada didn't bother to recognize us.[19]

Soroka was not alone. Master Cpl. John Edelman, who received NATO's Yugoslavia medal, said a military medal is far more than just a bauble. They afford their recipients recognition among their peers. Edelman said: "I guess you should take some solace in what you do but the only way that you can demonstrate what you've done in the military is to walk away with these $10 or $15 medals on your chest."[20]

Capt. Brett Glaeser, who flew seventeen missions and received NATO's Kosovo medal, said that it was "kind of weird" that the Canadians received essentially a peacekeeping medal for dropping bombs in Kosovo.

> I think when you're dropping 2,000-pound bombs on Serbians in Kosovo and they're shooting back with SAMs and triple-A, maybe the politicians don't want to call it war but for the fighter pilots that went there and for the ground crew that were there, it was a war for sure. Maybe if we lost an airplane or a pilot somewhere in there, I don't know, they'd probably call that peacekeeping, too.[21]

One Bagotville pilot, who flew nine missions and had twenty missions cancelled due to weather, didn't qualify for the Kosovo medal. Being awarded a medal never crossed his mind when he was flying into combat, but:

> I think it's something that catches up with you afterward. I don't think you realize the real potential of dying or being shot down until you're actually over there and you look down and you see people that are shooting at you. I firmly believe that people that crossed the line of fire and put their lives on the line for the country should be recognized. We

> were sent there by our Canadian government and should be recognized as much as the people did in World War I, World War II, and the Gulf War—either in the air or on the ground.²²

Jim Donihee thinks that the Canadian government needed to award the Canadians who were in Aviano with a medal. Without being specific, he argued the American government recognized some Canadians.

> I know for a fact that some of our Canadian pilots led in proportion a greater number of mass formations than any number of our NATO allies and were held in great respect and were mentioned in dispatches elsewhere. As Canadians, we seem loath to recognize them. I just think it's a failing on the part of our government. Quite frankly, I don't understand why we are loath to recognize men and women who dedicate their lives to the service of their country and do so, so professionally.²³

Lt. Col. Sylvain Faucher was awarded a chief of defence staff commendation for his role in commanding Bagotville's 425 Squadron at the beginning of the air campaign. He thinks everyone in the campaign should be recognized with a medal.

> Every one of the folks that I had the honour to work with and I'm saying everyone, the technician on the ramp, the admin support, the doctors, the engineers, the lawyers, they should all be recognized. They made sacrifices to go there and they were involved, some of them directly, some of them in support. A medal is a very, very little thing to give for that contribution.²⁴

"Hooker," awarded the Meritorious Service Medal in November 2000 for his role in Operation Allied Force, knew the hard feelings among his colleagues over the issue of a medal. He said:

> I can tell you that amongst the guys who flew in theatre, there's a certain amount of bitterness. We've encountered an awful lot of resistance to having the government cut a medal for Operation Allied Force, whereas medals for other things have happened it seems overnight. Something seems different and whether it was a function of us not dying or whether it was a function of a lack of UNSCR resolutions and the whole legality issue behind it and the whole political dirtiness associated with it, I don't know. Other operations seem to have been better sold to the public at home for whatever reason. Perhaps it is a function of the fact that we did our jobs well and brought everybody home, but you know, I would rather have it that we brought everybody home than we lost somebody and got patted on the back for it.[25]

David Jurkowski and Billie Flynn have both strong feelings about a special medal for the Kosovo campaign and some insight as to why such a medal has not been struck and why just two Meritorious Service Medals were awarded. Flynn, who wrote the twenty-two Meritorious Service Medal recommendations, thinks the air force did a poor job of making its case for awarding more than two them.

> The air force had a hard time articulating to those who were on the boards to decide why this was any different than just flying another mission. I mean, how hard is it? These guys drop bombs every day; they went and dropped bombs, what the big deal? No one understood the difference between day-to-day operations and this so-called combat. If you said these Canadian pilots planned the entire attacks and led seventy jets into a combat zone and brought them back safely that meant nothing to an army guy on an awards panel.[26]

Jurkowski, who was a National Defence Headquarters insider during the medal consideration medals, corroborated Flynn's version of events. The

Kosovo medals issue became mired in a swamp of interservice rivalry and politics in Ottawa.

> The process, as far as I'm concerned, is or was flawed. I had been part of that process previously. Gosh, someone on the board made a strong recommendation to present medals for the Oka crisis. I'm sitting on this board and I said: "Excuse me. This is in our own country. You want a medal for a military operation in your own goddamn country?" I would have no part of it and they were never given. There are a number of people roaming around who are on honors boards. They include the Governor-General's staff, for one thing. What overrides everything is: How is this particular conflict judged in the context of Vimy Ridge, in the context of WWII, in the context of the Korean War? Does giving a medal to this individual match the same kind of standard? So, there is a levelling and that's valid. I believe.
>
> But I still say that there were little cabals against issuing medals to our pilots. All they did was fly the planes you know, drop bombs, did what they were trained to do.' I got so pissed off I asked the chief of the air staff if he wouldn't mind appointing somebody to go ahead and independently judge whether or not his guys should get medals. I was for them quite frankly but I couldn't succeed. I mean you can't talk fast enough because an army guy will not understand the context of sitting there at night being shot at, ensuring you hit your target and trying to find your lead on radar. They think: "Well, that's what you're trained to do isn't it?" I couldn't talk fast enough to convince them so I said: "Take it out of my hands. Let the chief of the air force assign somebody independent in the air force and decide whether or not those medals should be requested and honors should be granted."[27]

Gen. Ray Henault was deputy chief of defence staff responsible for the Canadians' participation in Operation Allied Force and appreciated the controversy and the hard feelings in the air force over the absence of a made-in-Canada Kosovo medal. He explained:

> I'm very conscious of that issue as you would imagine. There is a tremendous amount of work that's been done to pursue that. There are recommendations that have been made to Government House to provide appropriate recognition for the campaign. I can't comment a whole lot more, to be perfectly honest, because it has been forwarded to Government House. But I can certainly attest to the fact that I'm aware of how strongly this recognition is felt and warranted from the fighter pilot community.[28]

Somewhere in an office at the Chancellery of Government House in Rideau Hall Ottawa sits a document of about 100 pages that contains the military's arguments for and against striking a medal for those members of the Canadian Forces who participated in the Kosovo air war. They are not available for inspection to ordinary Canadians because they are exempt from disclosure in their entirety under section 21 of the *Access to Information Act*.[29] That section exempts from disclosure consultation, deliberations, advice, or recommendations developed for a government institution or a minister of the Crown or positions or plans to be carried on by or on behalf of the Government of Canada if the record came into existence less than twenty years prior to the request.[30]

The Chancellery's director of honours, Mary de Bellefeuille-Percy, confirmed their exemption in writing:

> Regarding the striking of any new medal, I must first advise you that the process for developing new awards is considered "Honours in Confidence." That means that the entire process, from its initial proposal phase to its conclusion, including discussion and consultation with partners, is handled by the Chancellery of Honours at the Office of the Secretary to the Governor General and is not subject to release under the *Access to Information Act*.[31]

On 7 July 2004, Governor General Adrienne Clarkson announced that Queen Elizabeth II had approved the creation of the General Campaign Star and the General Service Medal that were to be awarded in an inaugural presentation ceremony at Rideau Hall at a later date. Veterans had to apply for it, but the star would be awarded to those deployed into a defined theatre to take part in operations in the presence of an armed enemy. The medal would also be awarded to those deployed outside Canada who provided direct support on a full-time basis, to operations in the presence of an armed enemy. The star had a 12-millimetre red stripe flanked by 2-millimetre white stripes and 8-millimetre green stripes. The medal had a 12-millimetre green stripe flanked by 2-millimetre white stripes and 8-millimetre stripes. On paper, that appeared to be a good solution to the medal issue eating away at the Balkan Rats and Balkan Bats war veterans. They finally appeared to have an alternate to the peacekeeping medal. The Government of Canada, however, lost an opportunity to create a medal specifically for Operation Allied Force, as opposed to one for general service. Canadian Forces veterans who served in Afghanistan in the International Security Assistance Force (ISAF) qualify for the General Campaign Star and General Service Medal.[32]

The only difference between the Allied Force campaign medal and the ISAF campaign medal was the bars on their ribbons signifying the campaign. Meanwhile, the standards for the ISAF version differed from those imposed on Kosovo veterans. The fighter pilots and airborne warning and control system crew members were awarded the Star and Allied Force Bar if they flew at least five sorties. Ground crews were awarded the Medal and Allied Force Bar if they served at least thirty days cumulative in direct support of Allied Force. The same stars and medals, but with a different ISAF bar, are awarded for thirty days' service in Afghanistan. The feelings among the Balkan Rats and Balkan Bats were mixed. Some were glad to have anything other than the Canadian Peacekeeping Service Medal; some were proud to wear the medal; some were sick and tired of the fight and have moved on; some were disillusioned, and some were bitter — very, very bitter — that they risked their lives and the government had been chintzy in return.

A Lieutenant Colonet, who was with 410 Fighter Squadron, initially was among those who thought they should have their own Allied Force medal but had given up. "We've beaten a dead horse long enough. It's time to move on to the next fifty dead horses," he said. "I'm happy with the medal. It recognizes that we are getting the same kind of medal as the guys getting shot at by the Taliban in Afghanistan."[33] Now retired commander of 441 Squadron Col. Flynn said he doubted that the Balkan Rats and Balkan Bats would ever get the recognition they deserve with their own medal:

> It's a lost battle. It was never going to happen. I could go into the apathy of the Canadian Forces and, by default, the Canadian government. We don't care until years and years later. I took on everyone I thought I could. I burned every bridge and got nowhere. Five years later we got the Campaign Star and that was as good as we were going to get. After all, it couldn't have been that hard; no one got killed. Now the army has lost guys in Afghanistan. It's hard to imagine that we could get people to rally behind our cause.[34]

As with most of the pilots and ground crews, there was no Rideau Hall ceremony for Flynn's Star presentation. He received his in the mail in May 2005 from the office of National Defence's Director of History and Heritage, which noted: "Sincere congratulations accompany this award, as well as our appreciation of your service to your country." Recipients of the campaign star or medal had to return their NATO peacekeeping medal, because they may not wear both medals. "Rambo"—now Lt. Col. Soroka, who had the star, said in 2004 he knew pilots who still were wearing the NATO medal because, having to apply for it, any lustre it might have had for them has worn off. "Quite honestly, it took so many years to get it, we don't even care anymore."[35]

Another serving pilot saw a simple solution that would avoid the disillusion among the very people the government thought they were honouring. Instead of bars, all that was needed were different ribbons on the star and the medal to acknowledge that Operation Allied Force was different from the ISAF mission in Afghanistan. The ISAF medal would have its own distinctive ribbon, as would Operation Allied Force. "That's what they did in World War Two for the different theatres of operations; four or five different campaigns. The Star was a brilliant idea, but they took a good idea and screwed it up. They just put different bars on it to save a buck."[36]

On 14 September 2007, Governor General Michaëlle Jean approved the creation of the Kosovo theatre Battle Honours for 441 and 425 Tactical Fighter Squadrons. This decision ought to have caused a celebration for the men and women in both units, but it did not. For 441 Squadron, Kosovo was added to the Battle Honours awarded for the Defence of Britain 1945; Fortress Europe 1944; Normandy France and Germany 1944-45; and Arnhem Walcheren. For 425 Squadron, Kosovo is added to the Battle Honours for the English Channel and North Sea 1942-1943; Fortress Europe 1942-1944; France and Germany 1944-1945; Biscay Ports 1943-1944; Ruhr 1942-1945; Berlin 1944; German Ports 1942-1945; Normandy 1944; Rhine Biscay 1942-1943; Sicily 1943; and Italy 1943 Salerno. As a result of their long histories, soldiers revere their regiments, sailors their ships, and air force members their squadrons, but there was no cause for celebration among the 441 and 425 Tactical Fighter Squadrons' aircrews. In the summer of 2005, the crews of 425 and 433 Tactical Fighter Squadrons were amalgamated to form 425 Tactical Fighter Squadron, the sole fighter squadron in 3 Wing at CFB Bagotville. The bitterness created in Bagotville by one fiercely proud squadron being disbanded while the other survived was wretched.

To avoid that fate at CFB Cold Lake, it was decided not to favour one squadron over another. Both 441 and 416 Squadrons were disbanded in July 2006 and amalgamated into 409 Tactical Fighter Squadron. Leave it to the Canadian Forces, however, to shoot itself in both feet, rather than just one, to make things better. As a result, one of two squadrons awarded the Kosovo Battle Honour—441 Squadron—no longer exists. Its colours have been laid to rest at city hall in its affiliated city, Sydney, NS. As if that weren't disheartening enough, as a result of the Battle Honours Committee taking so long to recommend allocation of the Kosovo Battle Honour, many—if not most—of the members who served with distinction in Aviano are out of the Forces.[37]

Finally, on 31 March 2010, Governor General Jean, on the recommendation of Prime Minister Stephen Harper, wrote a new ending to the sad saga of the Kosovo medals for the pilots and ground crew. It was announced that any pilot who flew five missions or more would qualify for a

12.1. 441 Squadron's Colours with Kosovo Battle Honours. Photo courtesy of the Department of National Defence.

General Campaign Star with their own Allied Force ribbon. The ground crew qualified for the General Service Medal with the Allied Force ribbon.[38] The Allied Force ribbon has a 12-millimetre light blue stripe flanked by 2-millimetre white stripes and 8-millimetre red stripes. With their own distinctive medals, as cheerless as the story is about the Battle Honours, the air force men and women who toiled in Aviano and fought over the skies of Serbia and Kosovo finally were recognized for earning their rightful place in Canadian history.

13

Context-Less Facts, Ambiguity, Half-Truths, and Outright Lies

The largest study on Canadian journalism, the *Royal Commission on Newspapers*, was published more than thirty years ago. Clearly, much has changed in the world since 1981, and it would take a whole series of books to chronicle the technological tools alone that media now have at their disposal: powerful desktop and tablet computers, cellular phones that take pictures rivalling some single-lens reflex cameras, digital photography, communications satellites, satellite phones, and the Internet, to name but a few. One thing, however, hasn't changed: the principle that the best journalism "has as its philosophical ideal the quest for what it is right and true."[1] At the same time, the commission admitted that it was difficult to turn that principle into a yardstick to measure the media's performance.[2] This book examined the performance of the media's coverage of the Kosovo air war and found it sorely wanting. But this wasn't the fault of some of Canada's best journalists, who did their best to determine what was right and true, but failed.

This book is also a study that goes far beyond Kosovo. Initially, it was based to a large degree on interviews with journalists who were open and forthright about the challenges they faced trying to cover Canadian operations in Aviano, Italy, in 1999. As such, it adds to our knowledge of media-military relations in Canada and contributes to this aspect of Canadian journalism history. Finally, this study assesses the nature of military policy in a democracy and the uses of secrecy and censorship. The hope is that it will stir debate about strategic and media studies and the lessons that can be learned. That is the ultimate goal. It was first driven by the research question: What could Canadians have learned from the national news about the Canadian air force's exercise of its military skill during the Kosovo air war? The answer is simple: not much at all.

There was a contention that the news media were drawn to the Canadian Forces during the bombing campaign simply for information they could package and sell. On one hand, that is a gross oversimplification of the state of the Canadian news media. The largest journalistic organization in Canada is the CBC, a public broadcaster. One of its stated mandates is to contribute to Canada's shared national consciousness and identity. There could have been no better way to raise Canadians' consciousness of their country's role in the world than by the CBC reporting on what the Canadian Forces were doing in Aviano and in the skies over Serbia and Kosovo. On the other hand, part of the argument that the news media were drawn to the war for information they could package and sell rings true: the majority of the journalistic organizations are commercial in nature, and it is true that profits drive news media in a free society. But that is a valuable democratic construct because it is what keeps the media at arm's length from government and enables it to hold governments and their institutions accountable. The reporters who travelled to Aviano were serious journalists who went there to do serious work. They simply should not have been dismissed so cavalierly by a commander who was trained to do otherwise but who rejected his training as a result of operational security considerations that were fundamentally flawed.

This book explores the operational security argument that the news media's identification of air force members during the 1991 Gulf War resulted in body bags being placed on the lawns of their families in Canada and that the Forces did not want a replication of such harassment. That story is an urban myth. The question remains: Why did that myth take on such importance in Canada and Aviano? The answers may be found in the news media policies of US General Wesley Clark in Belgium and in the half-baked public affairs plan developed by the Department of National Defence in Ottawa.

As SACEUR, Clark played an active role in NATO's public affairs activities, to the point of ordering his staff to call NBC on the first night of the bombing campaign to correct a report. He appeared before press briefings in Brussels on five separate occasions. Clark initially wanted as little information about the war to get out as possible in the interest of operational security. Despite that, some of the US military appeared on television and gave interviews allowing their names to be reported. That policy was amended within a few days to allow the identification of pilots by first names only.

A spokesman said the rationale for the restrictive public affairs policy was that American pilots who might be shot down preferred the news media not to publish or broadcast their names or identify their families or hometowns. The shooting down of an F-117 Stealth fighter on the fourth day of the war provided a rationale for that argument. The predisposition toward secrecy won the day. The identification of downed pilots became associated with a threat to their families. That threat had two effects. First, the policy stole the life from news reports on the bombing campaign in the way of names, faces, and points of reference such as hometown information. Second, it also softened the media exposure of the war's deadly consequences on Americans at home. Gen. Clark drew the lesson that attention to the news media is a must for future military commanders, because public support is necessary for sustained operations. As the bombing of the Chinese Embassy showed in stark contrast, an absence of criticism over the long term may also have important consequences.

Fortunately, and almost miraculously, no Canadian pilots were shot down during the war. Still, in the absence of a public affairs plan to handle media requests for interviews with air force members in Aviano, the half-remembered and false stories about harassment of air force families during the 1991 Gulf War spurred the military's disposition toward secrecy. During the Kosovo air war, the Canadian Forces were able to define the news through security measures based on a myth driven by slipshod military public affairs and sloppy media coverage during the 1991 war. If ever there was a myth, the 1991 body bag is it. Nonetheless, its use prohibited journalists, with rare exceptions, from talking to the pilots and prevented Canadians from identifying, even vicariously, with hometown heroes.

It is entirely conceivable that out of the ashes of other wars, new myths about security threats to pilots' families resulting from news postings on the Internet will emerge. The information highway offers newspaper readers, television viewers, and social media observers alternatives and opportunities to obtain more information and diversity of views. If the contents of a local newspaper could pose an operational security concern, then one posted on the Internet can be seen to pose an exponentially greater threat to operational security. The short combined history of militaries, the Internet, and the news media has borne that out. As the Kosovo air war showed, myths don't need to be true; they need only to be believed. Myths should not drive operational security considerations.

Due to a series of minor miracles, the combat operations had a relatively happy ending: no Canadian died. It was a minor miracle that one or more of the pilots strung out in single line formations weren't picked off by enemy fire. It was a minor miracle that one or more of the pilots weren't shot down because their radars were trained not on potential oncoming threats but on the CF-18s in front of them so they didn't collide in the fog of war. It was a minor miracle that the lack of night-vision goggles didn't have catastrophic consequences. As a result, there was no outpouring of emotion for the CF-18 crews as there was for Canadian soldiers when their losses began to mount in Afghanistan. Members of the Canadian Forces accept that they may be killed or harmed in the performance of their duty to their country. The corollary is that they should have the right tools to carry out their missions. The politicians and top military brass in the Canadian military insisted that the CF-18 squadrons in Aviano were well equipped and well trained. This book finds much differently. They weren't well equipped, and being well trained wasn't the issue: pilot performance was the issue. Some were on probation, more were under supervision. Some were even grounded and returned to Canada because, although they could fly warplanes, they came up short fighting a war. However, and remarkably, those who remained accomplished their mission.

It has been argued that the Forces' hastily developed public affairs policy during the Kosovo war was based on the best available information at the time given operational security concerns. But it merits examining the assumed source of the threats to air force families in Canada in 1999 that bolstered such concerns. There were thousands of anti-war protesters outside the gates at the Aviano air base and protests against the war in Canada. But in the eyes of the military, the protesters in Canada were linked not to those in Aviano but to war criminals in Serbia. An enduring feature of the *Canadian Charter of Rights and Freedoms* is the democratic right of freedom of association and speech. Even during a war, protesters have a right to gather within the legal limits as prescribed in Canadian law. They were protesters, not war criminals. Could the military have done more to ascertain the threat to military families in Canada in 1999? The answer is yes. Gen. Raymond Henault told the news media that the Forces were attempting to assess the threat to military families, but there is no documented evidence that a threat assessment was ever conducted.

Notwithstanding the best efforts of public affairs officers in Aviano who worked on their own to help the news media as much as they could—even when journalists were not present—their work resulted in the military controlling the news agenda. The only options for the news media were to take or to leave what was given to them. Once the TV outlets accepted the military's film footage—even when identified as military footage—public affairs effectively circumvented the media's function of gathering its own footage independently. The sanitized images provided could not possibly convey audio and visual actualities of the horrible business of humans bombing, killing, and maiming other humans. That brutal reality evaded Canadians during the Kosovo air war.

Political scientist Murray Edelman wrote that reality is socially constructed through shared meanings that shape patterns of belief and frame ideas and concepts. The strategic need, he said, is for leaders to either create support for their policies or to immobilize opposition. Prime Minister Jean Chrétien, Minister of Foreign Affairs Lloyd Axworthy and Minister of National Defence Art Eggleton never did call the Kosovo aerial bombardment a war. The closest Chrétien came was to say that it was a military action meant to force the Yugoslav president to accept a peace agreement. Axworthy said the bombing campaign was part of the international community's response to Yugoslavia's failure to protect the human rights of Kosovars. Eggleton called it a humanitarian mission. That was entirely in keeping with Edelman's writings on socially constructed reality and framing. It can't really be said that the Canadian population was mobilized to support the 78-day bombing campaign, but it can be said it remained largely quiescent, which met the strategic need.

Further, the military absolutely mastered the news media during the technical briefings at National Defence Headquarters. It scattered context-less facts, ambiguity, half-truths, and outright lies like chaff from a CF-18 trying to thwart a radar-guided missile. Communications scholar Daniel Hallin wrote about American president Lyndon Johnson lying to the American news media about his intention to increase the number of US troops in Vietnam in the 1960s. US journalists, Hallin wrote, had not been taught to question whether a president or government would lie and cheat. The same thing happened in Canada during the Kosovo air war, although it wasn't the US commander-in-chief lying, it was a handful of Canadian generals and colonels. Canadians simply deserve better from their military leaders. The military is not an island unto itself. The values of Canadian society, which include freedom of the press, must be reflected in the military's professional values. The *Canadian Charter of Rights and Freedoms*' guarantees must be embraced by the Canadian Forces in a way that includes more than the charade of openness and transparency perpetrated in Ottawa during the Kosovo air war. What took place in Aviano, Italy—far beyond the farce taking place in Ottawa—ought to be viewed as censorship.

Journalists accept the need for some military secrecy, but because of nebulous security concerns, the Canadian Forces undermined the media's democratic role in holding the Liberal government of Jean Chrétien accountable for its slashing and burning of military budgets in the 1990s. Its security policy also forbade pilots from disclosing anything but the vaguest details about their missions. But precisely the kind of information desired by reporters in Aviano and in Canada appeared later in great detail in the *Maple Leaf*. Similarly, in Ottawa, journalists were denied information about how much was being spent on bombs by Brig. Gen. Jurkowski for operational security reasons one day, yet it was released by Gen. Henault the next. Both examples indicate of how cavalierly and unnecessarily operational security was invoked in Aviano and Ottawa.

If Canadians were as unaware of what their Forces had done during the bombing campaign as Gen. Jurkowski claimed, then he must bear some of the responsibility for that fact. Gen. Jurkowski doubted the body bag story, but he let his subordinates undermine him. But, that being said, the restrictive media strategies that kept Canadians from knowing of the air force's role in the Kosovo air war were not the failures of a few men but of the Canadian Forces as an institution. This was an institutional failure for several reasons.

First, the Kosovo air war was only the second war the Canadian Forces had fought since the Korean War. The most recent war before Kosovo was the 1991 Persian Gulf War. After that war, the Forces compiled a voluminous lessons-learned report on how to improve its dealings with the media. The key lesson was that the Forces should learn from their more experienced allies and adopt more liberal policies regarding the release of operational information.

Second, the air force failed to learn from the navy and the army, both of which anticipated news media coverage in theatre and stipulated that commanders must prepare for that eventuality. As an institution, the Canadian Forces developed a guiding public affairs policy document, DAOD 2008, which was in place in 1998–1999. DAOD 2008 required national and operational public affairs plans in the event of escalating military tension or war. Astonishingly, the air force deployed in June 1998 with the intention of fighting an aerial bombing operation without considering the possibility that news media might want to interview pilots. The only guidelines developed were produced ad hoc and were founded on myth, not fact. This failure was not of men but of an institution that did not function as a whole.

University of Washington scholar Lance Bennett wrote that the level of domestic debate from Vietnam, the Falklands, Nicaragua, and the Persian Gulf wars was driven by journalistic routines driving them to official sources who were indexed within the political hierarchy. As a result, the prolonged debate in the media ended when official debate ended. The main official sources for information about Canadian involvement in the Kosovo air war were, in indexed order: Minister of National Defence Art Eggleton, Lt. Gen. Raymond Henault and Brig. Gen. David Jurkowski in Ottawa, and Lt. Col. Dwight Davies in Aviano, Italy. Eggleton revealed nothing in Parliament about the bombing campaign. When parliamentarians complained, they were told to attend the media technical briefings, where Henault and Jurkowski were evading reporters' questions and not telling the truth. As a result, there was neither prolonged official debate in Parliament nor in the media. There was nothing that affected the Liberal government's policy options.

It was argued there was no expectation that the Canadian air force would be fighting over Kosovo for five years or that the military would need Canadians to do without shoes in order to produce war materials to win, in which case the hearts and minds of Canadian people would be needed. That was true, but winning the hearts and minds of Canadians was not the point. The Liberal government sent the air force to fight from Italy because of the humanitarian crisis unfolding in Serbia, but there was no accountability to Parliament, the democratic source of that military action. Those who study the relationship of militaries to civilians in democracies hold that there ought to be an unbroken line of accountability from Canadian Forces commanders in the field, to the chief of the defence staff, to cabinet, to Parliament and, ultimately, to Canadian citizens, voters who pay for the troops with their taxes and whose sons, daughters, husbands, wives, brothers, sisters, fathers, and mothers participate in combat operations. During the Kosovo war, that unbroken line of accountability utterly failed, and with it the principles that give democracy meaning.

In absence of such institutional accountability, if the news media is to serve as an intermediary that informs Canadians about what the military does, how it does it, and why, in a meaningful way, there are several things that must happen in the future. The Canadian Forces must get beyond its empty, meaningless public affairs rhetoric that most Canadians will learn about the Forces in both peacetime and wartime through the news media. Militaries are being called upon more and more to resolve humanitarian and terrorist crises in failed and failing states. Canada is expecting to be one of these militaries, but what is to be learned from the Kosovo war?

Some of Canada's most accomplished and respected journalists travelled to Aviano to cover the Canadian Forces there and came away empty-handed. Would there have been more or better coverage of the air force if more media outlets had made greater efforts, spent more money, and committed journalists in greater numbers to the air war's coverage in Kosovo? The answer can only be speculative given the military's success in neutralizing the parliamentary press gallery in Ottawa and those who travelled to Aviano. Yet the evidence from this research is clear: most Canadian journalists do a poor job of covering the Canadian Forces. The journalism industry must shoulder the responsibility for that. Covering the military is a challenging undertaking that should be taught by journalism schools, yet Canadian universities are woefully deficient in this regard. Aspiring journalists ought to learn how to cover the Canadian military in the same way the best of them cover health, the arts, the courts, business, and municipal, provincial, and federal politics. The use of military force, after all, is the pursuit of politics by other means.

Journalists believe that a talented reporter can take on almost any topic and produce a good story, but there is more to responsible journalism than that. The best journalists approach their subject areas knowledgeably, critically, with an in-depth understanding developed over time. To argue that a general reporter, court reporter, police reporter, or legislature reporter can seamlessly be assigned to cover an organization as complex as the Canadian Armed Forces on a story-by-story basis—and do it well—is wrong.

It has been suggested that journalists train with the military and have exposure to it well before a crisis unfolds to build expertise in what the military is doing and why. There are many problems associated with that suggestion. The problems are not insurmountable, but they are significant. The first is that the journalists must be exposed to the Forces in garrison and in the field over time. They must observe and understand its training, understand its culture, and ultimately understand what they do and why they do it. All of that takes time and money. Given the increasingly profit-driven nature of the news media organizations in Canada, that may be a hard sell, but it shouldn't be. The editors and news directors who assign stories must understand the importance of military news when it comes to deciding which stories are to be covered. Senior editors and managers with an eye on budgets must be prepared to bear the costs associated with military journalism. News organizations should be more than a collection of writers, photographers, cameramen and women, editors, and news directors packaging information like sausage stuffers in a meat-packing plant as efficiently as possible in order to maximize owners' profits.

In a perfect world, profit-driven publishers and owners would learn from the great news organizations that they have a social responsibility of public service to their readers and viewers. One can be forgiven for not being overly optimistic that owners, already coping with the migration of advertisers to the Internet, will embrace the concept of an overhead-laden social responsibility and, more critically, the diminished profits that might go with it. Yet the best news organizations don't bleed to death by paying for quality journalism, they profit from it. Perhaps events after Kosovo—September 11, 2001; the Canadian missions in Afghanistan; Libya and Iraq—have changed journalists' attitudes toward the need to be better informed about national defence, security, and foreign affairs matters. Even if attitudes have changed, the entire parliamentary press gallery cannot be expected to become experts on the Canadian Armed Forces. How many should become military experts is unclear, but having more would enhance the diversity of news coverage.

The second problem with the suggestion that journalists train with the military and have exposure to them well before accompanying them on operations is that it would only work with the army and the navy. Journalists can accompany the army and the navy on exercises or missions. That is better than nothing, but covering the air force or tank regiments presents a much different set of problems. For example, even during training exercises like Maple Flag at CFB Cold Lake, there is little else for observers to do but watch scores of NATO aircraft thunder into the sky and disappear out of sight. Journalists can't accompany pilots in their one-seat fighter aircrafts like they can accompany soldiers in many of their fighting vehicles and sailors on their ships. With air forces, there is little for journalists to do but photograph jets taking off and landing or interview airmen before and after missions.

A third problem is operational security. Viewed through the prism of operational security, what needs to be considered is that which might jeopardize a mission at the secrecy end of the spectrum, what might not at the transparent other end, and where a balance can be struck in the subtle middle range. At the conservative end of the secrecy spectrum, it is not reasonable to expect that the Canadians should have revealed that flying without night-vision goggles forced them to fly in dangerous formations or reveal the tactics they developed in order to avoid colliding with each other during the Kosovo campaign. At the transparency end, disclosure of the costs of a bombing campaign to taxpayers would not have compromised operational security, despite what Brig. Gen. Jurkowski said. That much is intuitive.

In the subtle middle range of the operational security spectrum, it was argued in Aviano that the pilots' mission focus should not be needlessly jeopardized simply to satisfy information-starved journalists in pursuit of a story, any story. On one hand, Canadian historian Jack Granatstein is right: the public's right to know is not absolute and is not worth the life of one Canadian soldier. Freedom of the press simply does not trump the sanctity of life. On the other hand, there was no evidence that the pilots were concerned about news media reports or that their mission focus was compromised by them. The Task Force Aviano commander simply didn't like what was written in just one article. The news media can accept that operational security requirements will, at times, restrict the freedom of journalists to report on all aspects of operations. But the military should not use the comfort blanket of operational security to shut the door on media scrutiny of its operations in their entirety as it did during the Kosovo air war.

A balance needs to be struck that bridges the military's conservative value of discretion, if not secrecy, and the media's liberal value of openness. Journalists should be allowed to report on the challenges overcome, the dangers faced, the hardships endured, and the sacrifices made by military personnel without compromising operational security. Allowing journalists to see that the Canadians were retooling US bombs and that they relied on the Americans, in many ways and more than anyone knew, presents a case where a balance might be struck. On one hand, while such a revelation shedding new light on the state of the Canadian Forces would not have provided comfort to an enemy that wouldn't have cared where the bombs that were being dropped on them came from, there might well have been have political and diplomatic repercussions. On the other hand, revealing that the ground crews not only met the challenges of long hours; had little sleep and inappropriate footwear; slogged through the rain; and persevered through insufferable heat and injuries that debilitated crew members who were too old to do their jobs would have enabled Canadians to know about their commitment to duty and dedication to their country.

As a result, it is not unreasonable to suggest that the Canadian Forces and news media could learn from the Kosovo air war and that they should discuss aspects of future media coverage that would and would not constitute legitimate threats to operational security. To that end, it is suggested that military and journalistic leaders engage in dialogue to strike such a reasonable balance between their respective and competing imperatives. The likelihood of that happening in my lifetime, if ever, is remote. Although it is a highly romantic—if not idealistic—notion, the Canadian public does have the right, if not always the ability, to make informed decisions about the government and its policies. This includes the application of military skill in combat. For this reason, when operational security is invoked by the military to restrict, if not censor, the Canadian news media, the reasons for it must be based on empirical facts and must be explained in clear, concise terms.

The news media's coverage of the Kosovo air war presents the question: Could the media's readers and audiences have known about the Canadian military's participation in a war that wasn't covered by the media? The answer is they couldn't have. As mentioned earlier, Canadians could not have made informed judgments about the Canadian military's prosecution of the Kosovo air war in an information vacuum.

Afterword

Much has changed in the world since the 1999 Kosovo air war. The war ended when Serb president Slobodan Milosevic allowed United Nations peacekeepers into Kosovo and the United Nations to govern it. Kosovo eventually declared independence in 2008, which the Serbian government doesn't recognize but which a large majority of the international community does. Canada's strategic goal of seeing an independent Kosovo within Yugoslavia was sheer folly, but its use of military force alongside its NATO allies contributed to bringing a cessation to the brutal and bloody ethnic cleansing.

Also, since then, Canadian soldiers fought in Afghanistan from 2001 to 2011 after the terrorist incidents in the United States on 11 September 2001. Hundreds of Canadian journalists were embedded with them over the years, most for short periods of time. One hundred and fifty-eight Canadian soldiers along with seven civilians died, including *Calgary Herald* journalist Michelle Lang on 30 December 2009. Lang died with four Canadian soldiers when the armoured vehicle they were travelling in was struck by an improvised explosive device or bomb. In the context of her death, the notion that journalists travel to war zones and use military members merely to provide entertainment for their readers or audiences is appalling. Thousands of news stories were published and broadcast about Afghanistan, but the most authoritative source of information about that war comes from books written by journalists and academics, not the news.[1]

As a society, Canada in the late twentieth century and in the early twenty-first century will be judged by how it supported civil liberties and the democratic guarantees enshrined in the *Canadian Charter of Rights and Freedoms*, including freedom of the press and other media of communication, subject only to such reasonable limits as prescribed by law. In the case of Kosovo, the Canadian Forces failed to meet those *Charter* guarantees. Afghanistan was a much different war because it was a ground war, and journalists could go on patrol with the troops if their editors would let them leave the relative safety of the Kandahar Airfield so as not to miss the next Canadian soldier body bag story. There is, however, one parallel that can be made with Afghanistan: Kosovo. Canada had a squadron of Lord Strathcona's Horse (Royal Canadians) tanks in Afghanistan continuously since the fall of 2006 until 2010, when they were withdrawn. They were making history because it was the first time since the Korean War that Canadian tanks were sent to fight in an active war zone. There was nothing reported about them. Much as with the CF-18s, there is no room for journalists to ride along in tanks. The tanks in Afghanistan were even less visible in the media to Canadians than were the CF-18s in Kosovo. The Canadian air force participated in the Libya bombing campaign 2011 in Operation Mobile and in Operation Impact against the Islamic State (also known variously as Daesh, ISIL, and ISIS) in Iraq and Syria from October 2014 to February 2016. The stories of Operation Mobile and of Operation Impact have yet to be told.

Two shocking and tragic events involving Canadian soldiers provide ample reason to think there will be even greater media restrictions than those imposed by the Canadian military to date. On 20 October 2014, two Canadian soldiers were injured in a hit-and-run accident in Saint-Jean-sur-Richelieu, Quebec, that was thought to be a terrorist attack. There was a vehicle chase by police, and the driver was shot dead after his car crashed and he emerged brandishing a knife. One of the soldiers, Warrant Officer Patrice Vincent, died of his injuries. That terrorist-attack speculation was cemented in Parliamentary history by the prime minister later that day in the House of Commons when Member of Parliament Randy Hoback, of Prince Albert, Saskatchewan, rose in the House and asked a planted question. He said. "Mr. Speaker, there are unconfirmed reports of a possible terror attack against two members of the Canadian Armed Forces near Saint-Jean-sur-Richelieu. Can the Prime Minister please update the House on this matter?"[2] Prime Minister Stephen Harper replied:

> Mr. Speaker, we are aware of these reports and they are obviously extremely troubling. First and foremost, our thoughts and prayers are with the victims and their families. We are closely monitoring the situation, and we will make available all of the resources of the federal government.[3]

The attacker, Martin Couture-Rouleau, was identified as a Canadian-born radicalized Muslim convert. Couture-Rouleau had been stripped of his passport by Canadian authorities to prevent him from travelling abroad to join Islamic State fighters. Two days later, Canadian Forces Cpl. Nathan Cirillo was shot dead on 22 October 2014, while he stood on ceremonial guard at the National War Memorial in Ottawa. His killer, Michael Zehaf-Bibeau, who stormed into Parliament's Centre Block after he shot Cpl. Cirillo, was also a Canadian-born radicalized Muslim convert. After a fierce gunfight in the Centre Block's hallways, he was shot and killed by House of Commons security and the Parliamentary Sergeant-at-Arms, Kevin Vickers. Some ninety-three radicalized Canadians were said to be known to the RCMP as high-risk travellers, but Zehaf-Bibeau was not thought to be one of them. The son of a Libyan immigrant, he had attempted to renew his Libyan passport on 2 October 2014 but was turned down by Libyan embassy officials wary of his demeanour. Canadian officials were in the midst of processing his Canadian passport application, but it became delayed when the application was forwarded to the RCMP for a background check.[4] Following Zehaf-Bibeau's death, Prime Minister Harper spoke in a nationally televised address from his home at 24 Sussex Drive, calling the shooting a terrorist act. "In the days to come, we will learn more about the terrorist and any accomplices he may have had, but this week's events are a grim reminder that Canada is not immune to the types of terrorist attacks we have seen elsewhere around the world."[5]

It didn't take long for the Canadian Armed Forces to react. Within hours of the Ottawa shooting, military bases and armouries were locked down. Military members were told not to wear their uniforms in public unless they were driving to work. They were told to not gas up in uniform. A military police officer in Saint-Hubert asked the media not to publish pictures of soldiers' faces. The wife of a Montreal soldier feared military families could be targeted.[6] Military members feared their spouses were targets in their own country. Permission to wear their uniforms was restored a day later, and the honour guard resumed at the National War Memorial in Ottawa on October 25.[7] In the weeks following, Canadian Armed Forces members were advised to be vigilant and not to wear their uniforms when not on duty.

On 7 December 2014, Canadian television news ran a vitriolic video of Canadian John Maguire, a reported Islam convert. Maguire urged Canadian Muslims to either pack their bags and join ISIL or prepare explosive devices and carry out independent attacks on Canadian soil like those that killed Warrant Officer Vincent and Cpl. Cirillo.[8] Some in the Arab world dismissed the video as trumped-up Western propaganda aimed at bolstering public opinion for Prime Minister Harper's war agenda in the Middle East. It doesn't really matter. History is a teacher here. On 2 October 1924, the Canadian representative to the League of Nations, Raoul Dandurand, famously said of Canadians: "We live in a fire-proof house, far from inflammable materials."[9] The killings of Warrant Officer Vincent and Cpl. Cirillo on Canadian soil amply demonstrate that Canadians no longer live in a fire-proof house far from inflammable materials. The flames set and fanned by Muslim extremists threaten the houses of not just Canadian military families but potentially any Canadian. The events in the United States on 11 September 2001 showed how domestic airplanes hijacked by Muslim extremists could be turned into weapons of mass destruction. Couture-Rouleau showed how easily a car could be weaponized when he killed Warrant Officer Vincent. The problem is that there are far more cars in Canada than there are airplanes and people who know how to fly them. In other words, there are far more potential weapons readily available to those determined to use them.

It doesn't matter if Couture-Rouleau or Zehaf-Bibeau were acting as jihadi-wannabees; lone-wolf terrorists; micro-terrorists; were acting in concert with others in Canada or with terrorists abroad; were following a commander's intent; or, rather, were just deranged, heartless killers who just happened to be Muslim converts. What matters is that Canadian soldiers were deliberately killed on Canadian soil by homegrown radicalized Muslims. The Canadian Armed Forces themselves inextricably linked the fight against ISIL's Islamic extremists to Warrant Officer Vincent and Cpl. Cirillo by naming their Task Force Iraq facilities in Kuwait Camp Patrice

Vincent and Patrol Base Cirillo. The military public affairs specialists at National Defence Headquarters, this author argues, will surely conflate the tragic killings of Warrant Officer Vincent and Cpl. Cirillo and potential acts of retribution by those opposed to Canada's contribution to the war against ISIL, egged on by the likes of John Maguire. Out of an abundance of caution, they will build contingencies for direct and indirect terrorist threats to Canada, Canadians, and the Canadian Armed Forces and their families into their communications strategies. It is inconceivable to think they won't.

Clearly there was tension between the democratic need for open public discussion about the military's activities over Iraq and the secrecy and censorship needed to conduct dangerous operations. But within the discussion is a Russian nesting doll of moral equivalents and dilemmas. Writing comfortably in Canada, it is easy to call for more openness in military-media relations in keeping with The *Canadian Charter of Rights and Freedoms*. For example, US president Barack Obama said Sony Pictures Entertainment Inc. let down Americans when it censored itself and decided against releasing the movie *The Interview* on 25 December 2014. There had been threats of grave consequences regarding its release from North Korean leaders, which included terrorist attacks against movie theatres. Sony had been an earlier target of cyber-attacks by North Koreans upset with the comedy based on the mock assassination of North Korea's leader. The president said in part:

> We cannot have a society where some dictator someplace can start imposing censorship here in the United States. That's not what America's about. Again, I'm sympathetic that Sony, as a private company, was worried about liabilities and this and that and the other. I wish they'd spoken to me first. I would have told them, "Do not get into a pattern in which you're intimidated by these kinds of criminal attacks."[10]

The president also drew a parallel to the Boston Marathon bombing in April 2013 in which two radical Muslim brothers set off two pressure cooker bombs that killed three and injured hundreds of others. But that didn't stop Boston from running the marathon the next year. Even worse, the president said, would be a situation in which others began self-censoring themselves to ward off possible retribution. Yet the threats of ISIL against Canadians present precisely that self-censorship dilemma. ISIL is not North Korea, but it is a new enemy the likes of which Canadians have never faced. ISIL's threats have caused self-censorship and military censorship in Canada. This book on the Kosovo air war will surely offend many military sensibilities with its provocative censorship criticisms. Those who disagree will have their say and that is their right. But which author, journalist, or news organization is going to identify a Canadian pilot who dropped bombs on ISIL targets in Iraq and run the risk of potentially being personally responsible for a relative's or relatives' death at the hand of a radicalized Muslim extremist in Canada?

In the history of Canadian journalism, the Canadian government has only invoked military censorship twice, during the First and Second World Wars. Voluntary press censorship was set up early during the First World War under the Department of Militia and Defence with a deputy chief censor. Canada's communications facilities were meshed with a nationwide cable, radio-telegraph, telegraph, and telephone censorship. That network was tied in with Empire Cable and wireless censorship headed by the chief censor in London, England. A 12 September 1914 directive set out information useful to the enemy, and dealt with prevention of espionage, security of the armed forces, and the welfare of the Canadian people. In June 1915, regulations made press censorship mandatory, set out what matter was acceptable or unacceptable, and authorized censors who had the power to enter printing and press establishments.[11] This is how it worked: Far removed from the European theatres of war, Canadians were largely informed of the overseas events of the First World War by news reports from the front, which were heavily censored by British military authorities. Most of the news reports received were not about the more than 15,600 Canadians dying horribly in less than a month in the mud of Passchendaele, but of ridiculously upbeat versions of battle.[12] From the news media's perspective, apart from socialist, anti-imperialist, rural, and certain French Canadian publications, partisanship was the norm among the nation's major daily newspapers. Typically, the *Manitoba Free Press* proclaimed upon the news that 6,000 Canadians had died at the second battle of Ypres: "above the tears ... there rose steady and clear the voice of thankfulness to God . . . that they were permitted in their death to make so splendid a sacrifice."[13]

Censorship of the news media was set up during the Second World War under the *Defence of Canada Regulations*, which derived their authority from the *War Measures Act* as set out in Chapter 206 of the 1927 *Revised Statutes of Canada*. The censors were advisors only and could not prohibit the publication of articles. Newspapers' guilt or non-guilt for violations could only be decided upon by the court. The sole power possessed by the chief censor was to say that information was in non-violation, meaning that a newspaper could not be prosecuted if it had obtained censorship clearance. Possible penalties included fines, imprisonment, and suspension.[14] Legendary Canadian Press war correspondent Ross Munro's coverage of the Dieppe Raid illustrates how Canadian journalists who witnessed the carnage on 19 August 1942 reported the news under such censorship. Nearly 5,000 Canadian soldiers made up the vast majority of 6,000 Allied troops who stormed the heavily defended beach at Dieppe that day in a raid on the German-held French coast. By historical accounts, the action was a tactical disaster that some suggest should never have taken place. Of 4,963 Canadians embarking on their first live action in Europe, only 2,210 returned. Of them, 807 were killed in action, 100 died of wounds, 586 were wounded, and 1,874 were taken prisoner.[15]

Munro was among four Canadian journalists who accompanied the Canadian troops as they powered toward the beaches at Dieppe. From his vantage point on the landing craft, Munro could see sandbagged German positions from the top of the cliff at Puys, in houses, and in the cliffs' clefts raining machine gun fire down on the hapless Canadians. To his horror, he had to look no farther than his own craft to see its bottom covered with dead troops who had been machine-gunned. Later, from an escaping vessel, he watched a furious air battle overhead as landing craft after Allied landing craft was blown out of the water.[16] After the war, he wrote in retrospect that "on no other front have I witnessed such carnage. It was brutal and terrible and shocked you almost to insensibility to see the piles of dead and feel the hopelessness of the attack at this point."[17] But what did he write after his story cleared military censorship in England?

> There was heroism at sea and in the skies in those hours, but the hottest spot was ashore, where the Canadians fought at close quarters with the Nazis. They fought to the end, where they had to, and showed courage and daring. They attacked the Dieppe arsenal of coastal defence. They left Dieppe silent and afire, its ruins and its dead under a shroud of smoke.[18]

Munro knew that was malarkey, but he wrote it anyway. He wrote after the war: "I watched those boats in the warm sunshine going back to England empty when they should have been filled with the thousands of soldiers they'd taken to France."[19]

One might ask: What is worse, the war correspondents' drivel during the First and Second World Wars under government censorship or nothing at all during the Kosovo air war under military censorship? In reality, that is an entirely immoral choice and an insult to the concept of Canada's democracy and democratic institutions. This is not an abstract problem. If there is to be censorship in future wars, the censorship and operational security issues raised in this book on the Kosovo air war should be debated in the House of Commons by parliamentarians. They could, in their wisdom, exercise leadership in legislating censorship if they find it necessary. They should not leave it to the military to impose its own restrictions, which this work has shown it is more than ready, willing, and able to do in policy and in practice. If legislated, that parliamentary leadership could amount to a reasonable limit on press freedom and other media of communication by law, as envisioned by the *Canadian Charter of Rights and Freedoms.*

Canadian democracy deserves that debate at the very least.

Notes

Introduction

1. Desmond Morton, *A Military History of Canada*, 3rd ed. (Toronto: McClelland and Stewart, 1992), 250.

2. Janice Gross Stein and Eugene Lang, *The Unexpected War: Canada in Kandahar* (Toronto: Viking Canada, 2007), 19.

3. Robert W. Bergen, "Balkan Rats and Balkan Bats" (PhD diss., University of Calgary, 2005), 396-99.

4. Canada, *Royal Commission on Newspapers* (Ottawa: Minister of Supply and Services Canada, 1981), 30.

5. Bergen, "Balkan Rats and Balkan Bats," 48-50.

6. Murray Edelman, *Political Language: Words that Succeed and Policies that Fail* (New York: Academic Press, 1977), 11.

7. Murray Edelman, *Politics as Symbolic Action: Mass Arousal and Quiescence* (Chicago: Markham, 1971), 10.

8. Murray Edelman, *Constructing the Political Spectacle* (Chicago: University of Chicago Press, 1988), 102.

9. Edelman, *Constructing the Political Spectacle*, 103-4.

10. Edelman, *Constructing the Political Spectacle*, 104; Edelman, *Politics as Symbolic Action*, 4.

11. Daniel C. Hallin, *The "Uncensored War": The Media and Vietnam* (Berkeley: University of California Press, 1989) 60-63.

12. W. Lance Bennett, "Toward a Theory of Press-State Relations in the United States," *Journal of Communications* 40, no. 2 (Spring 1990): 106; W. Lance Bennett, "The News about Foreign Policy," in *Taken By Storm: The Media, Public Opinion and U.S. Foreign Policy in the Gulf War*, ed. W. Lance Bennett, and David L. Paletz (Chicago: University of Chicago Press, 1994), 24.

13. Bennett, "The News about Foreign Policy," 26.

14 Jay Rosen, *What Are Journalists for?* (New Haven, CT: Yale University Press, 1999), 299.

15 "How confidential sources help keep us free," *Globe and Mail*. 23 January 2004, A19.

16 David Akin, "In China, Trudeau said journalism that informs, challenges is vital. Bravo." Global News, online: https://globalnews.ca/news/3903127/trudeau-journalism-vital-china/.

17 Ibid.

18 Denis Stairs, "The Media and the Military in Canada," *International Journal* 53, no. 3 (Summer 1998): 544–53.

19 See Ross Munro, *Gauntlet to Overlord: The Story of the Canadian Army* (Toronto: Macmillan Canada, 1946); Dick Malone, *Missing from the Record* (Toronto: Collins, 1946); Phillip Knightley, *The First Casualty: The War Correspondent as Hero and Myth-Maker from the Crimea to Iraq* (New York: Harcourt Brace Jovanovich, 1975); Richard S. Malone, *A Portrait of War: 1939–1946* (Toronto: Collins, 1983); Richard S. Malone, *A World in Flames: 1944–1945* (Toronto: Collins, 1984); Jack Donoghue, *The Edge of War* (Calgary: Detselig, 1988); Jack Chahill, *Words of War* (Toronto: Deneau, 1987); Peter Stursburg, *The Sound of War: Memoirs of a CBC Correspondent* (Toronto: University of Toronto Press, 1993); Robert A. Hackett, *News and Dissent: The Press and the Politics of Peace in Canada* (Norwood, NJ: Ablex, 1995); Michael Benedict, ed., *Canada at War* (Toronto: Viking, 1997); Kathy Gannon, *I Is For Infidel: From Holy War To Holy Terror: 18 Years inside Afghanistan* (New York: PublicAffairs, 2005); Christie Blatchford, *Fifteen Days: Stories of Bravery, Friendship, Life and Death from inside the New Canadian Army* (Toronto: Doubleday, 2007); Adam Day, *Witness to War: Reporting on Afghanistan 2004–2009* (Kingston, ON: Canadian Defence Academy Press, 2010); Murray Brewster, *The Savage War: The Untold Battles of Afghanistan* (Mississauga, ON: Wiley, 2011); Graeme Smith, *The Dogs are Eating Them Now: Our War in Afghanistan* (Toronto: Alfred A. Knopf Canada, 2013).

20 Canada, House of Commons, *Debates*, vol. 135, no. 203 (25 March 1999), 13510 (hereafter *Debates*).

21 *Debates*, vol. 135, no. 203 (25 March 1999), 13443.

22 *Debates*, vol. 135, no. 134 (7 October 1998), 8914.

23 Carl von Clausewitz, *On War*, ed. Michael Howard and Peter Paret (Princeton, NJ: Princeton University Press, 1976), 87.

24 *Debates*, vol. 135, no. 134 (7 October 1998), 8914.

25 Roy Remple, *The Chatter Box: An Insider's Account of the Irrelevance of Parliament in the Making of Canadian Foreign and Defence Policy* (Toronto: Dundurn Press, 2002), 56.

26 *Debates*, vol. 135, no. 205A (12 April 1999), 13594.

27 Paul Koring, "Canadian war planes upgraded to launch precision weapons," *Globe and Mail*, 25 March 1999, A16.

28 *Debates*, vol. 135, no. 216 (27 April 1999), 14386.

29 *Access to Information Act*, R.S.C. 1985, c. A-1, s. 15.

30 Ibid., s. 23.

31 *Debates*, vol. 275 (30 June 1950), 4459; J. L. Granatstein, *Canada's Army: Waging War and Keeping the Peace* (Toronto: University of Toronto Press, 2002), 335.

32 Granatstein, *Canada's Army*, 335.

33 Ibid.

34 *Debates*, vol. 135, no. 203 (24 March 1999), 13445.

35 Michael Ignatieff, *Virtual War: Kosovo and Beyond* (Toronto: Viking Canada, 2000).

36 Canada, House of Commons, "Resolution Following Public Hearings On Canada's Role in the Kosovo Conflict and its Aftermath," *Report of the Standing Committee on Foreign Affairs and International Trade*, June 2000, ii.

37 Ibid., 1.

38 Gen. Wesley K. Clark, *Waging Modern War: Bosnia, Kosovo and the Future of Combat* (New York: PublicAffairs, 2002), xxxvii.

39 Bill Clinton, *My Life* (New York: Alfred A. Knopf, 2004), 787–854, 855–60.

40 John Shy, "Jominy," in *Makers of Modern Strategy: From Machiavelli to the Nuclear Age*, ed., Peter Paret (Princeton, NJ: Princeton University Press, 1986), 143.

41 Baron de Jomini, *The Art of War*, trans. G. H. Mendell, and W. P. Craighill (Westport, CT: Greenwood Press, 1862), 11. As it will be seen, during the Kosovo air war, politicians from many nations meddled with the manner in which the NATO commander, Gen. Wesley Clark, achieved the war's objective—including becoming involved, at the highest political levels, in the selection of targets—much to Clark's chagrin.

42 Giulio Douhet, *The Command of the Air*, trans. Dino Ferrari (New York: Arno Press, 1972), 23.

43 Douhet, *The Command of the Air*, 51. Like Jomini's principle of command, Douhet's major principle of inflicting the greatest damage in the shortest time possible would be abandoned during the Kosovo air war.

44 Douhet, *Command of the Air*, 140.

45 Peter W. W. Wijninga and Richard Szafranski, "Beyond Utility Targeting: Toward Axiological Air Operations," *Aerospace Power Journal* 14, no. 4 (Winter 2000): 45–59.

46 Paul Rexton Kan, "What Should We bomb? Axiological Targeting and the Abiding Limits of Airpower Theory," *Air & Space Power Journal* 18, no. 1 (Spring 2004): 25–32.

47 Brereton Greenhous et al., *The Crucible of War 1939–1945: The Official History of the Royal Canadian Air Force*, vol. 3 (Toronto: University of Toronto Press, 1994), 15, online: https://www.canada.ca/content/dam/themes/defence/caf/militaryhistory/dhh/popular/crucible-war-1939-1945-1.pdf.

Chapter 1

1. Maj. Alain Pelletier, telephone interview by author, 16 July 2003.
2. Pelletier, telephone interview.
3. Lt. Col. Sylvain Faucher, interview by author, Ottawa, Ontario, 29 October 2003.
4. Faucher, interview.
5. Faucher, interview.
6. Confidential interview by author. In accordance with an ethical agreement, names were withheld by mutual agreement if requested, Canadian Forces Base Bagotville, Quebec, 22 October 2003.
7. Maj. Mike Barker, interview with author, Canadian Forces Base Cold Lake, Alberta, 16 April 2003.
8. Maj. Alain Pelletier, email message to author, 15 October 2003.
9. A sortie is one flight by one plane. One mission involving four CF-18s would count as four sorties.
10. Robert Hewson et al., "Operation Allied Force: The First 30 Days," *World Air Power Journal* 38 (Autumn 1999): 16–29.
11. Lt. Col. Kirk Soroka, telephone interview by author, 2 October 2012.
12. Soroka, telephone interview.
13. Soroka, telephone interview.
14. Soroka, telephone interview.
15. Soroka, email message to author, 28 October 2012.
16. Pelletier, telephone interview.
17. Pelletier, telephone interview.
18. Pelletier, telephone interview.
19. "Dutch/Belgian Allied Force," *World Air Power Journal* 38 (Autumn 1999): 23.
20. The AWACS had told the Dutch flying four F-16s in two pairs that three MiG-29s had taken off from Batajnica air base near Belgrade. The pilot who engaged the MiG fired one AMRAAM missile at it from a distance of eleven miles. He watched the missile detonate thirty seconds after launch. United States Air Force F-15s downed two others that night. "Dutch/Belgian Allied Force," *World Air Power Journal* 38 (Autumn 1999): 16, 23.
21. Pelletier, telephone interview.
22. Pelletier, telephone interview.
23. Faucher, interview.
24. Faucher, interview.
25. Faucher, interview.
26. Confidential interview.

27 Confidential interview.
28 Confidential interview. Chaff is a countermeasure to distract radar-guided missiles from their targets. It can be strips of aluminum foil or aluminum-coated glass fibres scattered by pilots to form an electromagnetic cloud that temporarily hides aircraft from missiles' radars. See online: https://www.globalsecurity.org/military/systems/aircraft/systems/chaff.htm.
29 Confidential interview.
30 Confidential interview.
31 David L. Bashow et al., "Mission Ready: Canada's Role in the Kosovo Air Campaign," *Canadian Military Journal* 1, no. 1 (Spring 2000): 55–61.
32 Pelletier, telephone interview.
33 Faucher, interview.
34 Confidential interview.
35 Faucher, interview.
36 Lt. Col. (ret.) William Allen Flynn, author telephone interview, 9 April 2003.
37 Capt. Kirk Soroka, interview by author, Canadian Forces Base Cold Lake Alberta, 14 April 2003.
38 By ship, the pilots mean the CF-18. Ship is a derivative of airship.
39 Soroka, interview.
40 "Tubs," interview with author, Canadian Forces Base Cold Lake, Alberta, 15 April 2003.
41 Capt. Brett Glaeser, interview by author, Canadian Forces Base Cold Lake, Alberta, 15 April 2003.
42 Glaeser, interview.
43 Capt. Travis Brassington, interview with author, Canadian Forces Base Cold Lake, Alberta, 15 April 2003.
44 Brassington, interview.
45 Glaeser, interview.
46 Capt. Kirk Soroka, telephone interview by author, 10 October 2003.
47 Soroka, telephone interview, 10 October 2003.
48 Those Nomex flight suits can be ordered online for US$175 Online: http://aureusinternational.com (accessed October 11, 2003).
49 Soroka, telephone interview, 10 October 2003.
50 Soroka, telephone interview, 10 October 2003.
51 Soroka, telephone interview, 10 October 2003. The original manufacturer of the PRC-112 was Motorola, but General Dynamics has taken over as contractor. Online: http://www.pacificsites.com/~brooke/Survival.s/html (accessed 18 March 2004).
52 Brig. Gen. (ret.) David Jurkowski, interview by author, Ottawa, Ontario, 27 October 2003.

53 Soroka, telephone interview, 10 October 2003.
54 Soroka, telephone interview, 10 October 2003.
55 Confidential interview by author, Canadian Force Base Bagotville, Quebec, 21 October 2003.
56 Confidential interview by author, Canadian Forces Base Cold Lake, Alberta, 14 April 2003.

Chapter 2

1 David Bercuson, *Significant Incident: Canada's Army, the Airborne, and the Murder in Somalia* (Toronto: McClelland and Stewart, 1996); Peter Desbarats, Somalia Cover-Up: A Commissioner's Journal (Toronto: McClelland and Stewart, 1997).

2 Col. (ret.) Benoît Marcotte, telephone interview by author, 9 January 2004; Marcotte, email correspondence to author, 11 January 2004; Gen. Wesley K. Clark, *Waging Modern War: Bosnia, Kosovo and the Future of Combat* (New York: PublicAffairs, 2002), 120.

3 Operation Mirador was Canada's contribution to NATO's enforcement of a no-fly zone over Bosnia-Herzegovina.

4 Marcotte, telephone interview.

5 Marcotte, telephone interview.

6 Marcotte, telephone interview; email correspondence.

7 Canadian pilots did drop bombs during the 1991 Persian Gulf War but they were not engaged in protracted combat, as will be seen in Chapter 6.

8 Canada, Report of the Auditor General of Canada to the House of Commons, April 1998, chap. 3, 3–10.

9 The auditor general uses the term "strategic" in the same manner as the *Access to Information Act* guidelines, which involves intercontinental war plans, as opposed to the Clausewitzian purist Colin S. Gray, who would argue that terms like "strategic airlift" and "strategic tankers" are misnomers. Gray says such terms confuse capabilities with results, that is to say the achievement of policy goals. *Modern Strategy* (Oxford: Oxford University Press, 1999), 17. Similarly, Clausewitz might argue that the heavy lift function of an air-to-air refuelling tanker is the modern-day air force equivalent of the march, which, even though it is linked to the engagement, is only a means to carry out a strategic plan. Carl von Clausewitz, *On War*, ed. Michael Howard and Peter Paret (Princeton, NJ: Princeton University Press, 1976), 29. Nonetheless, for the sake of consistency in terms of the Canadian government's phraseology, the Canadian terms when used in such fashion have been left intact.

10 Canada, Report of the Auditor General of Canada to the House of Commons, April, 1998, chap. 3, 3-11 to 3-12.

11 Canada, Department of National Defence, Directorate of Air Public Affairs, CF-18 backgrounder, 31 October 2002.

12 Canada, Department of National Defence, Operation Echo – Lessons Learned Staff Action Directive, Annex A, 12 Jan. 2000, obtained by author under *Access to Information Act* request A-2003-00305/Team1.

13 Ibid.

14 Canada, Department National Defence, online: http://www.airforce.forces.gc.ca/equip1k_e.htm (accessed 17 February 2004).

15 See online: http://www.airforce.forces.gc.ca/equip1k_e.htm (accessed 17 February 2004).

16 Confidential interview by author, names were withheld by mutual agreement, Canadian Forces Base Bagotville, Quebec, 22 October 2003. A strategic tanker is a jet aircraft.

17 Confidential interview by author. A "snag" is a piece of broken equipment like a radar or hydraulic system.

18 For a detailed history of the Permanent Joint Board of Defence and its workings, see C. P. Stacey, *Arms, Men and Governments: The War Policies of Canada 1939–1945* (Ottawa: Minister of National Defence, 1974), 338–95.

19 Brig. Gen. (ret.) David Jurkowski, interview by author, Ottawa, Ontario, 27 October 2003.

20 Col. (ret.) Benoît Marcotte, telephone interview by author, 9 January 2004.

21 Col. (ret.) Benoît Marcotte, email message to author, 11 January 2004.

22 Canada, Department of National Defence, Operation Echo – Lessons Learned Staff Action Directive, Annex A, 12 Jan. 2000, obtained by author under *Access to Information Act* request A-2003-00305/Team1.

23 Cpl. Patrick Savoie, interview by author, Canadian Forces Base Bagotville, Quebec, 21 October 2003.

24 Savoie, interview.

25 Operation Echo – Lessons Learned Staff Action Directive, Annex A.

26 Marcotte, email message.

27 Marcotte, email message.

28 Col. (ret.) J. M. Donihee, interview by author, Calgary, Alberta, 22 April 2003.

29 Savoie, interview.

30 Savoie, interview.

31 Savoie, interview.

32 Savoie, interview.

33 Savoie, interview.

34 Jurkowski, interview.

35 Donihee, interview. This was Donihee's recollection and argument, which won the day. The author's personal experience in Bosnia in 1994 was that the soldiers were allowed two beers in the mess per day maximum. This doesn't obviate Donihee's recollection and argument. Also, from the author's personal experience, they weren't allowed to

drink at all at the Kandahar Air Field or at Forward Operating Base Nathan Smith in Afghanistan in 2007.

36   Donihee, interview.
37   Donihee, interview.
38   Jurkowski, interview.
39   Military Analysis Network, Operation Deliberate Force, online: http://www.fas.org/man/dod-101/ops/deliberate_force.htm (accessed 26 February 2004).
40   North Atlantic Treaty Organization, Regional Headquarters Allied Forces Southern Europe: SFOR Air Component, online: http://www.afsouth.nato.int/factsheets/sforaircomponent.htm (accessed 26 February 2004).
41   Canada, Department of National Defence, National Defence Headquarters, Secret System High Generated/Mediated Message, Message ID: 199827000147, 27 September 1998, obtained by author under *Access to Information Act* request A-2002-01182/Team 3-2. The precise quantities of munitions were exempted from release on the grounds the information could be injurious to international affairs and on advice or recommendations developed by or for a government institution or a minister of the Crown.
42   Allied Forces Southern Europe, "Operation Allied Force," online: http://www.afsouth.nato.int/operations/detforce/Force.htm; Canada, Department of National Defence, "Kosovo," online: http://www.dnd.ca/eng/archive/1999/apr99/Kosovo1_b_e.htm (both accessed 26 February 2004).
43   Confidential interview with author, names were withheld by mutual agreement, Canadian Forces Base Bagotville, Quebec, 22 October 2003.
44   Benjamin Lambeth, *The Transformation of America Airpower* (Ithaca, NY: Cornell University Press, 2000), 182.
45   United Kingdom, House of Commons Library, "Kosovo: NATO and Military Action." Research Paper 99/34, 24 March 1999, online: researchbriefings.files.parliament.uk/documents/RP99-34/RP99-34.pdf.
46   Lambeth, The Transformation of America Airpower, 182–83.
47   Savoie, interview.
48   Canada, Department of National Defence, National Defence Headquarters, Message ID 199827000147, 27 September 1998, 5 RXFGDFD.0394 Secret, obtained by author under *Access to Information Act* request A-2002-01182/Team 3-2.
49   Message ID 199827000147, 27 September 1998.
50   Clark, *Waging Modern War*, 164.
51   Maj. Stéphane Hébert, interview by author, Canadian Forces Base Bagotville, Quebec, 22 October 2003.
52   Marie-Janine Calic, "Kosovo in the Twentieth Century: A Historical Account," in *Kosovo and the Challenge of Humanitarian Intervention*, ed. Albrecht Schnabel and Ramesh Thakur (New York: United Nations University Press, 2000), 28.

53 Ibid., 29. For a personal account of the back and forth negotiations between NATO and Slobodan Milosevic, see Clark, *Waging Modern War*, 131–89.
54 Maj. Alain Pelletier, telephone interview by author, 6 July 2003.
55 Savoie, interview.
56 Confidential interview with author, names were withheld by mutual agreement, Canadian Forces Base Bagotville, Quebec, 22 October 2003.
57 Pelletier, telephone interview.
58 David L. Bashow et al., "Mission Ready: Canada's Role in the Kosovo Air Campaign." *Canadian Military Journal* 1, no. 1 (Spring 2000): 55–61.

CHAPTER 3

1 A Cold-War era successor exercise that practised air attacks against ground targets, defences, communications, and jamming personnel and defence against surface-to-air missiles. See online: "Mallet Blow Strikes Again," https://www.flightglobal.com/FlightPDFArchive/1986/1986%20-%200892.PDF
2 Semi-confidential interview with author, full names were withheld by mutual consent if requested and call signs used instead.
3 "Cookie," interview by author, Canadian Forces Base Cold Lake, Alberta, 14 April 2003.
4 "Cookie," interview.
5 Maj. Mike Barker, interview by author, Canadian Forces Base Cold Lake, Alberta, 16 April 2003.
6 Interview by author, Canadian Forces Base Cold Lake, Alberta, 15 April 2003.
7 Interview by author, Canadian Forces Base Cold Lake, Alberta, 16 April 2003.
8 Barker, interview.
9 Barker, interview.
10 Interview by author, Canadian Force Base Cold Lake, Alberta, 14 April 2003.
11 Interview by author, Canadian Force Base Cold Lake, Alberta, 14 April 2003.
12 "Cookie," interview.
13 Capt. John Edelman, interview by author, Canadian Forces Base Cold Lake, Alberta, 15 April 2003.
14 Interview by author, Canadian Forces Base Cold Lake, Alberta, 16 April 2003.
15 Brig. Gen. (ret.) James Cox, interview by author, Ottawa, Ontario, 27 October 2003.
16 Confidential interview with author, names were withheld by mutual consent if requested, Canadian Force Base Cold Lake, Alberta, 16 April 2003.
17 Interview by author, Canadian Forces Base Cold Lake, Alberta, 16 April 2003.
18 MJ loaders are forklift-like tractors that lift bombs hydraulically for loading on the CF-18s.
19 Edelman, interview.
20 "Cookie," interview.

21 Interview by author, Canadian Forces Base Cold Lake, Alberta, 15 April 2003.
22 Interview by author, Canadian Forces Base Cold Lake, Alberta, 15 April 2003.
23 Interview by author, Canadian Force Base Cold Lake, Alberta, 14 April 2003.
24 Interview by author, Canadian Forces Base Cold Lake, Alberta, 16 April 2003.
25 The CF-18's empty weight is 10455 kg, or nearly 12 tons. Fully loaded with fuel and armaments for an attack mission, the CF-18 weighs about 23,400. Online: https://www.airforce-technology.com/projects/boeingcf18hornetmult/.
26 Confidential interview.
27 Edelman, interview.
28 Interview by author, Canadian Forces Base Cold Lake, Alberta, 15 April 2003.
29 Interview by author, Canadian Force Base Cold Lake, Alberta, 14 April 2003.
30 Barker, interview.
31 Barker, interview.
32 Barker, interview.
33 G.W.L. Nicholson, *The Canadians in Italy 1943–1945* (Ottawa: Queen's Printer, 1957), 534; David Dancocks, *The D-Day Dodgers: The Canadians in Italy, 1943–1945* (Toronto: McClelland and Stewart, 1991), 327–29; W.A.B. Douglas and Brereton Greenhous, *Out of the Shadows: Canada in the Second World War* (Toronto: Dundurn Press, 1995), 141.
34 Edelman, interview.
35 Interview by author, Canadian Forces Base Cold Lake, Alberta, 16 April 2003.
36 G.W.L. Nicholson, *Canadian Expeditionary Force 1914–1919: Official History of the Canadian Army in the First World War* (Ottawa: Queen's Printer, 1962), 27.
37 Interview by author, Canadian Forces Base Cold Lake, Alberta, 15 April 2003.
38 Confidential interview.
39 Barker, interview.
40 Confidential interview.
41 Interview by author, Canadian Forces Base Cold Lake, Alberta, 16 April 2003.
42 Barker, interview.
43 Confidential interview.
44 Edelman, interview.

Chapter 4

1 Capt. Kirk Soroka, unpublished notes for a Geoff Bennett painting "On a date with the Iron Maiden," from Canadian Airpower for Peace and Freedom Collection, unveiled 1 February 2001, at 4 Wing, Canadian Forces Base Cold Lake, Alberta.
2 Ibid.
3 Ibid.

4   Capt. Brett Glaeser, interview by author, Canadian Forces Base Cold Lake, Alberta, 15 April 2003.
5   Maj. Alain Pelletier, telephone interview with author, 16 July 2002.
6   Glaeser, interview.
7   Glaeser, interview.
8   Interview by author, Canadian Forces Base Cold Lake, Alberta, 15 April 2003.
9   Canada, Department of National Defence, Operation Echo – Lessons Learned Staff Action Directive. Annex A, 12 January 2000. Released under *Access to Information Act* request A-2003-00305/Team1.
10 Lt. Col. (ret.) Don Matthews, interview by author, Calgary, Alberta, 21 November 2003; telephone interview by author, 30 March 2004; Richard P. Hallion, *Storm over Iraq: Air Power and the Gulf War* (Washington: Smithsonian Institution Press, 1992), 289–90.
11 Canada, Department of National Defence, Historical and Comparative Overview of Canadian Defence Spending, online: http://www.forces.gc.ca/site/reports/cds_report/english/anxc_e.htm (accessed 29 December 2004).
12 Canada, Department of National Defence, 1994 White Paper on Defence, 48.
13 1994 White Paper on Defence, 48.
14 Matthews, interview.
15 "Canadian Contribution," *World Air Power Journal* 38 (Autumn 1999): 26.
16 Online: http://www.raytheon.com/products/paveway (accessed 14 October 2003).
17 Bob Bergen, "Calgary Salutes 75th Anniversary of the RCAF," *Calgary Herald*, 9 May 1999, D1.
18 Matthews, interview.
19 Col. (ret.) J. M. Donihee, interview with author, Calgary, Alberta, 22 April 2003; David L. Bashow et al., "Mission Ready: Canada's Role in the Kosovo Air Campaign," *Canadian Military Journal* 1, no. 1 (Spring 2000): 60.
20 Donihee, interview.
21 Lt. Col. (ret.) William Allen Flynn, telephone interview by author, 9 April 2003.
22 Bashow et al., "Mission Ready," 55–61.
23 "Tubs," interview by author, Canadian Forces Base Cold Lake, Alberta, 15 April 2003.
24 Confidential interview with author, names were withheld by mutual agreement if requested, Canadian Forces Base Bagotville, Quebec, 21 October 2003.
25 Confidential interview.
26 Confidential interview.
27 Canada, Evidence of Proceedings, House of Commons Standing Committee on National Defence and Veterans Affairs, 28 April 1999, online: http://www.parl.gc.ca/InfoCom/Doc/36/1/NDVA/Meetings/Evidence/ndvaev106-e.htm (accessed 10 August 2003).

28   Canada, Department of National Defence Daily Technical Briefing, 25 March 1999, online: http://dgpa-dgap.mil.ca/Transcr/1999Mar/99033007.htm, p. 8 of 11 (accessed 16 January 2003), provided by the National Defence Public Affairs Office – Calgary (Prairie Region & Northern Area). Henault's remarks were published the next day in the *Globe and Mail*, the *Toronto Sun*, the *Vancouver Sun* and the *Windsor Star*. See Brian Laghi, "Canada now waging high-tech warfare," *Globe and Mail*, 26 March 1999, A19; Anne Dawson and Stephanie Rubec, "Brass on Cloud 9 over hi-tech bomb; Laser-guided GBU-12 deadly," *Toronto Sun*, 26 March 1999; Mike Blanchfield, "Top weaponry puts Canada at front line: The state-of-the-art GBU-12 missiles—each with a $25,000 price tag—keep country 'in the club,'" *Vancouver Sun*, 26 March 1999, A13; Mike Blanchfield, "Canada's 'Top Guns': CF-18s launch missiles, rejoining NATO 'club,'" *Windsor Star*, 26 March 1999, A1.

29   Patrick Martin, "Balkan Rats," *Air Forces Monthly* (November 1999): 56–61.

30   Canada, Department of National Defence, National Defence Headquarters, Secret Memo DAEPMMFT028, CF-18 Weapons Augmentation Request, 5 October 1998, obtained by author under *Access to Information Act* request A-2002-01182/Team 3-2.

31   Flynn, telephone interview.

32   During the 1991 Gulf War, the Americans dropped 1,181 of the US$55,600 GBU-24s. See online: http://www.globalsecurity.org/military/systems/munitions/gbu-24.htm.

33   Flynn, telephone interview.

34   Flynn, telephone interview.

35   Flynn, telephone interview.

36   "Mur," interview with author, Canadian Forces Base Cold Lake, Alberta, 25 April 2003.

37   Flynn, telephone interview. A second consideration is collateral damage, which will be more fully explored later in the chapter. Flynn, telephone interview by author, 5 July 2005.

38   Canada, Department of National Defence, Operation Echo – Lessons Learned Staff Action Directive. Annex A, 12 January 2000, obtained by author under *Access to Information Act* request A-2003-00305/Team 1.

39   It was not possible to obtain records regarding 1 Canadian Air Division requests for war stocks for the years 1997 and 1998 that quantified anticipated war stock requirements in precise numbers using the *Access to Information Act*. The records were exempt from disclosure on the grounds the information could be injurious to the conduct of international affairs. From declassified secret documents obtained under the Act, however, it appears there were requirements for 30-day basis and 30-day additional sustained stocks of GBU-12 and GBU-24s. Canada, Department of National Defence, 1 CAD HQ Winnipeg, Secret A3 OPS RDNS 226, September 1997. Obtained by author under *Access to Information Act* request A-2003-00606/Team 1.

40   Interview by author, Canadian Forces Base Cold Lake, Alberta, 14 April 2003.

41   Martin, "Balkan Rats."

42   Brig. Gen. (ret.) James Cox, interview by author, Ottawa, Ontario, 27 October 2003.

43   Cox interview.

44 Canada, Public Works and Government Services Canada, Eugene B. Rizok, Letter from Public Works and Government Services Canada in Canadian Embassy in Washington to the Deputy Under-Secretary of the Air Force in the Pentagon, 8 April 1999, PWGSC file number W8484-6-WA09, obtained by author under *Access to Information Act* request A-2002-01182/Team 3-2.

45 Brig. Gen (ret.) David Jurkowski, interview by author, Ottawa, Ontario, 27 October 2003.

46 Confidential interview.

47 Evidence of Proceedings, House of Commons Standing Committee on National Defence and Veterans Affairs, Canada, 28 April 1999, online: http://www.parl.gc.ca/InfoCom/Doc/36/1/NDVA/Meetings/Evidence/ndvaev106-e.htm (accessed 10 August 2003).

48 Confidential interview.

49 Confidential interview.

50 Interview by author, Canadian Forces Base Cold Lake, Alberta, 14 April 2003.

51 Bashow et al., "Mission Ready."

52 Interview by author, Canadian Forces Base Cold Lake, Alberta, 14 April 2003.

53 Martin, "Balkan Rats."

54 Martin, "Balkan Rats."

55 Author's observation made during a tour of Canadian Forces Base Cold Lake's CF-18 hangars.

56 Gen. Wesley K. Clark, *Waging Modern War: Bosnia, Kosovo and the Future of Combat* (New York: PublicAffairs, 2002), 193–96.

57 Ibid., 198.

58 Ibid., 224.

59 Ibid., 201.

60 Steven Lee Myers, "All in Favor of This Target, Say Yes, Si, Qui, Ja." *New York Times*, 25 April 1999, Wk. 4.

61 David G. Haglund, ed., *New NATO, New Century: Canada, the U.S., and the Future of the Atlantic Alliance* (Kingston, ON: Centre for International Relations, 2000), viii.

62 Ibid., 425.

63 Lt. Col. Sylvain Faucher, interview by author, Ottawa, Ontario, 29 October 2003.

64 Ivan H. Daalder and Michael E. O'Hanlon, *Winning Ugly: NATO's War to Save Kosovo* (Washington, DC: Brookings Institution Press, 2000), 117.

65 Benjamin Lambeth, "Lessons from the War in Kosovo," *Joint Force Quarterly* (Spring 2002): 12–19.

66 Canada, Department of National Defence, Lt. Gen. R. R. Henault, National Targeting Process for OP Echo, Letter by then-Deputy Chief of Defence Staff to the Chief of Defence Staff et al., 6 July 1999, obtained by author under *Access to Information Act* request A-2003-00305/Team 1.

67 Canada, Department of National Defence, Lt. Gen. R. R. Henault, Operation Echo Lessons Learned Staff Action Directive, Annex A 3453-20 (DLLS), 12 January 2000, obtained by author under *Access to Information Act* request A-2003-00305/Team 1.

68 Ibid.

69 The precision required in modern aerial warfare is a far cry from the indiscriminate bombing discussed by one of the first aerial theorists, Giulio Douhet, who wrote in 1942 that civilian centres should be deliberately targeted in order to spread terror though the nation, advocating "ten, twenty, fifty cities," aiming at the "breakdown of social structure." See Giulio Douhet, *The Command of the Air* (North Stratford, UK: Ayer, 2002), 58–59.

70 "Chimp," interview by author, Canadian Forces Base Cold Lake, Alberta, 14 April 2003.

71 "Midas." Semi-confidential interview by author, full names were withheld by mutual consent if requested and call signs used instead, Canadian Forces Base Cold Lake, Alberta, April 14, 2003.

72 "Mur," interview by author, Canadian Forces Base Cold Lake, Alberta, 15 April 2003.

73 "Willie," interview by author, Canadian Forces Base Cold Lake, Alberta, 15 April 2003.

74 Capt. Kirk Soroka, interview by author, Canadian Forces Base Cold Lake, Alberta, 14 April 2003.

75 Confidential interview.

76 Confidential interview.

Chapter 5

1 Carl von Clausewitz, *On War*, trans. and ed. Michael Howard and Peter Paret (Princeton, NJ: Princeton University Press, 1976), 181.

2 Benjamin S. Lambeth, "Lessons from the War in Kosovo," *Joint Force Quarterly* (Spring 2002): 12–19.

3 Bill Clinton, *My Life* (New York: Alfred A. Knopf, 2004), 851.

4 For eyewitness testimony of the Serbian military's continued ethnic cleansing after the bombing campaign began on 24 March 1999, see Tim Judah, *Kosovo: War and Revenge*, 2nd ed. (New Haven, Ct.: Yale University Press, 2002): 227–64.

5 Judah, *Kosovo: War and Revenge*, 229.

6 Gen. Wesley K. Clark, *Waging Modern War: Bosnia, Kosovo and the Future of Combat* (New York: PublicAffairs, 2002), 221, citing Baron De Jomini, *The Art of War*, trans. G. H. Mendell, and W. P. Craighill (Westport, CT: Greenwood Press, 1862), 63.

7 Ibid., 221; Michael Russell Rip and James M. Hasik, *The Precision Revolution: GPS and the Future of Aerial Warfare* (Annapolis, MD: Naval Institute Press, 2003), 391.

8 Capt. Travis Brassington, interview by author, Canadian Forces Base Cold Lake, Alberta, 14 April 2003.

9 Rip and Hasik, *The Precision Revolution*, 393–99.

10 Capt. Todd Sinclair, interview by author, Canadian Forces Base Cold Lake, Alberta, 14 April 2003.

11 "Chimp," interview by author, Canadian Forces Base Cold Lake, Alberta, 14 April 2003.

12 "Tubs," interview by author, Canadian Forces Base Cold Lake, Alberta, 15 April 2003.

13 Lt. Col. (ret.) William Allen Flynn, telephone interview by author, 9 April 2003.

14 David L. Bashow et al., "Mission Ready: Canada's Role in the Kosovo Air Campaign," *Canadian Military Journal* 1, no. 1 (Spring 2000): 55–61.

15 Dense cloud cover over Serbia and Kosovo for much of the war would have resulted in the Paveway III guided bombs missing their targets and the pilots not knowing where they would have landed. That would have greatly increased the risk of unacceptable collateral damage.

16 Canada, Department of National Defence, National Defence Headquarters, Secret Memo, Message ID 199827000147, CF-18 Weapons Augmentation Request, 27 September 1998, obtained by author under *Access to Information Act* request A-2002-01182/Team 3-2. The relevant declassified secret Canadian Forces documents are heavily vetted, and major portions are exempt on the grounds they could be injurious to the defence of Canada or its allies.

17 Canada, Department of National Defence, National Defence Headquarters. Secret Memo DAEPMFT028, Weapons Augmentation Request, 20 October 98, obtained by author under *Access to Information Act* request A-2002-01182/Team 3-2.

18 Flynn, telephone interview.

19 Canada, Department of National Defence, National Defence Headquarters, Jim Judd, Letter to the Defence Minister, 20 April 99, obtained by author under *Access to Information Act* request A-2002-01182/Team 3-2.

20 Canada, Department of National Defence, National Defence Headquarters, Synopsis Sheet: Ammo Requirement OP Echo – Guided Bomb Unit (GBU) bombs, 20 April 1999, obtained by author under *Access to Information Act* request A-2002-01182/Team 3-2.

21 Bombs don't come fully assembled. The tail fins, for example, come in a can, the guidance system comes in a box or "coffin," and the bomb itself comes on a pallet.

22 Confidential interview with author, names were withheld by mutual consent if requested, Canadian Forces Base Cold Lake, Alberta, 16 April 2003.

23 Canada, Supply and Services Canada, Contract with the government of the U.S. of America, DSS file No. W8484-9-WA01 PT.2, 3 June 1999, obtained by author under *Access to Information Act* request A-2002-01182/Team 3-2.

24 Flynn, telephone interview.

25 Bashow et al., "Mission Ready," 58.

26 Maj. Kirk Soroka, interview by author, Canadian Forces Base Cold Lake, Alberta, 14 April 2003.

27 Maj. Alain Pelletier, telephone interview by author, 13 August 2003.

28 Brig. Gen. (ret.) David Jurkowski, interview by author, Ottawa, Ontario, 27 October 2003.

29   Gen. Raymond Henault, telephone interview by author, 22 September 2003.
30   Flynn, telephone interview. Night-vision capability was added to the CF-18s between 2003 and 2009.
31   Canada, Department of National Defence, Concepts of Operations for the Use of Night-vision Goggles in the CF-18, 441 TFS, 20 November 1997, obtained by author under *Access to Information Act* request A-2003-00139/Team 2-3.
32   Canada, Department of National Defence, Minute to Wing Commander from Wing Operations officer Lt. Col. J. M. Ouellet, 6 October 1997, obtained by author under *Access to Information Act* request A-2003-00139/Team 2-3.
33   Canada, Department of National Defence, Col. R. W. Guidinger, Wing Commander, 4 Wing Cold Lake, letter to National Defence Headquarters, 27 October 1997, obtained by author under *Access to Information Act* request A-2003-00139/Team 2-3.
34   Canada, Department of National Defence, Concepts of Operations for the Use of Night-vision Goggles in the CF-18, 441 TFS, 20 November 1997, obtained by author under *Access to Information Act* request A-2003-00139/Team 2-3.
35   Canada, Department of National Defence, Minutes of the CF-18 NVG Project Committee Meeting, 28 April 1998, obtained by author under *Access to Information Act* request A-2003-00139/Team 2-3. Details of cockpit light issues to be addressed at that time in order to accommodate the use of night-vision goggles were exempted from disclosure under the *Access to Information Act*, citing trade secrets, confidentiality, and potential for loss of material gain provisions.
36   Canada, Department of National Defence, 441 OT&E Proposal, undated, obtained by author under *Access to Information Act* request A-2003-00139/Team 2-3.
37   Flynn, telephone interview.
38   Flynn, telephone interview.
39   Soroka, interview.
40   Confidential telephone interview by author, names were withheld by mutual consent if requested, 10 October 2003.
41   Capt. Brett Glaeser, interview by author, Canadian Forces Base Cold Lake, Alberta, 15 April 2003.
42   Glaeser, interview.
43   Glaeser, interview.
44   "Hooker," telephone interview by author, 24 April 2003.
45   "Hooker," telephone interview.
46   "Hooker," telephone interview.
47   Soroka, interview.
48   Brassington, interview.
49   Capt. Neil McRury, interview by author, Canadian Forces Base Cold Lake, Alberta, 16 April 2003.
50   Confidential interview.

51 Glaeser, interview.

52 Soroka, interview

53 McRury, interview.

54 Brassington, interview.

CHAPTER 6

1   Justine Hunter, "Harassment: Navy wife finds body bag on her lawn in a series of incidents in Victoria area," *Vancouver Sun*, 21 January 1991, B1.

2   Ibid.

3   "Gulf's cruelties here and there," *Vancouver Sun*, 21 January 1991, A10.

4   Canada, House of Commons, *Debates*, vol. 13 (22 January 1991), 17567–17568.

5   Vietnam is often thought to be the first "television war" because its film showed audiences worldwide war's brutality. Daniel C. Hallin, *The "Uncensored War": The Media and Vietnam* (Berkeley: University of California Press, 1989); Todd Gitlin, *The Whole World Is Watching: Mass Media in the Making & Unmaking of the New Left* (Berkeley: University of California Press, 1980). But most of its footage was shown days or weeks after it was taken because it had to be physically transported to the United States, as opposed to the real time television that satellite technology enabled.

6   W. Lance Bennett and David L. Paletz, eds., *Taken By Storm: The Media, Public Opinion, and U.S. Foreign Policy in the Gulf War* (Chicago: University of Chicago Press, 1994); John J. Fialka, *Hotel Warriors: Covering the Gulf War* (Washington, DC: Woodrow Wilson Centre Press, 1992).

7   Canada, Department of National Defence, Operation Friction: Canadian Forces Operations in the Persian Gulf Communications Plan, 15 August 1990, obtained by author under *Access to Information Act* request A-2003-00394.

8   Operation Friction: Canadian Forces Operations in the Persian Gulf Communications Plan.

9   Ibid.

10 Ibid.

11 Ibid.

12 Canada, Department of National Defence, After Action Report, Operation Friction: Director General Public Affairs, 24 July 1991, obtained by author under *Access to Information Act* request A-2003-00394.

13 Ibid.

14 Operation Friction: Canadian Forces Operations in the Persian Gulf Communications Plan.

15 Ibid.

16 Ibid.

17 Canada, Department National Defence, Communications Plan: Rotation of Ships' Companies CTG 302.3, 4 December 1990, obtained by author under *Access to Information Act* request A-2003-00394.

18 Communications Plan: Rotation of Ships' Companies.

19 Ibid.

20 Canada, Department of National Defence, Briefing Note Concerning Agenda Item X, CDS meeting with Group Principals, 0900 Hrs., 2 January 1991, obtained by author under *Access to Information Act* request A-2003-00394.

21 Canada, Department of National Defence, Canadian Forces Headquarters Middle East Public Affairs War Operations Plan, 14 January 1991, obtained by author under *Access to Information Act* request A-2003-00394.

22 Ibid.

23 Canada, National Defence Headquarters, Priority Message from NDHQ Ottawa// CDS//, Op Friction MSN and Roles/Official Spokespersons, 15 January 1991, obtained by author under *Access to Information Act*: request A-2003-00394.

24 Canada, House of Commons, *Debates*, vol. 13 (16 January 1991), 17164 (Mr. Mulroney, Prime Minister).

25 Online: http://members.lycos.co.uk/Hornet/index-20 (accessed 8 March 2004).

26 Brig. Gen. (ret.) Ed McGillivray, interview by author, Calgary, Alberta, 12 August 2003.

27 Pat Brennan, "'I'm heading out,' pilot tells mom," *Toronto Star*, 18 January 1991, A20; Anna-Maria Galante, "Kentville parents worried about son in Gulf," *Chronicle-Herald* (Halifax), 21 January 1991, A3; Janice Tibbetts, "Peace protests upset families of Gulf troops," *Chronicle-Herald* (Halifax), 21 January 1991, A3; Anna-Maria Galante, "Kentville native tapped for first CF-18 mission," *Chronicle-Herald* (Halifax), 22 January 1991, A4; Kelly Shiers, "War bonds women across the miles," *Chronicle-Herald* (Halifax), 22 January 1991, A1.

28 McGillivray, interview. Also see: "Pilot's wife faced with helping children cope," *Chronicle-Herald* (Halifax), 19 January 1991, A2; George Oake, "Cold Lake supports its fliers," *Toronto Star*, 24 January 1991, A20; Sylvia Lee and Terry Johnson, "A town at war," *Report*, 28 January 1991, online: http://report.ca/classics/o1281991/p12i910128f.html (accessed 10 August 2003).

29 "Persian Gulf war recreates spirit of simple soldier," *Fort Worth Star Telegram*, reprinted in the *Chronicle-Herald* (Halifax), 21 January 1991, A7.

30 "Canadian soldiers watch deadline pass, 'waiting for war,'" *Chronicle-Herald* (Halifax), 17 January 1991, A3; Jim Gowen, "Field hospital posting frightening – N.S. technician," *Chronicle-Herald* (Halifax), 19 January 1991, D21; Stephen Ward, "Bad weather scrubs CF-18s' first mission," *Gazette* (Montreal), 21 January 1991, A5; "Weather scrubs two Canadian jet sorties," *Vancouver Sun*, 21 January 1991, A6; Michael Hanlon, "Weather delays combat by Canadian fighters," *Toronto Star*, 21 January 1991, A14; Stephen Ward, "Bad weather keeps CF-18s out of the danger zone," *Gazette* (Montreal), 22 January 1991, A9; Stephen Ward, "Cloud keeps Canadians grounded," *Calgary Herald*, 23

January 1991, A6; Michael Hanlon, "Canadian jet pilots 'psyched up' for war," *Toronto Star*, 23 January 1991, A19.

31 Charles H. Brown, *Informing the People* (New York: Holt, Rinehart and Winston, 1957), 73.

32 *Stylebook: A Guide for Writers and Editors* (Toronto: Canadian Press, 1983), 156. Canadian university textbooks on news writing and reporting are silent on military coverage. See Carmen Cumming and Catherine McKercher, *The Canadian Reporter: News Writing and Reporting* (Toronto: Harcourt Brace, 1994); Maxine Ruvinsky, *Investigative Reporting in Canada* (Don Mills, On: Oxford University Press, 2008).

33 Mary Gooderham, "Noisy crowd blocks traffic: Protestors angry over Gulf attack," *Globe and Mail*, 17 January 1991, A10; Rosie DiManno, "Political agendas on the march as wartime hits the peace front," *Toronto Star*, 18 January 1991, A7; David Shoalts and Mary Gooderham, "Sanctions given no time to work, protestors say," *Globe and Mail*, 18 January 1991, A10.

34 Shoalts and Gooderham, "Sanctions"; Paul Moloney, "Marchers burn flags in protest," *Toronto Star*, 20 January 1991, C7; Keith Damsell and Susan Chung, "Anti-war demonstrations build," *Toronto Star*, 21 January 1991, A4; "Halifax, Amherst sites of anti-war protests," *Chronicle-Herald* (Halifax), 21 January 1991, A1.

35 "Ottawa tightens water plant security," *Toronto Star*, 22 January 1991, A16.

36 "Police disrupt Ottawa protest," *Toronto Star*, 22 January 1991, A16.

37 Robert MacLeod, "Police increase security against terrorist attacks," *Globe and Mail*, 18 January 1991, A7.

38 Bruce Erskine, "Local authorities increase vigilance," *Chronicle-Herald* (Halifax), 18 January 1991, A4; Tom Peters and Barry Dorey, "Security beefed up at Halifax airport," *Chronicle-Herald* (Halifax), 23 January 1991, A5.

39 Andre Picard, "Quebec preparing to increase security," *Globe and Mail*, 19 January 1991, A9.

40 Maureen Murray and Bob Brent, "Police issue nationwide security alert," *Toronto Star*, 17 January 1991, A17.

41 Keith Damsell and Susan Chung, "Anti-war demonstrations build," *Toronto Star*, 21 January 1991.

42 "Censorship guidelines to restrict war reporting." *Globe and Mail*, 19 January 1991, A10.

43 Sally Ritchie, "News censorship follows a pattern: Rules similar to Second World War," *Globe and Mail*, 21 January 1991, 9.

44 Ritchie, "News censorship follows a pattern."

45 House of Commons, *Debates*, vol. 13 (21 January 1991), 1750 (Mr. Mulroney, Prime Minister).

46 Ibid. (Mr. McKnight, Minister of Defence).

47 Hunter, "Harassment: Navy wife finds body bag on her lawn in a series of incidents in Victoria area."

48 Tim Harper, "Military sure of public support despite harassing calls to wives," *Toronto Star*, 24 January 1991, A20.

49 William Walker, "Police probing threats to military families," *Toronto Star*, 25 January 1991, A18.

50 Ibid.

51 Don MacDonald, "Forces families harassed," *Chronicle-Herald*, 25 January 1991, A3.

52 "CF-18s to 'sweep and escort,'" *Vancouver Sun*, 23 January 1991, A4; William Walker, "Canadian pilots sent into combat," *Toronto Star*, 20 January 1991, A1; as an aside, pilots often refer to their formations as "four-ship" formations, as opposed to "four-jet" formations.

53 Galante, "Kentville native tapped for first CF-18 mission."

54 Michael Hanlon, "Canadian jet pilots 'psyched up' for war," *Toronto Star*, 23 January 1991, A19.

55 Michael Hanlon, "Canadian pilots join first bombing mission," *Toronto Star*, 25 January 1991, A16.

56 Tony Wong, "Canadian fighter pilot a 'bit of a daredevil,'" *Toronto Star*, 26 January 1991, A10.

57 Hanlon, "Canadian pilots join first bombing mission."

58 Lt. Col. (ret.) Dave Matthews, interview by author, Calgary, Alberta. 21 November 2003.

59 Scott White, "Canadian troops fear harassment of families back home," *Gazette* (Montreal), 28 January 1991, A7.

60 Alan Ferguson, "CF-18 pilots shun limelight: Crank threats to families may have turned pilots shy," *Toronto Star*, 28 January 1991, A12.

61 Hugh Winsor and Ross Howard, "Ottawa moves to gain support for Gulf role, boost troop morale," *Globe and Mail*, 5 February 1991, A9.

62 Ibid.

63 Geoffrey York, "Weaponry on CF-18s not changing, military says," *Globe and Mail*, 30 January 1991, A12.

64 "Crank calls lead military to request media help," *Chronicle-Herald* (Halifax). 28 January 1991, A5.

65 Terrance Wills, "Canadian Forces brass put zipper on information about the war," *Gazette* (Montreal), 23 January 1991, A5.

66 "Censors: Shh . . . there's a war on," *Calgary Herald*, 24 January 1991, A5; "Canadian journalists say they are frustrated by censorship," *Vancouver Sun*, 24 January 1991, A6.

67 "Canadian journalists say they are frustrated by censorship," *Vancouver Sun*, 24 January 1991, A6. Also see: "CF-18 mission reports under strict censorship," *Vancouver Sun*, 23 January 1991, A8; Tim Harper, "Military puts new restrictions on information," *Toronto Star*, 23 January 1991, A19; "Canadian reporters blocked from media pools, editors say," *Toronto Star*, 23 January 1991, A20; Allan McRae, Canadian journalists want access to front," *Gazette* (Montreal), 24 January 1991, A6; "Canadian media

protest exclusion," *Globe and Mail*, 24 January 1991, A14; Evans Lipton, "Military censorship has become an issue in Persian Gulf," *Toronto Star*, 28 January 1991, A18.

68 Paul Koring, "Media army covers wars from hotels," *Globe and Mail*, 24 January 1991, A1.
69 Ibid.
70 Linda Hossie, "All quiet on the news front: Lack of war information 'very undemocratic,'" *Globe and Mail*, 24 January 1991, A15.
71 William Walker, "Does Ottawa get news of Gulf war from TV?" *Toronto Star*, 25 January 1991, A16.
72 Ibid.
73 Geoffrey York, "U.S. only source of war details, MPs told," *Globe and Mail*, 26 January 1991, A10.
74 Canada, Department of National Defence, Directorate of Public Affairs Operations, Media Guidelines, 20 February 1991, obtained by author under *Access to Information Act* request A-2003-00394.
75 Ibid.
76 Matthew Fisher, "Pilots glad to switch to bombing," *Globe and Mail*, 22 February 1991, A12.
77 Matthew Fisher, "Canada launches bombing," *Globe and Mail*, 25 February 1991, A11.
78 Alan Ferguson, "CF-18s pilots shun limelight," *Toronto Star*, 28 January 1991, A12.
79 Robert Mason Lee, "First shots: CF-18 pilots asked to join attack on Iraqi boats," *Gazette* (Montreal), 31 January 1991, A8.
80 Ross Howard, "Pilots reprimanded for firing at Iraqi ship," *Globe and Mail*, 6 February 1991, A11.
81 "Canadian pilots commended," *Chronicle-Herald* (Halifax), 7 February 1991, A4.
82 "Servicewomen in Gulf coping in male-dominated environment," *Chronicle-Herald* (Halifax), 4 February 1991, A3.
83 "*Huron* wives' trek worth it," *Chronicle-Herald* (Halifax), 16 February 1991, A4.
84 "CF-18s to assume offensive in ground attacks," *Chronicle-Herald* (Halifax), 21 February 1991, A1.
85 Fisher, "Pilots glad to switch to bombing."
86 Fisher, "Canada launches bombing."
87 Alan Ferguson, "Owen Sound pilot leads CF-18s jets on first bombing run," *Toronto Star*, 25 February 1991, A14.
88 Brian Kennedy, "CF-18s carry out bombing missions," *Chronicle-Herald* (Halifax), 25 February 1991, A1.
89 Canada, Department of National Defence, After Action Report: Gulf War Public Affairs, Director General Public Affairs. 23 April 1991, obtained by author under the *Access to Information Act* request A-2003-00394.

90 Online: http://members.lycos.co.uk/Hornet/index-20 (accessed 8 March 2004).
91 Matthews, interview.
92 Alan Ferguson, "Owen Sound pilot leads CF-18 jets," *Toronto Star*, 25 February 1991, A14.
93 Online: http://news.bbc.co.uk/1/shared/spl/hi/middle_east/03/v3_iraq_timeline/html/ground_war.stm.
94 Matthews, interview.
95 Canada, Department of National Defence, After Action Report: Gulf War Public Affairs, Director General Public Affairs, 23 April 1991, obtained by author under the *Access to Information Act* request A-2003-00394.
96 Canada, Department of National Defence, After Action Report: Gulf War Public Affairs, Director General Public Affairs, 23 April 1991, obtained by author under the *Access to Information Act* request A-2003-00394.
97 Ibid.
98 Ibid.
99 Terrance Wills, "Female soldiers told to wear civilian clothes," *Gazette* (Montreal), 25 January 1997, A7.
100 William Walker, "Police probing threats to military families," *Toronto Star*, 25 January 1991, A18.
101 Deborah Wilson, "Military wives harassed: Phone calls, letters say husbands killed," *Globe and Mail*, 22 January 1991, A10.
102 The author was a journalist at the *Calgary Herald* writing about events and issues in Canada involving the war effort. I called the civilian police in Victoria and the civilian and military police in Esquimalt after the *Globe and Mail*'s story was published. The same information was received from the police: they had no evidence that the incidents took place.
103 Canada, Department of National Defence, Judith A. Mooney, Director of Access to Information and Privacy, letter to author, 7 October 2003, in response to *Access to Information Act* request A-2003-00704/Team 3-6.
104 Lt. Cmdr. (N) Paul Seguna, telephone interview by author, 16 October 2003; telephone calls by author to 11 Medical Company, 16 October and 5 November 2003.
105 Wilson, "Military wives harassed."
106 Tim Harper, "Military sure of public support despite harassing calls to wives," *Toronto Star*, 24 January 1991, A20.
107 Wilson, "Military wives harassed."
108 Ibid.
109 CHEK 6 was bought by CanWest Global in 2000 and became for a time CH TV in Victoria. Its news archives were searched for stories relating to the 1991 harassment of Esquimalt military families for this study by CH TV journalist Hudson Mack on 3 October 2003. Mack had worked at the television station since 1985. His archive search failed to discover any such stories.

110 Seguna, telephone interview.

111 McGillivray, interview.

112 Matthews, interview.

113 Bill Cleverley, "Armbands to protest 'glorifying' of Gulf War," *Times Colonist* (Victoria), 2 January 1991, A1.

114 "Here are the crewmembers of Gulf bound HMCS *Huron*," *Times Colonist* (Victoria), 4 January 1991, A10. The headline writer got it wrong. It was the crew that was bound for the Gulf, not the ship.

115 Judith Lavoie, "Military wives march to back husbands," *Times Colonist* (Victoria), 16 January 1991, B1.

116 Ibid.

117 Bill Cleverley, "Esquimalt base tightens checks," *Times Colonist* (Victoria), 18 January 1991, A7.

118 "Hoax bomb call at HMC Dockyard sparks evacuation," *Times Colonist* (Victoria), 18 January 1991, A7.

119 Judith Lavoie, "Victoria peace activists being harassed, says woman," *Times Colonist* (Victoria), 19 January 1991, A6.

120 Ibid.

121 Judith Lavoie, "Service wives 'reluctant' to report harassment to police," *Times Colonist* (Victoria), 27 January 1991, A6.

122 Ibid.

123 Ibid.

124 Ibid.

125 Murray Edelman, *Politics as Symbolic Action: Mass Arousal and Quiescence* (Chicago: Markham, 1971), 14.

126 Ibid., 157.

Chapter 7

1 Joy Malbon, interview by author, Ottawa, Ontario, 28 October 2003.

2 Phillip Knightley, The First Casualty: The War Correspondent as Hero and Myth-Maker from the Crimea to Iraq (New York: Harcourt Brace Jovanovich, 1975), 12–13.

3 Jeffrey A. Keshen, *Propaganda and Censorship during Canada's Great War* (Edmonton: University of Alberta Press, 1996), 31–32.

4 W. H. Kesterton, *A History of Journalism in Canada* (Toronto: McClelland and Stewart, 1967), 210.

5 Robert Bergen, "Censorship; The Canadian News Media and Afghanistan: A Historical Comparison with Case Studies," Calgary Papers in Military and Strategic Studies, Occasional Paper no. 3 (Calgary: University of Calgary Press, 2009), 6–10.

6   Kesterton, A History of Journalism in Canada, 214.

7   *The Charter of Rights and Freedoms: A Guide for Canadians* (Ottawa: Minister of Supply and Services Canada, 1983), 3.

8   The origins of the characterization of the news media as the "fourth estate," the guardians of democracy serving the public interest in its oversight of the workings of government, are widely misunderstood. The most common reference to the press as the "fourth estate" is found in the nineteenth-century works of author Thomas Carlyle. Carlyle wrote on the business of government, saying that far more comprehensive debate about the government's business took place outside Parliament thanks to the fourth estate that sat in the reporters' gallery. Carlyle wrote: "Burke said there were Three Estates in Parliament; but, in the Reporters' Gallery yonder, there sat a *Fourth Estate* more important far than they all. It is not a figure of speech, or a witty saying; it is a literal fact, – very momentous to us in these times. Literature is our Parliament too. Printing, which comes necessarily out of Writing, I say often, is equivalent to Democracy: invent Writing, Democracy is inevitable. Writing brings Printing; bring universal every-day extempore Printing, as we see present. Whoever can speak, speaking now to the whole nation, becomes a power, a branch of government, with inalienable weight in law making, in all acts of authority." Thomas Carlyle, *Sartor Resartus; On Heroes and Hero Worship* (London: Dent Dutton, 1965), 392. It has been widely accepted that Burke penned all those words. In fact, the term "fourth estate" appears in none of Burke's published works. See Paul Langford, ed., *The Writings and Speeches of Edmund Burke*, vols. 1–12 (Oxford: Clarendon Press, 1996). The term "Fourth Estate" is actually found in an essay by Lord Macaulay published in the *Edinburg Review* in 1828 and reprinted in Hallam's *Constitutional History of England*. Macaulay wrote: "The gallery in which the reporters sit has become the fourth estate of the realm. The publication of debates, a practice which seemed to the most liberal statesmen of the old school full of danger to the great safeguards or public liberty, is now regarded by many persons as a safeguard tantamount, and more than tantamount, to all the rest together." "Lord Macaulay on Hallam's Constitutional History of England," in Henry Hallam, *The Constitutional History of England*, vol. 2 (London: Alex Murray & Co., 1872), 930.

9   Canada, Department of National Defence, After Action Report, Operation Friction, Director General Public Affairs, Memorandum (Draft) 1350-3350 (DGPA), 24 July 1991, obtained by author under *Access to Information Act* request A-2003-00394/Team 3.

10 Ibid.

11 Ibid.

12 Canada, Department of National Defence, After Action Report: Gulf War Public Affairs. Lt. Col. R. C. Coleman, Memorandum 3350-OF-3 (DND PA), 25 April 1991, obtained by author under *Access to Information Act* request A-2003-00394/Team 3.

13 Ibid.

14 Canada, Department of National Defence, *Adjusting Course: A Naval Strategy for Canada*, April 1997, 7.

15 Canada, Department of National Defence, Army Lessons Learned Centre, "Media Relations," Dispatches, vol. 4, no. 3 (March 1997), 6.

16 Ibid.

17 Bob Bergen, "Soldiers offer journalists a true taste of war," *Calgary Herald*, 2 June 1997, B2.

18 Canada, Department of National Defence, The Land Force Strategic Guidance and Direction. pt. 1, chap. 2, 1–16. Online: http://army.dwan.dnd.ca/dlsp/LFSDG_e/Part1/Chapter_2.htm (accessed 16 September 1998).

19 Canada, Department of National Defence, DAOD 2008-4, Public Affairs, Military Doctrine and Canadian Forces Operations, online: http://admfincs.forces.gc.ca/admfincs/subjects/daod/2008/4_e.asp (accessed 23 June 2005).

20 Ibid. Due to changes in titles, the 2005 website document makes the Assistant Deputy Minister for Public Affairs ADM (PA) responsible for the development of a national public affairs plan, but in 1999 the person responsible for the plan was the Director General Public Affairs (DGPA).

21 Ibid.

22 Ibid.

23 Malbon, interview.

24 Malbon, interview.

25 Malbon, interview.

26 "Gagging the Media," *National Post*, 25 March 1999, A13.

27 Mark Henderson and Carol Midgley, "Belgrade steps up expulsion of press 'spies,'" *Times* (London), 26 March 1999, 2.

28 Juliette Terzieff, "Journalists threatened, beaten in Kosovo," *National Post*, 26 March 1999, A13.

29 Olivia Ward, "Bombs spark Serb fury: Western journalists expelled at gunpoint in capital," *Toronto Star*, 26 March 1999, A1.

30 Canada, House of Commons, *Debates*, vol. 135, no. 234 (31 May 1999), 15501.

31 Canada, Evidence of Proceedings, House of Commons Standing Committee on National Defence and Veterans Affairs, 31 March 1999, online: http://www.parl.gc.ca/InfoCom/Doc/36/1/NDVA/Meetings/Evidence/ndvaev99-e.htm (accessed 10 August 2003).

32 Ibid.

33 Lt. Cmdr. Jeff Agnew, telephone interview by author, 30 June 2005.

34 Canada, Department of National Defence, Transcript of briefing by DCDS – Media Q, 24 March 99, obtained by author from National Defence Public Affairs Office – Calgary (hereafter Transcript of briefing by DCDS), online: http://dgpa-dgpa.mil.ca/Transcr/1999Mar/99032409.htm (accessed 8 July 2003).

35 Transcript of briefing by DCDS, 24 March 1999.

36 Ibid.

37 Ibid.

38 Brig. Gen. (ret.) James Cox, interview by author, Ottawa, Ontario, 27 October 2003.
39 Transcript of briefing by DCDS, 24 March 1999.
40 Ibid.
41 Gen. Wesley K. Clark, *Waging Modern War: Bosnia, Kosovo and the Future of Combat* (New York: PublicAffairs, 2002), 195.
42 NATO, NATO's role in Kosovo, Press conference transcript, 25 March 1999, online: http://www.nato.int/kosovo/press/p990325a.htm.
43 Ibid.
44 "War with Yugoslavia" *Vancouver Sun*, 25 March 1999, A19; "NATO blasts Yugoslavia." *Calgary Herald*, 25 March 1999, A1; John Ward, "Canada's CF-18s given baptism of fire," *Calgary Herald*, 25 March 1999, D4; "Yugoslavia pounded by NATO," *Province* (Vancouver), 25 March 1999, A2; Aileen McCabe and John Nadler, "The bombing begins," *Edmonton Journal*, 25 March 1999, A1; Aileen McCabe and John Nadler, "Serbs under fire," *Gazette* (Montreal) 25 March 1999, A1; Tim Naumetz, "PM says report proves he's clean on 'Shawinigate,'" *Ottawa Citizen*, 25 March 1999, A9; William Walker, "Canadian jets attack targets," *Toronto Star*, 25 March 1999, A11; John Ward, "CF-18s strike at Kosovo: Planes return safe from raid," *Hamilton Spectator*, 25 March 1999, C1; "NATO pounds Serb targets," *Daily News* (Halifax), 25 March 1999, 8; "NATO missiles pummel Yugoslavia," *Toronto Sun*, 25 March 1999, 2; Joel-Denis Bellevance, "Canadian fighters join risky battle against Yugoslavia," *National Post* (Toronto), 25 March 1999, A14; John Ward, "Canadian jets join NATO onslaught," *Times Colonist* (Victoria), 25 March 1999, A3; "Canadian jets safe after NATO strikes," *Guardian* (Charlottetown), 25 March 1999, B7; Graham Fraser, "Canadians in first wave of strikes on Serbia," *Globe and Mail*, 25 March 1999, A1.
45 Bob Gilmore, "Canadian fighter pilots in good spirits after raid," *Edmonton Journal*, 25 March 1999, A6; John Ward, "CF-18 pilots return safely," *Gazette* (Montreal), 25 March 1999, B1.
46 Kate Jaimet, "Home base proud of Canadian crews," *Ottawa Citizen*, 25 March 1999, A4.
47 "Canadian warplanes in action," The National, CBC-TV, 25 March 1999, Broadcast transcript, Canadian NewsDisc.
48 Transcript of briefing by DCDS, 25 March 99. online: http://dgpa-dgpa.mil.ca/Transcr/1999Mar/99032509.htm (accessed 7 July 2003).
49 Clark, *Waging Modern War*, 442.
50 Transcript of briefing by DCDS, 25 March 99.
51 Ibid.
52 Ibid.
53 Ibid.
54 Joy Malbon, email correspondence to author, 24 June 1999.
55 Malbon, email correspondence.
56 Malbon, email correspondence.

57 James Landale and John Phillips, "Two Serb Jets shot down over no-fly zone," *Times* (London), 27 March 1999, 2.
58 Malbon, interview.
59 Neil Macdonald, telephone interview by author, 5 September 2003.
60 Macdonald, telephone interview.
61 Macdonald, telephone interview.
62 Malbon, interview.
63 Canada, Department of National Defence, Capt. Mietzner, email correspondence with Lt. Col. S. Wills, Director of Air Force Public Affairs, 19 March 1999, obtained by author under *Access to Information Act* request A-2002-01184/Team 2.
64 Canada, Department of National Defence, Lt. L. Wilson, email correspondence with Lt. Col. S. Wills, Director of Air Force Public Affairs, 25 March 1999, obtained by author under *Access to Information Act* request A-2002-01184/Team 2.
65 Canada, Department of National Defence, Lt. Cmdr. Jeff Agnew, email correspondence, Distribution list, 26 March 1999, obtained by author under *Access to Information Act* request A-2002-01184/Team 2.
66 Transcript of briefing by DCDS, 26 March 1999.
67 Confidential interview with author, names were withheld by mutual agreement if requested, Canadian Forces Base Cold Lake, 16 April 2003.
68 Transcript of briefing by DCDS, 26 March 1999.
69 Col. (ret.) Jim Donihee, interview by author, Calgary, Alberta, 22 April 2003.
70 Capt. Travis Brassington, interview by author, Canadian Forces Base Cold Lake, Alberta, 14 April 2003.
71 Vicki Hall, "Cold Lake pilots head for conflict; Families watch as loved ones thunder into sky," *Edmonton Journal*, 27 March 1999, A8.
72 Ibid.; Kenny Eoin, "Families bid farewell to pilots," *Calgary Herald*, 27 March 1999, D1; "A tearful farewell to Canadian pilots," *Ottawa Citizen*, 27 March 1999, A10; "4 Wing Command prepares for mission over Yugoslavia: 4 jets take off for Italy," *National Post* (Toronto), 27 March 1999, A13.
73 Brassington, interview.
74 Transcript of briefing by DCDS, 27 March 1999.
75 William Walker, "Canadian pilots miss military targets," *Toronto Star*, 27 March 1999, A15.
76 Rosie DiManno, "Canadian jets change targets: Serb troops now in the line of fire in NATO attacks," *Toronto Star*, 30 March 1999, A9.
77 Transcript of briefing by DCDS, 28 March 1999.
78 Transcript of briefing by DCDS, 31 March 1999.
79 Canada, Department of National Defence, Briefing Note prepared for CAS: Op Echo – Communications Approach Issue by Lt. (N) John D. Coppard, D Air PA 2-2. 31 March 1999, obtained by author under *Access to Information Act* request A-2002-01184/Team 2.

80 Ibid.
81 Ibid.
82 Ibid.
83 Ibid.
84 Lt. Cmdr. Jeff Agnew, telephone interview by author, 30 June 2005.
85 Confidential telephone interview with author, names were withheld by mutual agreement if requested, 8 September 2003.
86 Confidential telephone interview.
87 Confidential telephone interview.
88 Confidential telephone interview.
89 "In this country, most MPs on the Commons Defence and Foreign Affairs committees endorsed Canada's role in the NATO air campaign," CTV National News, CTV, 31 March 1999, Canadian NewsDisc.

Chapter 8

1 Neil Macdonald, telephone interview by author, 5 September 2003.
2 Macdonald, telephone interview.
3 "A Canadian pilot's story," The National, CBC-TV, 2 April 1999, Canadian NewsDisc.
4 Canada, Department of National Defence, Transcript of briefing by DCDS – Media Q, 2 April 1999, obtained by author from National Defence Public Affairs Office – Calgary (hereafter Transcript of briefing by DCDS). online: http://dgpa-dgpa.mil.ca/Transcr/1999Apr/99040207.htm (accessed 16 July 2003).
5 Transcript of briefing by DCDS, 2 April 1999.
6 "Canadian pilots based in Aviano, Italy, have been flying combat missions into Yugoslavia and now we have a Canadian pilot's eyewitness account," CTV National News, CTV, 2 April 1999, Canadian NewsDisc; Tim Harper, "Canadian pilot tells of mission into enemy skies," *Toronto Star*, 3 April 1999, A23; "NATO cruise missile attack shakes Yugoslavia's capital," *Vancouver Sun*, 3 April 1999, A1; Joan Bryden, "Canadian pilot nervous and proud," *Edmonton Journal*, 3 April 1999, A1; Joan Bryden, "I admit, sometimes I wanted to cry," *Ottawa Citizen*, 3 April 1999, A5; Joan Bryden, "For CF-18 pilots, fear, excitement and pride," *Gazette* (Montreal), 3 April 1999, A19; Joan Bryden, "People are going to shoot at you," *Daily News* (Halifax), 3 April 1999, 10; Stephanie Rubec, "Missiles and MiGs all in a day's work," *Toronto Sun*, 3 April 1999, 5; Leanne Yohemas-Hayes, "'Sometimes I wanted to cry," *Hamilton Spectator*, 3 April 1999, B1; Geoffrey York, "Human factor never in my mind," *Globe and Mail*, 3 April 1999, A1.
7 Lt. Cmdr. Jeff Agnew, telephone interview by author, 30 June 2005.
8 Lt. Col. Sylvain Faucher, interview by author, Ottawa, Ontario, 29 October 2003.
9 Geoffrey York, email correspondence to author, 11 August 2003.
10 Transcript of briefing by DCDS, 4 April 1999.

11 United States, Department of Defence, Office of the Assistant Secretary of Defense (Public Affairs), DoD News briefing, 6 April 1999 (hereafter DoD News briefing). Online: http://www.pentagon.mil/transcripts/1999/t04061999_t0406asd.html (accessed 4 July 2005).

12 Transcript of briefing by DCDS, 6 April 1999.

13 Ibid.

14 Ibid.

15 Rosie DiManno, "Aviano: The counterpoint to chaos," *Toronto Star*, 8 April 1999, A9.

16 Geoffrey York, "Canadian operations kept under wraps," *Globe and Mail*, 9 April 1999, A18.

17 Ibid.

18 Geoffrey York, email correspondence to author, 11 August 2003.

19 Transcript of briefing by DCDS, 14 April 1999.

20 Ibid.

21 Ibid.

22 Transcript of briefing by DCDS, 17 April 99.

23 "My first combat mission," *Maple Leaf*, vol. 2, no. 7, 15 April 1999. Online: http://www.forces.gc.ca/site/community/mapleleaf/html (accessed 9 September 2003).

24 "Pilots tell of combat stress," *Gazette* (Montreal), 26 April 1999, A12; "CF-18 pilot recounts first combat mission," *Daily News* (Halifax), 6 April 1999; "Military journal reveals pilot's brush with Serbs," *Times Colonist* (Victoria), 26 April 1999, A3; "Canadian pilot details harrowing mission," *Globe and Mail*, 26 April 1999, A12.

25 Faucher, interview.

26 DoD News briefing, 16 April 1999.

27 Ibid.

28 Ibid.

29 DoD News briefing, 2 April 1999.

30 Transcript of briefing by DCDS, 17 April 1999.

31 Transcript of briefing by DCDS, 18 April 1999.

32 Ibid.

33 Phillip Knightley, The First Casualty: The War Correspondent as Hero and Myth-Maker from the Crimea to Iraq (New York: Harcourt Brace Jovanovich, 1975).

34 Robert Bergen, "Censorship; the Canadian News Media and Afghanistan: A Historical Comparison with Case Studies," Calgary Papers in Military and Strategic Studies, Occasional Paper no. 3 (Calgary: University of Calgary Press, 2009).

35 "Canada on the attack," CBC News, online: http://www.cbc.ca/news/indepth/canadaattack/military.html (accessed 17 June 2003).

36 Gen. (ret.) Maurice Baril, telephone interview by author, 3 November 2003.

37 Baril, telephone interview.
38 Joe Warmington, telephone interview with author, 15 September 2003.
39 Robert W. Bergen, "Balkan Rats and Balkan Bats" (PhD diss., University of Calgary, 2005), 312
40 NATO, NATO's role in Kosovo, Press conference transcript, 31 March 1999, online: http://www.nato.int/kosovo/all-frce.htm.
41 Joy Malbon, interview by author, Ottawa, Ontario, 28 October 2003.
42 Malbon, interview.
43 Malbon, interview.
44 Lt. Cmdr. (N) John Larsen, interview by author, Calgary, Alberta, 19 June 2003.
45 Larsen, interview.
46 Larsen, interview.
47 Larsen, interview.
48 "A Canadian pilot's view of Canada's role in the NATO bombing raid," *CTV National News*, CTV, 18 April 1999, Canadian NewsDisc.
49 Malbon, interview.
50 "In their own words, Canada's troops describe their mission," *CTV National News*, CTV, 24 April 1999, Canadian NewsDisc.
51 Malbon, interview.
52 Larsen, interview.
53 The story didn't explain the difference between the two types of computers or what might be the problem with a 1980s-vintage computer technology. The Commodore 64 was originally developed as a video game engine that could be programmed for a different game when the previously installed one became old hat. See online: http://www.old-computers.com/museum/computer.asp?c=98. The main problem with the 1980s technology was that it was both difficult to find software for and was so limited in what it could do in terms of multi-tasking that some of the CF-18s' capabilities were lost when modified to accommodate precision-guided munitions.
54 Joe Warmington, "CF-18s showing their age; Canadian pilots urge spending on new warplanes," *Toronto Sun*, 18 April 1999, 4.
55 Sault Ste. Marie, Ontario.
56 Joe Warmington, telephone interview by author, 15 September 2003.
57 Warmington, telephone interview.
58 Warmington, telephone interview.
59 Warmington, telephone interview.
60 Sean Durkan, "DND says CF-18s OK; but pilot quips they're like 'Commodore 64,'" *Toronto Sun*, 19 April 1999, 34.
61 Transcript of briefing by DCDS, 18 April 1999.

62 Ibid.
63 "B roll" is additional footage shot by a television cameraman or woman that is secondary and augments the main video of a story.
64 Larsen, interview.
65 Larsen, interview.
66 Malbon, interview.
67 Malbon, interview.
68 DoD News briefing, 19 April 1999.
69 NATO, NATO's role in Kosovo Press Conference, 25 March; 1 April; 13 April 1999, online: http://www.nato.int/kosovo/press/p990325a.htm; http://www.nato.int/kosovo/press/p990401c.htm; http://www.nato.int/kosovo/press/p990413a.htm.

CHAPTER 9

1   Lt. Col. Sylvain Faucher, interview by author, Ottawa, Ontario, 19 October 2003.
2   Faucher, interview.
3   Faucher, interview.
4   Interview by author, Canadian Forces Base Cold Lake, Alberta, 16 April 2003.
5   Confidential interview by author, names were withheld by mutual consent if requested, Canadian Forces Base Bagotville, Quebec, 22 October 2003.
6   Confidential interview.
7   Confidential interview.
8   "Midas," Semi-confidential interview with author, full names were withheld by mutual consent if requested and call signs used instead, Canadian Forces Base Cold Lake, Alberta, 14 April 2003.
9   Maj. Kirk Soroka, interview by author, Canadian Forces Base Cold Lake, 14 Alberta, April 2003.
10 Soroka, interview.
11 Confidential interview.
12 Interview by author, Canadian Forces Base Cold Lake, Alberta, 16 April 2003.
13 Interview by author, Canadian Forces Base Cold Lake, Alberta, 15 April 2003.
14 Col. (ret.) J. M. Donihee, interview by author, Calgary, Alberta, 22 April 2003.
15 Defence spending accounted for 2.2 per cent of the Canadian Gross Domestic Product in 1985–1987. By 1994, defence spending was 1.7 per cent of the GDP. By 2003 it had dropped to about 1.1 per cent, representing a 50 per cent drop since the 1980s. See Douglas Bland, ed., *Canada without Armed Forces* (Kingston: Queen's University School of Policy Studies, 2003), 105–6.
16 Bob Bergen, "Trouble in the marriage: Man and machine need to bridge trust and fear," *Calgary Herald*, 29 April 1990, C2.

17 Ibid.
18 Ibid.
19 Ibid.
20 Donihee, interview.
21 Donihee, interview.
22 "Hooker," telephone interview by author, 24 April 2003.
23 Ibid.
24 Ibid.
25 Lt. Col. (ret.) William Allen Flynn, telephone interview by author, 9 April 2003.
26 Flynn, telephone interview.
27 Flynn, telephone interview.
28 Flynn, telephone interview.
29 Bob Bergen, "Cause of recent crashes still up in the air," *Calgary Herald*, 29 April 1990, C2; Bergen, "Trouble in the marriage."
30 Capt. Neil McRury, interview by author, Canadian Forces Base Cold Lake, Alberta, 16 April 2003.
31 Donihee, interview.
32 "Hooker," telephone interview.
33 Donihee, interview.
34 Canada, Department of National Defence, Operation Echo – Lessons Learned Staff Action Directive. Annex A, 12 January 2000, Released informally to author under *Access to Information Act* request A-2001-00308 and formally to author under request A-2003-00305/Team1.
35 Tim Judah, *Kosovo: War and Revenge* (New Haven, CT: Yale University Press, 2000), 259.
36 Ivo H. Daalder and Michael E. O'Hanlon, *Winning Ugly: NATO's War to Save Kosovo* (Washington, DC: Brookings Institution Press, 2000), 144–45.
37 Daalder and O'Hanlon, *Winning Ugly*, 103.
38 Daalder and O'Hanlon, *Winning Ugly*, 103. It has been observed that the Kosovo air war shocked western Europeans into a grim realization of just how much they and NATO were completely dependent on the United States military. As a result, European leaders announced on 3 June 1999 that they would build their own self-sufficient military. David Fromkin, *Kosovo Crossing: American Ideals Meet Reality on the Balkan Battlefields* (New York: The Free Press, 1999), 185.
39 Carl von Clausewitz, *On War*, trans. and ed., Michael Howard and Peter Paret (Princeton, NJ: Princeton University Press, 1984), 119.

Chapter 10

1. Canada, Department of National Defence, Transcript briefing by DCDS – Media Q, 20 April 1999, obtained by author from National Defence Public Affairs Office – Calgary (hereafter Transcript briefing by DCDS). online: http://dgpa-dgpa.mil.ca/Transcr/1999April/99042006.htm (accessed 16 July 2003).
2. Lt. Cmdr. Jeff Agnew, telephone interview by author, 30 June 2005.
3. Transcript briefing by DCDS, 22 April 1999.
4. Transcript briefing by DCDS, 22 April 1999.
5. Ibid.
6. Department of National Defence, Col. D. A. Davies, Commander, Task Force Aviano, Letter to the Chief of Staff J3, Mislabelled Video Purporting to be a CF-18 Mission, 22 April 1999, obtained by author under *Access to Information Act* request A-2003-00396/Team 3-5.
7. NATO Meeting, The National, CBC TV, 22 April 1999; "Canadian fighter pilots received some unwelcome praise and publicity from Washington today," CTV National News, CTV, 22 April 1999, Canadian NewsDisc.
8. Julian Beltrame, "Ottawa says war video is plane-ly wrong; Attack on Yugoslavia," *Edmonton Journal*, 23 April 1999, A1; Julian Beltrame, "DND officials in a flap over release of bomb video," *Ottawa Citizen*, 23 April 1999, A8; "Milosevic sites hit by NATO," *Hamilton Spectator*, 23 April 1999, C4; "Sometimes even praise can be an unwelcome thing," *National Post* (Toronto), 23 April 1999, A5; "UN solution unlikely, Chrétien says," *Times Colonist* (Victoria), 23 April 1999, A4; Brian Laghi and Murray Campbell, "Ottawa tops up Kosovo relief," *Globe and Mail*, 23 April 1999, A15; Sean Durkan, "Canada beefs over NATO bombing video," *Toronto Sun*, 23 April 1999, 51. On 23 April 1999, US Assistant Secretary of Defence (Public Affairs) Kenneth Bacon told journalists attending the Pentagon's press briefing that the previous day's identification of the F-18 in the Pentagon video as Canadian was a mistake.
9. Transcript briefing by DCDS, 23 April 1999.
10. Ibid.
11. Ibid. It was not possible to learn the names of the journalists attending the briefing that day from transcripts. Unlike in the transcripts from some other days, no journalists were identified.
12. NATO, NATO's role in Kosovo, Press conference transcript, 15 May 1999, online: http://www.nato.int/kosovo/all-frce.htm.
13. Transcript briefing by DCDS, 6 May 1999.
14. Eric Schmitt, "More Anti-U.S. Protests in Beijing as Officials Study Bombing," *New York Times*, 10 May 1999, 1.
15. NATO, NATO's role in Kosovo, Press conference transcript, 15 May 1999, online: http://www.nato.int/kosovo/all-frce.htm.
16. Michael R. Gordon, "NATO Admits Village Attack and Casualties," *New York Times* International, 16 May 1999, 1.

17 Felicity Barringer, "Editors Seek More Information on the Air War," *New York Times*, 16 April 1999, 11.

18 Ibid.

19 Gen. Wesley K. Clark, *Waging Modern War: Bosnia, Kosovo and the Future of Combat* (New York: PublicAffairs, 2002), 444–45.

20 Ibid., 444.

21 R. W. Apple, Jr., "Clinton Tailors Legacy but Kosovo Isn't Fabric," *New York Times International*, 10 June 1999, A20. On 12 June 1999, two days after the bombing campaign ended, a *New York Times* journalist eventually was able to get aboard an American Jstars surveillance aircraft on a flight over Albania and report on the difficulties in flying such missions. But from a journalistic perspective, by the time the story was published two days after that, its timeliness and, in the process, its relevance were compromised.

22 Maj. Stéphane Hébert, interview by author, Canadian Forces Base Bagotville, Quebec, 22 October 2003.

23 Hébert, interview.

24 Hébert, interview.

25 Paul Workman, telephone interview by author, 13 August 2003.

26 Workman, telephone interview.

27 "Canadians in combat," The National, CBC-TV, 13 May 1999, Canadian NewsDisc.

28 Transcript briefing by DCDS, 14 May 1999.

29 Ibid.

30 Ibid.

Chapter 11

1 Allan Thompson, "Canada earns air stripes in Kosovo, but our top soldier fears the strain of a ground war," *Toronto Star*, 29 May 1999, A1.

2 "Canadian planes led missions," *Daily News* (Halifax), 17 June 1999, 8; Eileen McCabe, "Chretien thanks air crews in Italy," *Ottawa Citizen*, 21 June 1999, A6.

3 "Most Canadian CF-18s begin long journey home," *Toronto Star*, 26 June 1999, A24; "Most of Canada's CF-18 crews about to begin journey home," *Calgary Herald*, 26 June 1999, A17.

4 Maj. Alain Pelletier, telephone interview by author, 16 July 2003.

5 Pelletier, telephone interview.

6 Cpl. Patrick Savoie, interview by author, Canadian Forces Base Bagotville, Quebec, 21 October 2003.

7 "Chimp," interview by author, Canadian Forces Base Cold Lake, Alberta, 14 April 2003.

8 Ibid.

9 Lt. Col. (ret.) William Allen Flynn, telephone interview by author, 9 April 2003.
10 Gen. Raymond Henault, telephone interview by author, 22 September 2003.
11 Lt. Cmdr. (N) John Larsen, interview by author, Calgary, Alberta, 19 June 2003.
12 Ibid.
13 Ibid.
14 Ibid.
15 Telephone interview by author, 8 September 2003.
16 Ibid.
17 The parliamentary press gallery was initially composed only of newspaper journalists and remained that way until 1959, when broadcasters were admitted. Television camera and sound crews were admitted in 1982. *Canadian Parliamentary Guide* 1998–1999, ed. Kathryn O'Handy (Farmington Hills, MI: Gale Group Inc., 1999), 547–51.
18 Telephone interview by author, 8 September 2003.
19 Peter W. W. Wijninga and Richard Szafranski, "Beyond Utility Targeting: Toward Axiological Air Operations," *Aerospace Power Journal* 14, no. 4 (Winter 2000): 45–59.
20 Paul Rexton Kan, "What Should We bomb? Axiological Targeting and the Abiding Limits of Airpower Theory," *Air & Space Power Journal* 18, no. 1 (Spring 2004): 25–32.
21 James Kitfield, "Lessons from Kosovo: Bad Things Happen When the Media and the Military Butt Heads Yet Again," *Media Studies Journal* 15, no. 1 (Summer 2001): 34–39.
22 NATO, NATO's role in Kosovo, Press conference transcript, 22 May 1999, online: http://www.nato.int/kosovo/all-frce.htm.
23 Ibid.
24 Department of National Defence, Transcript briefing by DCDS – Media Q, 22 May 1999, obtained by author from National Defence Public Affairs Office – Calgary (hereafter Transcript briefing by DCDS), online: http://dgpa-dgpa.mil.ca/Transcr/1999Jun/99052204.htm (accessed 16 July 2003).
25 Transcript briefing by DCDS, 1 June 1999.
26 Transcript briefing by DCDS, 1 June 1999.
27 Transcript briefing by DCDS, 2 June 1999.
28 Transcript briefing by DCDS, 2 June 1999.
29 Dean Beeby, "Error forces CF-18 repairs," *Toronto Star*, 2 June 1999, A11.
30 Dean Beeby, "Maintenance mistake weakened engine blades on all CF-18s," *Gazette* (Montreal), 2 June 1999, A13.
31 Transcript briefing by DCDS, 4 June 1999.
32 Transcript briefing by DCDS, 4 June 1999.
33 Allan Thompson, "Fighting defended Canadian values, Chrétien says; but some say peacekeeping image is sullied," *Toronto Star*, 11 June 1999, A10.

34 John Ward, "Canadian crews happy air war is over," *Hamilton Spectator*, 16 June 1999, D2; "Canadian crews grateful," *Daily News* (Halifax), 16 June 1999, 11; "Weary air crews ready to celebrate," *Times Colonist* (Victoria), 16 June 1999, A5.

35 Transcript briefing by DCDS, 16 June 1999.

36 "Canadian planes led missions," *Daily News* (Halifax), 17 June 1999, 8.

37 Lt. Col. (ret.) William Allen Flynn, in Bob Bergen, "Balkan Rats and Balkan Bats: The Untold Story Of Canada's Air Force during the Kosovo Air War," Paper presented at the Conference of Defence Associations Institute 6th Annual Graduate Student Symposium, Kingston, ON, October 2003.

38 Paul Workman, telephone interview by author, 13 August 2003.

39 "Twelve Canadian Fighter Pilots Return Home from War," Canada AM, CTV, 29 June 1999, Canadian NewsDisc.

40 "View from the jets," The National, CBC-TV, 29 June 1999, Canadian NewsDisc.

41 Canada, National Defence Headquarters, Defence Ethics Program, "Ethics and Operations Project: Project Report," 9 March 2000, p. 8, online: http://www.dnd.ca/ethics/pages/kdocs_e.htm (accessed 25 September 2003).

42 Brig. Gen. (ret.) David Jurkowski, interview by author, Ottawa, Ontario, 27 October 2003.

43 Larsen, interview.

Chapter 12

1 See NATO, NATO's role in Kosovo, online: http://www.nato.int/kosovo/docu/u990610a.htm.

2 Duska Anastasijevic, "The Closing of the Kosovo Cycle: Victimization versus Responsibility," in *Kosovo and the Challenge of Humanitarian Intervention*, ed. Albrecht Schnabel and Ramesh Thakur (New York: United Nations University Press, 2000), 57.

3 Lt. Col. (ret.) William Allen Flynn, telephone interview by author, 9 April 2003.

4 Canada. National Defence. News Release, 25 June 1999, online: http://www.forces.gc.ca/site/newsroom/view_news_e.asp?id=706 (accessed 12 April 2004).

5 Confidential interview by author, names were withheld by mutual consent if requested, Canadian Forces Base Bagotville, Quebec. 22 October 2003.

6 Interview by author, Canadian Forces Base Cold Lake, Alberta. 15 April 2003.

7 Confidential interview.

8 Capt. Travis Brassington, interview by author, Canadian Forces Base Cold Lake, Alberta, 14 April 2003.

9 Maj. Kirk Soroka, interview by author, Canadian Forces Base Cold Lake, Alberta, 14 April 2003.

10 David L. Bashow et al., "Mission Ready: Canada's Role in the Kosovo Air Campaign," *Canadian Military Journal* 1, no. 1 (Spring 2000): 59.

11 Bashow et al., "Mission Ready."
12 Patrick Martin, "Balkan Rats," *Air Forces Monthly* (November 1999): 56–59.
13 David Bercuson, *Blood on the Hills: The Canadian Army in the Korean War* (Toronto: University of Toronto Press, 1999), 11.
14 Canada, Governor General of Canada, Meritorious Service decorations, online: https://www.gg.ca/honour.aspx?id=221&t=16&ln=Davies.
15 Canada, Governor General of Canada, Meritorious Service decorations, online: https://www.gg.ca/honour.aspx?id=222&t=16&ln=Parker.
16 Soroka, interview.
17 For a complete list of the Canadian orders, decorations, medals, and their precedence, see the Governor General of Canada's website at: https://www.gg.ca/document.aspx?id=5&lan=eng.
18 Soroka, interview.
19 Soroka, interview.
20 Capt. John Edelman, interview by author, Canadian Forces Base Cold Lake, Alberta, 15 April 2003.
21 Capt. Brett Glaeser, interview by author, Canadian Forces Base Cold Lake, Alberta, 15 April 2003.
22 Interview by author, Canadian Forces Base Cold Lake, Alberta. 15 April 2003.
23 Col. (ret.) Jim Donihee, interview by author, Calgary, Alberta, 22 April 2003.
24 Lt. Col. Sylvain Faucher, interview with author, Ottawa, Ontario, 29 October 2003.
25 "Hooker," telephone interview by author, 9 April 2003.
26 Flynn, telephone interview, 5 July 2005.
27 Brig. Gen. (ret.) David Jurkowski, interview by author, Ottawa, Ontario, 27 October 2003.
28 Gen. Raymond Henault, telephone interview by author, 22 September 2003.
29 Canada, National Defence Headquarters, Judith A, Mooney, Director of Access to Information and Privacy, letter on behalf of to author, 30 September 2003, in response to *Access to Information Act* request A-2003-00486/Team 1.
30 *Access to Information Act*, s. 21.
31 Canada, Rideau Hall, The Chancellery, Mary de Bellefeuille-Percy, letter to author, 31 October 2003, in response to *Access to Information Act* request A-2003-00486/Team 1.
32 Bob Bergen, "Air Force men and women deserve more than a better than nothing medal," 6 March 2007, online: http://www.cdfai.org/bergenarticles/Air%20force%20men%20and%20women%20deserve%20more%20than%20a%20better%20than%20nothing%20medal.pdf (accessed 6 March 2007).
33 Telephone interview by author, 27 March 2007.
34 Flynn, telephone interview, 5 July 2005.

35 Maj. Kirk Soroka, telephone interview by author.
36 Confidential telephone interview by author.
37 Bob Bergen, "New Historic Battle Honour for Canadian Fighter Jet Squadrons Bittersweet," 12 December 2007, online: http://www.cdfai.org/bergenarticles/New%20historic%20Battle%20Honour%20for%20Canadian%20jet%20fighter%20squadrons%20bittersweet.pd (accessed 12 December 2007).
38 Government of Canada. Order Awarding of the General Campaign Star with the ALLIED FORCE RIBBON. online: http://gazette.gc.ca/rp-pr/p2/2010-03-31/html/si-tr19-eng.htm (accessed 9 September 2012).

Afterword

1 Canada, *Royal Commission on Newspapers* (Minister of Supply and Services Canada, 1981), 21.
2 Ibid.
1 Robert W. Bergen, "Censorship; the Canadian News Media and Afghanistan: A Historical Comparison with Case Studies," Calgary Papers in Military and Strategic Studies, Occasional Paper no. 3 (Calgary: University of Calgary Press, 2009).
2 Canada, House of Commons, *Debates*, vol. 147, no. 128 (20 October 2014), 8583.
3 Ibid.
4 Michael Friscolanti, "Uncovering a Killer," *Maclean's*, 10 November 2014, 36–42.
5 Stephen Harper, Prime Minister of Canada, "Statement by the Prime Minister of Canada in Ottawa," online. https://cija.ca/prime-minister-ottawa/.
6 Graeme Hamilton, "No uniforms in public for Quebec troops," *National Post*, 23 October 2014, A11.
7 Erin Anderson, "Canadian Forces uniform 'is not a costume,'" *Globe and Mail*, 25 October 2014, A4.
8 John McGuire, online: https://nationalpost.com/news/world/israel-middle-east/john-maguire-an-isis-fighter-from-ottawa-appears-on-video-warning-canada-of-attacks-where-it-hurts-you-the-most.
9 Raoul Dandurand, in *Historical Documents of Canada, vol. 5: The Arts of War and Peace*, ed. C. P. Stacey (New York: St. Martin's Press, 1972), 511.
10 Barack Obama, President of the United States, online: https://www.rollingstone.com/movies/movie-news/barack-obama-sony-made-a-mistake-canceling-the-interview-241123/.
11 W. H. Kesterton, *A History of Journalism in Canada* (Toronto: McClelland and Stewart, 1967), 246.
12 Jeffrey A. Keshen, *Propaganda and Censorship during Canada's Great War* (Edmonton: University of Alberta Press, 1996), xiii.
13 Ibid., 12–13.

14 Kesterton, *A History of Journalism in Canada*, 248.

15 David J. Bercuson, *Maple Leaf against the Axis: Canada's Second World War* (Toronto: Stoddart, 1995), 61.

16 Ross Munro, *Gauntlet to Overlord: The Story of the Canadian Army* (Toronto; Macmillian Canada, 1946), 326–37.

17 Ibid., 326.

18 Ross Munro, "I saw Canadian Heroes Die at Dieppe," *Vancouver Sun*, 21 August 1942.

19 Munro, *Gauntlet to Overlord*, 337.

Bibliography

Primary Sources—Unpublished

Canada. Department of National Defence. 1 CAD HQ Winnipeg, Secret A3 OPS RDNS 226, September 1997. Obtained by author under Access to Information Act request A-2003-00606/Team 1.

———. 441 OT&E Proposal, Undated, obtained by author under *Access to Information Act* request A-2003-00139/Team 2-3.

———. After Action Report: Gulf War Public Affairs. Director General Public Affairs. 23 April 1991. Obtained by author under *Access to Information Act* request A-2003-00394.

———. After Action Report: Gulf War Public Affairs. Lt. Col. R. C. Coleman. Memorandum 3350-OF-3 (DND PA). 25 April 1991. Obtained by author under *Access to Information Act* request A-2003-00394/Team 3.

———. After Action Report, Operation Friction. Director General Public Affairs. Memorandum (Draft) 1350-3350 (DGPA). 24 July 1991. Obtained by author under *Access to Information Act* request A-2003-00394/Team 3.

———. After Action Report. Operation Friction: Director General Public Affairs, 24 July 1991. Obtained by author under *Access to Information Act* request A-2003-00394.

———. Agnew, Jeff, Lt. Cmdr. (N). Email correspondence, Distribution list, 26 March 1999. Obtained by author under *Access to Information Act* request A-2002-01184/Team 2.

———. Assistant Deputy Minister of Public Affairs. J5PA, Instruction 0301. 12 November 2003. Obtained by author under *Access to Information Act*: request A-2003-00394.

———. Briefing Note Concerning Agenda Item X, CDS meeting with Group Principals 0900Hrs. 2 January 1991. Obtained by author under *Access to Information Act* request A-2003-0394.

———. Briefing Note prepared for CAS: Op Echo – Communications Approach Issue by Lt. (N) John Coppard, D Air PA 2-2. 31 March 1999. Obtained by author under *Access to Information Act* request A-2002-01184/Team 2.

———. Canadian Forces Headquarters Middle East Public Affairs War Operations Plan. 14 January 1991. Obtained by author under *Access to Information Act* request A-2003-00394.

———. Communications Plan: Rotation of Ships' Companies CTG 302.3. 4 December 1990. Obtained by author under *Access to Information Act* request A-2003-00394.

———. Concepts of Operations for the Use of Night Vision Goggles in the CF-18. 441 TFS, 20 November 1997. Obtained by author under *Access to Information Act* request A-2003-00139/Team 2-3.

———. Davies, D. A., Col. Commander, Task Force Aviano. Letter to the Chief of Staff J3, Mislabelled Video Purporting to be a CF-18 Mission. 22 April 1999. Obtained by author under *Access to Information Act* request A-2003-00396/Team 3-5.

———. Directorate of Public Affairs Operations. Media Guidelines. 20 February 1991. Obtained by author under *Access to Information Act* request A-2003-00394.

———. Guidinger, R. W., Col. Wing Commander, 4 Wing Cold Lake. Letter to National Defence Headquarters. 27 October 1997. Obtained by author under *Access to Information Act* request A-2003-00139/Team 2-3.

———. Henault, Lt. Gen. R. R. National Targeting Process for OP Echo. Letter to the Chief of Defence Staff et al. 6 July 1999. Obtained by author under *Access to Information Act* request A-2003-00305/Team 1.

———. Henault, Lt. Gen. R. R. Operation Echo Lessons Learned Staff Action Directive. Annex A 3453-20 (DLLS). 12 January 2000. Obtained by author under *Access to Information Act* request A-2003-00305/Team 1.

———. Mietzner, Capt. E-mail correspondence to Lt. Col. S. Wills, Director of Air Force Public Affairs. 19 March 1999. Obtained by author under *Access to Information Act* request A-2002-01184/Team 2.

———. Minute to Wing Commander from Wing Operations officer Lt. Col. J. M. Ouellet. 6 October 1997. Obtained by author under *Access to Information Act* request A-2003-00139/Team 2-3.

———. Minutes of the CF-18 NVG Project Committee Meeting. 28 April 1998. Obtained by author under *Access to Information Act* request A-2003-00139/Team 2-3.

———. Mooney, Judith A. Director of Access to Information and Privacy. Letter on behalf of to author. 30 September 2003. In response to *Access to Information Act* request A-2003-00486/Team 1.

———. Mooney, Judith A. Director of Access to Information and Privacy. Letter on behalf of to author. 4 July 2003. In response to *Access to Information Act* request A-2003-00372/Team 1.

———. Mooney, Judith A. Director of Access to Information and Privacy. Letter to author. 21 July 2003. In response to *Access to Information Act* request A-003 00434/Team 1.

———. Mooney, Judith A. Director of Access to Information and Privacy. Letter to author. 7 October 2003. In response to *Access to Information Act* request A-2003-00704/Team 3-6.

———. National Defence Headquarters. Jim Judd. Letter to the Defence Minister. 20 April 1999. Obtained by author under *Access to Information Act* request A-2002-01182/Team 3- 2.

———. National Defence Headquarters. Memo. Message ID. 199827000147. Secret. CF-18 Weapons Augmentation Request. 27 September 1998. Obtained by author under *Access to Information Act* request A-2002-01182/Team 3-2.

———. National Defence Headquarters. Secret Memo DAEPMMFT028. CF-18 Weapons Augmentation Request. 5 October 1998. Obtained by author under *Access to Information Act* request A-2002-01182/Team 3-2.

———. National Defence Headquarters. Synopsis Sheet: Ammo Requirement OP Echo – Guided Bomb Unit (GBU) bombs. 20 April 1999. Obtained by author under *Access to Information Act* request A-2002-01182/Team 3-2.

———. Operation Echo – Lessons Learned Staff Action Directive. Annex A. 12 January 2000. Released informally to author under *Access to Information Act* request A-2003-00305/Team 1.

———. Operation Friction: Canadian Forces Operations in the Persian Gulf Communications Plan. 15 August 1990. Obtained by author under *Access to Information Act* request A-2003-00394.

———. Operation Friction: Canadian Forces Operations in the Persian Gulf Communications Plan. 9 November 1990. Obtained by author under *Access to Information Act* request A-2003-00394.

———. Priority Message from NDHQ Ottawa//CDS//. Op Friction MSN and Roles/Official Spokespersons. 15 January 1991. Obtained by author under *Access to Information Act* request A-2003-00394.

———. Secret System High Generated/Mediated Message. Message ID: 199827000147. 27 September 1998. Obtained by author under *Access to Information Act* request A-2002- 01182/Team 3.

———. Transcripts of briefings by DCDS – Media Q, March–June 1999, obtained by author from National Defence Public Affairs Office – Calgary.

———. Wilson, L., Lt. E-mail correspondence to S. Wills, Lt.-Col., Director of Air Force Public Affairs. 25 March 1999. Obtained by author under *Access to Information Act* request A-2002-01184/Team 2.

Canada. Public Works and Government Services Canada. Eugene B. Rizok, Letter from Public Works and Government Services Canada in the Canadian Embassy in Washington to the Deputy Under-Secretary of the Air Force in the Pentagon. 8 April 1999. PWGSC file number W8484-6-WA09. Obtained by author under *Access to Information Act* request A-2002-01182/Team 3-2.

Canada. Rideau Hall. The Chancellery. Mary de Bellefeuille-Percy. Letter to author. 31 October 2003. In response to *Access to Information Act* request A-2003-00486/Team 1.

Canada. Supply and Services Canada. Contract with the government of the U.S. of America, DSS file No. W8484-9-WA01 PT.2. 3 June 1999. Obtained by author under *Access to Information Act* request A-2002-01182/Team 3-2.

Soroka, Kirk. Unpublished notes for a Geoff Bennett painting "On a date with the Iron Maiden," fromCanadian Airpower for Peace and Freedom Collection, unveiled 1 February 2001, at 4 Wing, Canadian Forces Base Cold Lake, Alberta.

Primary Sources—Published

Canada, Auditor General. Report of the Auditor General of Canada to the House of Commons. April 1998. Chapter 3.

Canada, Department of National Defence. Adjusting Course: A Naval Strategy for Canada. April 1997.

———. Department of National Defence. A Role of Pride and Influence in the World—Defence. Canada's International Policy Statement, 2005.

———. Army Lessons Learned Centre. "Media Relations." Dispatches, vol. 4, no. 3 (March 1997).

———. Atkinson, Peter, Brig. Gen. ADM(PA) Transcript, "Government Officials hold technical briefing to provide an update on Canada's activities in Afghanistan." Media Q, 14 February 2008. Obtained by author from National Defence Public Affairs Office, Prairies and NWT, 15 February 2008.

———. Bland, Douglas L. "National Defence Headquarters Centre for Decision." A study prepared for the Commission of Inquiry into the Deployment of Canadian Forces to Somalia. 1997.

———. Canada's Soldiers: Military Ethos and Canadian Values in the 21st Century Army. Report to the Commander Land Force Command. January 2005.

———. Canadian Expeditionary Force Command. Canadian Forces Media Embedding Program, Guidelines, Ground Rules and Documentation for Her Majesty's Canadian Ships.

———. Directorate of Air Public Affairs. CF-18 backgrounder. 31 October 2002.

———. Transcripts of Daily Kosovo Technical Briefings. 24 March 1999 to 16 June 1999.

Obtained by author from National Defence Public Affairs Office – Calgary.

———. 1994 White Paper on Defence.

Canada. Parliament. House of Commons. Debates, vol. 275, 1950.

———. Debates, vol. 13, 1991.

———. Debates, vol. 135, no. 134, 1998, and nos. 203, 204, 205A, and 234, 1999.

———. Debates, vol. 147, no. 128, 2014.

———. "Resolution Following Public Hearings On Canada's Role in the Kosovo Conflict and its Aftermath." Report of the Standing Committee on Foreign Affairs and International Trade. June 2000.

———. The Senate. The New NATO and the Evolution of Peacekeeping: Implications for Canada. Report of the Standing Senate Committee on Foreign Affairs. April 2000.

———. Treasury Board of Canada. Interim Policy Guide, Access to Information and Privacy Acts. Circular No. 1983-35.

NATO Handbook. Brussels: NATO Office of Information and Press, 2001.

Newspapers and Magazines

Calgary Herald
National Post (Toronto)
Ottawa Citizen
Daily News (Halifax)
Edmonton Journal
Gazette (Montreal)
Globe and Mail
Hamilton Spectator
New York Times
New York Times Magazine.
Telegram (St. John's)
Times (London, England)
Toronto Star
Toronto Sun
Vancouver Sun
Times Colonist (Victoria)

Personal Interviews

All interviews were conducted by the author. Those listed below are directly cited in notes. Confidential interviewees have not been listed. Some interviewees are identified by their military call signs only.

Barker, Mike, Maj., Canadian Forces Base Cold Lake, Alberta.
Brassington, Travis ("Brass"), Capt., Canadian Forces Base Cold Lake, Alberta.
Cox, James, retired Brig. Gen., Ottawa, Ontario.
Donihee, Jim, retired Col., Calgary, Alberta.
Edelman, John, Capt., Canadian Forces Base Cold Lake, Alberta.
Faucher, Sylvian, Lt. Col., Ottawa, Ontario.
Glaeser, Brett ("Laser"), Capt., Canadian Forces Base Cold Lake, Alberta.
Hébert, Stéphane, Maj., Canadian Forces Base Bagotville, Quebec.
Jurkowski, David, retired Brig. Gen., Ottawa, Ontario.
Larsen, John, Lt. Cmdr., Calgary, Alberta.
Malbon, Joy, CTV News, Ottawa, Ontario.
Matthews, Don, retired Lt. Col., Calgary, Alberta.
McGillivray, Ed, retired Brig. Gen., Calgary, Alberta.
McRury, Neil ("Hoss"), Capt., Canadian Forces Base Cold Lake, Alberta.
Savoie, Patrick, Cpl., Canadian Forces Base Bagotville, Quebec.
Soroka, Kirk, ("Rambo") Maj., Canadian Forces Base Cold Lake, Alberta.

Telephone Interviews

Agnew, Jeff, Cmdr., from Ottawa, Ontario.
Baril, Maurice, retired Gen., from Ottawa, Ontario.
Flynn, William Allen ("Billie"), retired Lt. Col., from Toronto, Ontario.
Henault, Ray, Gen., from Ottawa, Ontario.
Macdonald, Neil, CBC TV, from Washington, D.C., United States of America.
Marcotte, Benoît, retired Col., from Longueuil, Quebec.
Pelletier, Alain, Maj., from Ottawa, Ontario.
Seguna, Paul, Lt. Cmdr., from Vancouver, British Columbia.
Soroka, Kirk ("Rambo"), Maj., from Canadian Forces Base Cold Lake, Alberta.
Warmington, Joe, *Toronto Sun*, from Toronto, Ontario.
Workman, Paul, CBC TV, from Paris, France.

Email Correspondence

Baril, Maurice, retired Gen., Ottawa, Ontario.
Marcotte, Benoît, retired Col., Longueuil, Quebec.
Malbon, Joy, CTV News, Aviano, Italy.
Soroka, Kirk ("Rambo"), Maj., Canadian Forces Base Cold Lake, Alberta.
York, Geoffrey, *Globe and Mail*, Beijing, China.

Books, Articles, and Theses

Anastasijevic, Duska. "The Closing of the Kosovo Cycle: Victimization versus Responsibility." In *Kosovo and the Challenge of Humanitarian Intervention*, edited by Albrecht Schnabel and Ramesh Thakur, 44–63. New York: United Nations University Press, 2000.

Bain, George. *Gotcha*. Toronto: Key Porter Books, 1994.

Bashow, David L. "Reconciling the Irreconcilable? Canada's Foreign and Defence Policy Linkage." *Canadian Military Journal* 1, no. 1 (Spring 2000): 17–26.

———, et al. "Mission Ready: Canada's Role in the Kosovo Air Campaign." *Canadian Military Journal* 1, no. 1 (Spring 2000): 55–61.

Benedict, Michael, ed. *Canada at War*. Toronto: Viking, 1997.

Bennett, W. Lance. "The News about Foreign Policy." In *Taken By Storm: The Media, Public Opinion and U.S. Foreign Policy in the Gulf War*, edited by W. Lance Bennett and David L. Paletz, 12–40. Chicago: University of Chicago Press, 1994.

———. "Toward a Theory of Press-State Relations in the United States." *Journal of Communications* 40, no. 2 (Spring 1990): 103–26.

———. and David L. Paletz, eds. *Taken By Storm: The Media, Public Opinion, and U.S. Foreign Policy in the Gulf War*. Chicago: University of Chicago Press, 1994.

Bercuson, David. *Blood on the Hills: The Canadian Army in the Korean War*. Toronto: University of Toronto Press, 1999.

———. *Maple Leaf against the Axis: Canada's Second World War*. Toronto: Stoddart, 1995.

———. *Significant Incident: Canada's Army, the Airborne, and the Murder in Somalia*. Toronto: McClelland and Stewart, 1996.

Bergen, Robert W. "Balkan Rats and Balkan Bats." PhD diss., University of Calgary, 2005.

———. "Balkan Rats and Balkan Bats: The Untold Story of Canada's Air Force during the Kosovo Air War." Paper presented at the Conference of Defence Associations Institute 6th Annual Graduate Student Symposium. Kingston, ON, October 2003.

———. "Censorship; the Canadian News Media and Afghanistan: A Historical Comparison with Case Studies." Calgary Papers in Military and Strategic Studies, Occasional Paper no. 3. Calgary: University of Calgary Press, 2009.

Bland, Douglas L. "The Government of Canada and the Armed Forces: A Troubled Relationship." In *The Soldier and the Canadian State: A Crisis in Civil-Military Relations?*, edited by David A. Charters and Brent J. Wilson, 27–45. Proceedings of the Second Annual Conflict Studies Workshop. Fredericton: University of New Brunswick, October 1995.

———. "Parliament's Duty to Defend Canada." *Canadian Military Journal* 1, no. 4 (Winter 2000–2001): 35–43.

———, ed. *Canada without Armed Forces*. Kingston: Queen's University School of Policy Studies, 2003.

Blatchford, Christie. *Fifteen Days: Stories of Bravery, Friendship, Life and Death from inside the New Canadian Army*. Toronto: Doubleday, 2007.

Brewster, Murray. *The Savage War: The Untold Battles of Afghanistan*. Mississauga, ON: Wiley, 2011.

Brown, Charles H. *Informing the People*. New York: Holt, Rinehart and Winston, 1957.

Calic, Marie-Janine. "Kosovo in the Twentieth Century: A Historical Account." In *Kosovo and the Challenge of Humanitarian Intervention*, edited by Albrecht Schnabel and Ramesh Thakur, 19–31. New York: United Nations University Press, 2000.

Canada. *Dishonored Legacy: The Lessons of the Somalia Affair: The Report of the Commission of Inquiry into the Deployment of the Canadian Forces to Somalia*, vol. 5. Ottawa: Minister of Public Works and Government Services Canada, 1997.
Canada. *Royal Commission on Newspapers*. Ottawa: Supply and Services Canada, 1981.

———. *The Charter of Rights and Freedoms: A Guide for Canadians* (Ottawa: Minister of Supply and Services Canada, 1983).

"Canadian contribution." *World Air Power Journal* 38 (Autumn 1999).

Canadian Press. *Stylebook: A Guide for Writers and Editors*. Toronto: Canadian Press, 1983.

Carlyle, Thomas. *Sartor Resartus; On Heroes and Hero Worship*. London: Dent Dutton, 1965.

Chahill, Jack. *Words of War*. Toronto: Deneau, 1987.

Clark, Gen. Wesley K. *Waging Modern War: Bosnia, Kosovo and the Future of Combat*. New York: PublicAffairs, 2002.

Clausewitz, Carl von. *On War*. Translated and edited by Michael Howard and Peter Paret. Princeton, NJ: Princeton University Press, 1976.

Clinton, Bill. *My Life*. New York: Alfred A. Knopf, 2004.

Cumming, Carmen, and Catherine McKercher. *The Canadian Reporter: News Writing and Reporting*. Toronto: Harcourt Brace, 1994.

Daalder, Ivan H., and Michael E. O'Hanlon. *Winning Ugly: NATO's War to Save Kosovo*. Washington: Brookings Institution Press, 2000.

Dancocks, David. *The D-Day Dodgers: The Canadians in Italy, 1943–1945*. Toronto: McClelland and Stewart, 1991.

Day, Adam. *Witness to War: Reporting on Afghanistan 2004–2009*. Kingston, ON: Canadian Defence Academy Press, 2010.

Desbarats, Peter. *Somalia Cover-Up: A Commissioner's Journal*. Toronto: McClelland and Stewart, 1997.

Donoghue, Jack. *The Edge of War*. Calgary, Detselig, 1988.

Douglas, W.A.B., and Brereton Greenhous. *Out of the Shadows: Canada in the Second World War*. Toronto: Dundurn Press, 1995.

Douhet, Giulio, *The Command of the Air.* Translated by Dino Ferrari. New York: Arno Press, 1972.

———. *The Command of the Air.* North Stratford, UK: Ayer, 2002.

Edelman, Murray. *Constructing the Political Spectacle.* Chicago: University of Chicago Press, 1988.

———. *Political Language: Words that Succeed and Policies that Fail.* New York: Academic Press, 1977.

———. *Politics as Symbolic Action: Mass Arousal and Quiescence.* Chicago: Markham, 1971.

Fialka, John J. *Hotel Warriors: Covering the Gulf War.* Washington, DC: Woodrow Wilson Centre Press, 1992.

Fromkin, David. *Kosovo Crossing: American Ideals Meet Reality on the Balkan Battlefields.* New York: The Free Press, 1999.

Gannon, Kathy. *I Is For Infidel: From Holy War To Holy Terror: 18 Years inside Afghanistan.* New York: PublicAffairs, 2005.

Gitlin, Todd. *The Whole World Is Watching: Mass Media in the Making & Unmaking of the New Left.* Berkeley: University of California Press, 1980.

Granatstein, J. L. *Canada's Army: Waging War and Keeping the Peace.* Toronto: University of Toronto Press, 2002.

Gray, Colin S. *Modern Strategy.* Oxford: Oxford University Press, 1999.

Greenhous, Brereton, et al. *The Crucible of War: The Official History of the Royal Canadian Air Force*, vol. 3. Toronto: University of Toronto Press, 1994.

Hackett, Robert A. *News and Dissent: The Press and the Politics of Peace in Canada.* Norwood, NJ: Ablex, 1995.

Haglund, David G., ed. *New NATO, New Century: Canada, the U.S., and the Future of the Atlantic Alliance.* Kingston, ON: Centre for International Relations, 2000.

Hallam, Henry. *The Constitutional History of England*, vol. 2. London: Alex Murray & Co., 1872.

Hallin, Daniel C. *The "Uncensored War": The Media and Vietnam.* Berkeley: University of California Press, 1989.

Hallion, Richard P. *Storm over Iraq: Air Power and the Gulf War.* Washington, DC: Smithsonian Institution Press, 1992.

Haydon, Peter. "The Changing Nature of Canadian Civil Military Relations in the Aftermath of the Cold War." In *The Soldier and the Canadian State: A Crisis in Civil-Military Relations?*, edited by David A. Charters and Brent J.Wilson, 46–64. Proceedings of the Second Annual Conflict Studies Workshop. Fredericton: University of New Brunswick, October 1995.

Hewson, Robert, et al. "Operation Allied Force: The First 30 Days." *World Air Power Journal* 38 (Autumn 1999): 16–29.

Ignatieff, Michael. *Virtual War: Kosovo and Beyond.* Toronto: Viking Canada, 2000.

Jomini, Baron de. *The Art of War.* Translated by G. H. Mendell, and W. P. Craighill. Westport, CT: Greenwood Press, 1862.

Judah, Tim. *Kosovo: War and Revenge*, 2nd ed. New Haven, CT: Yale University Press, 2002.

Kan, Paul Rexton. "What Should We Bomb? Axiological Targeting and the Abiding Limits of Airpower Theory." *Air & Space Power Journal* 18, no. 1 (Spring 2004): 25–32.

Keshen, Jeffrey A. *Propaganda and Censorship during Canada's Great War.* Edmonton: University of Alberta Press, 1996.

Kesterton, W. H. *A History of Journalism in Canada.* Toronto: McClelland and Stewart, 1967.

Kitfield, James. "Lessons from Kosovo: Bad Things Happen When the Media and the Military Butt Heads Yet Again." *Media Studies Journal* 15, no. 1 (Summer 2001): 34–39.

Knightley, Phillip, *The First Casualty: The War Correspondent as Hero and Myth-Maker from the Crimea to Iraq.* New York: Harcourt Brace Jovanovich, 1975.

Lambeth, Benjamin. "Lessons from the War in Kosovo." *Joint Force Quarterly* (Spring 2002): 12–19.

———. *The Transformation of America Airpower.* Ithaca, NY: Cornell University Press, 2000.

Liddell Hart, B. H. *Strategy.* 2nd ed. New York: Meridian, 1991.

Malone, Richard S. *Missing from the Record.* Toronto: Collins, 1946.

———. *A Portrait of War: 1939-1946.* Toronto: Collins, 1983.

———. *A World in Flames: 1944-1945.* Toronto: Collins, 1984.

Martin, Patrick. "Balkan Rats." *Air Forces Monthly* (November 1999): 56–61.

McKercher, Catherine. *The Canadian Reporter: News Writing and Reporting.* Toronto: Harcourt Brace, 1994.

Morton, Desmond. *A Military History of Canada.* 3rd ed. Toronto: McClelland and Stewart, 1992.

Munro, Ross. *Gauntlet to Overlord: The Story of the Canadian Army.* Toronto: Macmillan Canada, 1946.

Nicholson, G.W.L. *The Canadians in Italy 1943-1945.* Ottawa: Queen's Printer, 1957.

———. *Canadian Expeditionary Force 1914-1919: Official History or the Canadian Army in the First World War.* Ottawa: Queen's Printer, 1962.

O'Handy, Kathryn, ed. *Canadian Parliamentary Guide 1998-1999.* Farmington Hills, MI: Gale Group, 1999.

Remple, Roy. *The Chatter Box: An Insider's Account of the Irrelevance of Parliament in the Making of Canadian Foreign and Defence Policy.* Toronto: Dundurn Press, 2002.

Rip, Michael Russell, and James M. Hasik. *The Precision Revolution: GPS and the Future of Aerial Warfare*. Annapolis, MD: Naval Institute Press, 2003.

Rosen, Jay. *What Are Journalists for?* New Haven, CT: Yale University Press, 1999.

Ruvinsky, Maxine. *Investigative Reporting in Canada*. Don Mills, ON: Oxford University Press, 2008.

Shy, John. "Jominy." In *Makers of Modern Strategy: From Machiavelli to the Nuclear Age*, edited by Peter Paret, 143–85. Princeton, NJ: Princeton University Press, 1986,.

Smith, Graeme. *The Dogs are Eating Them Now: Our War in Afghanistan*. Toronto: Alfred A. Knopf Canada, 2013.

Stacey, C. P. *Arms, Men and Governments: The War Policies of Canada 1939–1945*. Ottawa: Minister of National Defence, 1974.

———, ed. *Historical Documents of Canada, vol. 5: The Arts of War and Peace*. New York: St. Martin's Press, 1972.

Stairs, Denis. "The Media and the Military in Canada." *International Journal* 53, no. 3 (Summer 1998): 544–53.

Stein, Janice Gross, and Eugene Lang. *The Unexpected War: Canada in Kandahar*. Toronto: Viking Canada, 2007.

Stursburg, Peter. *The Sound of War: Memoirs of a CBC Correspondent*. Toronto: University of Toronto Press, 1993.

van Crevald, Martin. *The Transformation of War*. New York: The Free Press, 1991.

Wijninga, Peter W.W., and Richard Szafranski. "Beyond Utility Targeting: Toward Axiological Air Operations." *Aerospace Power Journal* 14, no. 4 (Winter 2000): 45–59.

Winter, James. *Democracy's Oxygen: How Corporations Control the News*. Montreal: Black Rose Books, 1997.

Index

A

Air Force. *See* Royal Canadian Air Force

B

Bagotville, QC. *See* Canadian Forces bases, Bagotville

body bag incidents, 119-20, 128, 130-31, 137-43, 140, 211, 224-25, 235, 254, 255, 258, 266

Britain, 16, 18, 38, 41, 90, 125, 132, 134, 135, 137, 151, 155, 158, 167, 233, 250, 270. *See also* news media outlets, *Times* of London

C

Canada. *See* Canadian Forces bases; Canadian Forces personnel; Canadian news media personnel; *Charter of Rights and Freedoms*; Government of Canada; news media outlets; operational security; Patrol Base Cirillo; public affairs (Canada); Royal Canadian Air Force; Royal Canadian Navy

Canadian Forces bases.
Bagotville, xv, 16, 27, 28, 32, 42-47, 54-55, 57, 59-60, 67, 82, 85, 98-99, 105, 107, 110, 113, 116, 125, 155, 159, 195, 198, 199, 206, 216-17, 221, 222, 238-39, 243-44, 250

Cold Lake, xv, 7, 14, 16, 18, 27, 28, 30, 32, 41, 48, 57, 59-61, 66-67, 71, 88, 106, 115, 125-26, 133, 139, 159-62, 195, 199, 204, 206, 217, 221, 224, 235, 238, 240, 250, 262

Edmonton, 230

Esquimalt, 138-41

Canadian Forces. *See* Canadian Forces bases; Canadian Forces personnel; operational security; Patrol Base Cirillo; Royal Canadian Air Force; Royal Canadian Navy

Canadian Forces personnel, 6, 118, 152
Baril, Gen. Maurice, 46, 86, 96, 165, 179-80, 238
Barker, Capt. Mike, 16, 60, 62-63, 71-72, 75-76
Brassington, Capt. Travis, iv, 30-31, 61, 64, 80, 103, 114, 118, 161-63, 240
Cirillo, Cpl. Nathan, 267, 268, 269
Davies, Col. Dwight, 151, 154, 156, 159, 163, 165, 172, 182, 218-19, 222, 240-41, 259
Donihee, Lt. Col. Jim, 48-51, 84, 191, 200, 206-7, 244, 249n35
Edelman, Master Cpl John, 67, 70, 73, 75, 77, 243
Faucher, Lt. Col. Sylvain, 14-15, 23-27, 95, 170-71, 180, 191-92, 232, 244

325

Flynn, Lt. Col. William Allen, ix, 27-28, 30, 87-89, 105-6, 109-11, 202-4, 224, 237-38, 245, 249
Glaeser, Capt. Brett, 29-31, 79-82, 112-13, 116-17, 243
Hébert, Maj. Stéphane, 54, 216-17
Henault, Lt. Gen. Raymond, xvi, 46, 86, 91, 108, 152-56, 161, 163-65, 176, 179, 224, 230-32, 238, 246, 257-59, 284
Jurkowski, Brig. Gen. David, 33, 46, 50-52, 91, 108, 164, 179, 188, 200, 211-14, 219, 221, 227, 230, 235, 245, 258-59, 262
Kendall, Maj. Dave, 126, 133, 224
Marcotte, Col. Benoît, 40-43, 47-48
Matthews, Lt. Col. Don, 82-84, 129, 135-36, 139
McGillivray, Brig. Gen. Ed, 125-26, 139
McRury, Capt. Neil, 115-16, 117, 206
Pelletier, Maj./Col. Alain, 13-16, 20-26, 29, 55-56, 81, 106-7, 222
Savoie, Cpl. Patrick, 47, 49-50, 53, 55, 222
Sinclair, Capt. Todd, 104
Soroka, Capt./Lt. Col. Kirk, 18-19, 28, 31-35, 59, 99, 106, 111, 114, 117, 197-98, 240-41, 242-43, 249
Vincent, WO Patrice, 266, 268-69
Canadian news media. *See* Canadian news media personnel; news media outlets
Canadian news media personnel.
  Macdonald, Neil, xvi, 158-59, 169-70, 218
  Malbon, Joy, xvi, 145-46, 150-51, 156-59, 167, 181-87, 189, 236
  Warmington, Joe, 180, 186-88
  Workman, Paul, xvi, 218, 233-34
  York, Geoffrey, xvi, 171, 173-75
CFB. *See* Canadian Forces bases
Charter of Rights and Freedoms, 146, 257-58, 266, 269, 272
Chrétien, Jean, 2, 7-8, 39, 200, 237-38, 257-58
Clark, Gen. Wesley, 8, 54, 90-91, 94-95, 103, 154, 156, 176, 178, 187, 190, 216-17, 248, 254-55
Clausewitz, Carl von, 6, 209, 278n9
Clinton, Bill, 9, 38, 41, 94, 103

Cold Lake, AB. *See* Canadian Forces bases, Cold Lake

D

Dandurand, Raoul, 268

E

Edelman, Murray, 3, 142, 257
Eggleton, Art, 5-8, 59, 71, 105, 152, 155, 160-61, 165, 173, 178-79, 204, 237
Esquimalt, BC, 119, 124, 128, 130, 134, 138-42, 294n102, 294n109

G

Government of Canada, 247-48
  House of Commons, 5, 42, 54, 86, 122, 125, 128, 152, 266, 267, 272
  Ministers of National Defence. *See* Eggleton, Art; McKnight, William
  official censorship, 5, 11, 123-24, 127, 131-33, 254, 262, 269-72
  Official Opposition, 151
  Prime Ministers. *See* Chrétien, Jean; Harper, Stephen; Mulroney, Brian; Trudeau, Justin
Granatstein, Jack, 8, 127, 127-28, 263

H

Harper, Stephen, 250, 266, 267, 268

I

Internet threat, 217
Italy.
  Aviano, xvi, 6, 11-12, 13, 16-18, 26-31, 33-34, 42-57, 59-60, 63-67, 69-73, 75, 77, 81-82, 84-85, 88, 90-93, 95-97, 105-6, 108, 110, 145-46, 150-51, 153-56, 158-61, 163-67, 170-83, 187-90, 192, 197-98, 204, 206, 214, 216-19, 222, 225, 227-28, 231-32, 234-35, 237-39, 241-42, 244, 250-51, 253-60
  Piancavallo, 43, 60-66, 106
  Vicenza, 17, 43, 47, 96, 199

J

Korean War, 2, 8, 146, 241, 242

K

Kosovo, xv-xvi, 1-3, 6-12, 17-18, 21-22, 40-42, 44-46, 52-56, 59, 75-76, 79, 81-82, 84-85, 87-88, 95, 105, 108, 112,116, 118, 120, 143, 146, 151-52, 162, 165, 167, 171, 173, 179, 192, 196, 200-201, 206, 209, 212, 215, 224, 229, 231, 233-35, 237, 239, 241-43, 247, 250-51, 253-60, 262-64, 265-66, 270, 272, 275n41, 275n43, 287n15, 304n38

M

Maguire, John, 268-69
McKnight, William, 127-28, 135
Milosevic, Slobodan, 2, 6, 8, 10, 17, 41, 94-95, 103-4, 196, 208, 228-29, 237, 265, 281n53
Mulroney, Brian, 83, 125-26, 128

N

Navy. *See* Royal Canadian Navy
news media. *See* body bags; Canadian news media personnel; news media outlets
news media outlets.
   Calgary Herald, 162, 221, 265, 294n102
   Canadian Press, 127, 129, 134, 147, 155, 177, 221, 227-28, 230-31, 271
   CBC, xvi, 147, 151, 155, 158-59, 169, 179, 213, 218, 225, 226, 233-34, 254
   CTV, Canada AM, 234
   CTV, National News, 146-47, 150, 159, 167, 170, 181, 189, 190, 213, 234
   Daily News, The (Halifax), 221, 231-32
   Edmonton Journal, The, 159, 162
   Gazette, The (Montreal), 231
   Globe and Mail, The, xvi, 40-41, 127, 130, 133-35, 138-39, 142, 147, 171, 173, 294n102
   National Post, 162
   New York Times, The, 154, 215, 229, 306n21
   Ottawa Citizen, 155, 162, 221
   Times Colonist (Victoria), 140-42, 231
   Times of London, 151, 157, 215

   Toronto Star, The, 129, 134, 139, 142, 147, 163, 173, 221, 231
   Toronto Sun, The, 147, 180, 186-87, 213
   Vancouver Sun, The, 40, 119, 138, 141

O

operational security, 11, 121-24, 132, 137, 149-50, 152-54

P

Patrol Base Cirillo, 269
Persian Gulf War, 1991, xvi, 2, 10, 82, 118, 120, 146, 174, 211-12, 259, 278n7. *See also* Royal Canadian Air Force operations, Desert Storm, Persian Gulf War, and Friction, Persian Gulf War
Personnel. *See* Canadian Forces personnel; Canadian news media personnel
public affairs (Canada), 120-21, 123-24, 127, 132, 135, 137-39, 147-50, 152, 154-55, 159-60, 165, 170, 174, 177-78, 180-83, 189, 212, 218, 222, 225, 234-36, 254-57, 259-60, 269
   command prerogative, 149
   personnel
      Agnew Lt.Cmdr. (Navy) Jeff, 152, 160, 165, 170, 212
      Larsen, Lt./Lt.Cmdr. (Navy) John, 182-83, 185, 189, 218, 225-27, 231, 235
      Seguna, Lt. (Navy) Paul, 139-42

R

Royal Canadian Air Force.
   aircraft.
      C-130, Hercules, 16, 30, 44-45, 238
      CC-137, Boeing Tanker, 137
      CC-150, Polaris, 47
      CF-18, McDonnell Douglas Hornet, 6-7, 13, 15-16, 18, 21-22, 24-25, 27, 29-30, 32, 35, 40-46, 48, 51-52, 54, 56, 59-60, 67, 70-73, 77, 79-80, 82-87, 93-94, 96, 106-9, 111-15, 117-18, 120, 125, 129-31, 133-35, 137, 139, 142-43, 150, 153, 155-57, 159, 161-64, 171-72, 174, 176-79, 181, 183,

186-88, 193-94, 200-201, 204-6, 208, 212-13, 215-16, 219, 221, 223, 227, 229, 231-32, 234, 237-38, 240-41, 256, 258, 266, 276n9, 282n25; Forward Looking Infrared, 24, 83, 114, 206; mission computers, 84; radios, 56, 117-18, 209, 227

bombs.
   GBU-10, 105-7, 214, 241
   GBU-12, 34, 80, 87, 89-91, 105-6, 214, 241, 284n39
   GBU-24, 87-88, 105, 284n32, 284n39
   total dropped, 208, 230-32, 241

bombing, morality of, 6-10, 77, 195

squadrons.
   409 Tactical Fighter Squadron, 250
   425 Tactical Fighter Squadron, 2, 14, 16, 27, 82, 171, 191, 250
   433 Tactical Fighter Squadron, 15-16, 28, 85, 105, 216, 250
   441 Tactical Fighter Squadron, 16, 27, 67, 88, 90, 104, 109, 114, 224

Camp Patrice Vincent, Dubai, 268-69
Canadian Airborne Regiment, 37, 50, 148
Lord Strathcona's Horse (Royal Canadians), 230, 233, 266
See also Canadian Forces bases; Royal Canadian Air Force operations

Royal Canadian Air Force operations.
   Desert Storm, Persian Gulf War, 88, 120
   media policy, 122, 136, 160, 182
   Echo, 2, 42, 44, 46, 66, 89, 96, 163, 227, 230, 234, 235-36, 254-55
   credit card, 33, 60, 91, 106, 161, 227
   equipment deficiencies, 2, 44-45, 47, 70-71, 75, 86, 90-91, 105-6, 108-12, 188, 206-9, 227, 239
   pilots performance, 99, 202-4, 206-8, 199-202, 204, 256
   pilot training, 13, 16, 22-23, 26, 31-34, 48, 50, 53-54, 81, 83-85, 99, 106, 109-12, 154, 161, 170, 177, 192, 199-200, 202, 204, 206-8, 241, 261-62

Friction, Persian Gulf War, 1991, xvi, 2, 10, 82, 118, 120, 146, 174, 211-12, 259, 278n7
   media policy, 120-23, 131-38, 259
   pilots' families, 119, 126, 128, 130-31, 138-42, 162, 164, 178, 181, 211, 217, 224, 254-57, 267; Forsythe, Reg, 129; Kendall, Marion, 133, 126, 224; McNeil, Gus, 129

Royal Canadian Navy.
   HMCS *Athabaskan*, 120, 140
   HMCS *Huron*, 119, 124, 134, 139-42, 295n114
   HMCS *Preserver*, 124
   HMCS *Protecteur*, 120
   HMCS *Restigouche*, 124
   HMCS *Terra Nova*, 120

S
Supreme Headquarters Allied Powers Europe, 66, 215

T
Trudeau, Justin, 4-5

U
United Nations, 38-39, 41, 119, 127, 157, 196, 237, 265
United Nations Security Council, 41
United States. *See* Clark, Gen. Wesley; Clinton, Bill; news media outlets, *New York Times, The*; van Crevald, Martin

V
Vickers, Kevin, 267

Z
Zehaf-Bibeau, Michael, 267, 268

www.ingramcontent.com/pod-product-compliance
Lightning Source LLC
Chambersburg PA
CBHW042223250426
43661CB00081BA/2892